RACHEL

A beautiful young woman
abducted and murdered

The Search for her Killer
A True Story

Former Detective Superintendent
Paul Davison

'Sleep tight now and stay close by me,
until we meet again.
The song has ended but the melody lingers on'

Wanda Moran

To the memory of Rachel,
Her surviving family,
And all the victims of the
Evil perpetrated by others

Acknowledgements

I wish to thank:

David Hilditch, John Gaskin, Sam, Jack and Cal Davison for reading the early drafts, for the positive and constructive feedback, and for giving me the courage to publish RACHEL.

Ray and Wanda Moran for their humble, inspirational dignity in the face of unimaginable heartache and loss.

My team of outstanding detectives who went way beyond the call of duty for Rachel. They know who they are. I couldn't have done it without them.

All the officers and support staff who gave up their time to search for Rachel.

The HOLMES team for their forensic attention to detail and for providing the investigation with clear direction.

Lisa Hodson for handling the world's press with compassion, dedication and commendable resilience.

The Underwater Search Team for their outstanding work in discovering Rachel's belongings in atrocious circumstances.

The Dog, Horse Section and Helicopter Unit officers for their invaluable help in the search for Rachel.

Forensic officers and staff. Sometimes forgotten but they were outstanding. They know who they are.

Gary Shaw for his wit and invaluable assistance in the interviewing of Michael Little.

Dean at G T Graphics, Pocklington for the inspired and creative book cover art work.

Jack and Cal Davison for their invaluable help with formatting the book content.

My family - Fiona, Sam, Jack and Cal - for staying with me and supporting me, through some dark times.

Abbreviations

SIO: Senior Investigating Officer
DCI: Detective Chief Inspector
DI: Detective Inspector
DS: Detective Sergeant
DC: Detective Constable
HOLMES: Home Office Large Major Enquiry System
FLO: Family Liaison Officer
POLSA: Police Search Advisor
DCS: Detective Chief Superintendent
SOCO: Scenes of Crime Officer
DCC: Deputy Chief Constable
ACC: Assistant Chief Constable
JARIC: Joint Air Reconnaissance Centre
RIPA: Regulation of Investigatory Powers Act 2000
ONB: Officer Note Book
REGULATION 15 NOTICE: To advise an officer that a
complaint has been made that warrants an investigation by
the professional standards department.
PACE: Police and Criminal Evidence Act 1984

CONTENTS

Always ready to think the worst'
10: 'I've absolutely no idea'
11: 'Go with that gut instinct and see where it takes
you'

PART 2: IF IT SEEMS TOO GOOD TO
BE TRUE, IS PROBABLY IS

12: 'I must be evil. A normal person wouldn't do that'
13: 'It's hard to hold a candle in the cold November
rain'
14: 'I felt like I'd just opened a door that led to a further
dimension of despair and desolation'
15: 'Everybody has experienced the defeat of their own
lives'
16: 'Finally, it was here, what we'd all been waiting for'
17: 'Tasmanian devils by any chance?'

PART 3: THE CRIMINAL JUSTICE SYSTEM
ON TRIAL

18: 'There was something about him that was deeply
unsettling'
19: 'As he uttered the denial, tears rolled down his face'
20: 'I will sit through it all, as it's the very least I can do
for her'
21: 'I wouldn't protect a murderer'
22: 'It'd been an accident. I was drunk. It was an
argument that went wrong'
23: 'Eyes blinking, mouth dry, beads of sweat rolling
down his forehead, he looked like he was about to

PART 1

THE SEARCH

FOR RACHEL

ONE

'I've got a bad feeling about this one. Doesn't look good to me'

It was early January 2003. From my office overlooking Queens Gardens situated on the third floor of police HQ, I could see a covering of snow on the ground. I'd begun my career at the station back in 1982, as a constable, and now I'd achieved my dream job - Detective Superintendent. Not bad for a kid from an east Hull council estate, I thought, as the winter afternoon sunshine faded. But even though I'd a brilliant job, I'd changed from the person I used to be not having a care in the world, to the person I no longer recognised when I looked in the mirror. It'd been a bitter and lonely journey to get to this place and, at times, I felt like the old familiar voice of negativity chattering away in my head, telling me to pluck up the courage to end it all, would finally win. I found myself constantly wondering how it'd happened, how I'd been humiliated and treated with a complete lack of empathy by the force. Billy Connolly was spot on when he came to the conclusion that you could do pretty much anything to a human being and they'd recover their dignity, apart from humiliating them, and then they'd be scarred for life. He was, of course, speaking from experience

1

and I understood exactly what he meant.

Thankfully, though, I'd a loving family who'd stuck by me. I don't know why, because I'd behaved like an absolute bastard towards the people that I loved the most in this world. But during those dark days of being accused of something I hadn't done, I couldn't cope, and my way of dealing with the aftermath was to literally go off the rails. Right now, I'd give anything to go back to my old life but I knew that it could never happen.

Over the past year, Hull had experienced a substantial increase in murders and going from one case to another as SIO, had caught up with me. I was exhausted. Time for home. But just as I was about to leave, the phone rang and I instantly recognised the respectful voice of DI Alan Dorning.

"Boss, this missing female Rachel Moran. I know you're aware but I've got a bad feeling about this one. Doesn't look good to me. Done everything I can think of and there's no trace of her at all."

I'd not worked with Alan before but from the times when our paths had crossed on duty, I'd always liked him. Tall and solidly built, he'd a reputation for being able to sink a pint or two, which made him OK in my book. He also had a reputation for being extremely competent and so I trusted his judgement. I got hold of Chief Superintendent Peter Steel, the officer in overall command of Hull, and within half an hour, DI Dorning was briefing us both on what action he'd taken so far.

He'd done an excellent job with limited resources, but the problem was that Rachel had simply vanished after she'd left her parents' home on Hall Road in the early hours of New

Year's Day. There was no activity on her mobile phone or bank accounts, no contact with her boyfriend Mark Sheppard with whom she lived, no contact with friends or relatives, and house to house enquiries along the route she'd have taken, proved negative. Rachel left her parents' house against her mother's wishes intending to walk back to her home about a mile away. According to her mother, Wanda, she was angry with Mark for leaving their two kittens alone. They'd agreed that she'd go out with her brother to celebrate the New Year, whilst he stayed in to look after them. But despite her mother's concern for her daughter walking home alone in the dark and freezing cold, she could do nothing to stop her. And so, at 5.30pm on Monday, 6 January, the decision was made to step up significantly the scale of the investigation into Rachel's disappearance. I'd take over from DI Dorning as the SIO and DCI Redmore would be my deputy.

Driving to the Force Training Centre at Courtland Road, where the major incident team would be based, I welcomed the challenge that lay ahead because I knew that the feeling of leading the investigation would be like meeting up with an old friend again. Maybe I was addicted to the life of a SIO and all that came with it: forming and building a team, machine gun–like decision making, never giving up no matter how big the challenge, . and the satisfaction of putting murderers where they belonged - in prison. Or maybe it was the adrenalin that numbed the feeling of depression, working for an organisation that couldn't care less about me.

I passed Rachel's parents' address, 56 Hall Road, heading in the direction she would've walked in the early hours of New Year's Day. It was an area that bordered North Hull

Estate known for its high levels of crime and social deprivation. Although it was dark, the road was brightly lit and if Rachel had intended to walk home to Saxcourt, she'd have walked almost the whole way on the footpath by the side of the main road. The more I thought about it the more I realised that I hadn't dealt with anything like this before. I was used to starting with a dead body but this was different. I'd no way of knowing whether there was still a chance that Rachel was alive. Abduction couldn't be ruled out and if she had been, then I knew the investigation would have to move at lightning pace. I couldn't bring myself to think about what Rachel's Mum and Dad would be going through. If I were in their position, I'd want to know whether the police knew what they were doing and whether they cared about finding their youngest daughter.

By coincidence, the Force Training Centre was situated in the heart of Orchard Park Estate and only a few hundred yards from Rachel's home. I knew the area well from my days as a uniformed patrol sergeant. Regrettably, the fifties style semi-detached red-brick homes that gave Hall Road a solid and respectable feel, had been surrounded with poor quality concrete-built council flats and houses arranged in a warren of desolate streets and roads. Even the shops and pubs looked bleak and unwelcoming with their metal shutters and reinforced front doors. It wasn't difficult to understand why it was a breeding ground for crime and violence and, if chief officers imagined that the forces' flagship training facility would act as some kind of deterrent to local villains, they were very much mistaken. They hadn't bargained for having to spend a fortune on security to keep the criminals from breaking in, either. Nevertheless, on the plus side, it did have a canteen and a huge car park.

The makeshift incident room was situated on the third floor. It was deserted, apart from the familiar figure of Detective Sergeant Trev Watts. He looked absolutely exhausted - tie slackened, top shirt button undone, and his hair stood on end as if he'd received an electric shock. His desk was creaking under the strain of supporting a mountain of paper.

"Good to see you again, Trev. Looks like you've been busy."

"Sir, good to see you too. Are you the SIO now?"

"Yes, I am. Maly Redmore's going to be deputy. I see there's not much in your 'should do', and 'could do' trays."

DS Watts had been the HOLMES office manager pretty much from the beginning and, as experienced as he was, he hadn't expected such a massive response from the public over Rachel's disappearance. As a consequence, HOLMES had subsequently gone into overdrive and that's why his 'must do' tray was almost touching the ceiling.

"There's just so much stuff coming in and not enough staff to do the work. Coffee or tea, Sir?"

He disappeared to make me a coffee. Although tempted, I decided against taking a look at his 'must do' tray. It appeared to be on the verge of collapsing at any time, and I was sure that DS Watts wouldn't have thanked me for interfering. It wasn't long before the dire state of the force raised its ugly head. It was pretty much the only topic of conversation these days.

"How's life on Division?"

"With all due respect, Sir, don't get me started on bloody LPTs. I used to be a proud detective sergeant and now I'm classed as a community sergeant with detective skills. Absolute joke. There's no CID anymore. Crying shame. That's why I jumped at the chance to come on this job."

I had to agree with him. The Chief Constable had dismantled the structure of the force so that it could never be put back to its former state, and in July 2001, geographically based Local Policing Teams (LPTs), each headed by a uniform Inspector, were introduced. In order to create so many LPTs - and there were many - chief officers disbanded the CID, Traffic, and any other specialised department they could think of. I remember when they announced their plans. A special meeting was arranged for Chief Inspectors and above. You had to attend without exception. As the scale of their radical ideas began to unfold, we were all literally speechless. The gathering momentum that'd begun with the previous Chief to reduce the size of the CID, had finally run its course. There would be no CID, just a few Detective Superintendents like me to act as SIOs and Detective Inspectors to be on call. The great irony was that the vision of delivering a local service to the public by local officers via LPTs was, in many ways, ahead of its time but it simply didn't work.

"It's just ridiculous. Crime's going through the roof. There're no bloody systems. Everybody just does what they want. Nobody has a clue what they're doing. Don't the bosses worry about the force falling to pieces?"

I didn't have an answer for him. It was all I could do to keep my own head above water, but there was no doubt that the once proud force had a downtrodden feel about it now, and morale amongst junior officers had suffered as a consequence. Trev brought me up to speed with what had been done so far.

"I agree with Al Dorning. It doesn't look good. We've done all the HOLMES fast track actions and there's nothing, absolutely nothing. We've been at it twelve hours a day since her mother reported her daughter missing."

On my way home, in my heart I knew that I'd have to plan for the worst. Tomorrow would be a long and exhausting day, and I'd no idea who'd been seconded onto the investigation. All detectives had been posted out of the CID to LPTs, and Chief Superintendent Steel was struggling to stem the avalanche of crime in the city. I thought about just how fortunate I was to inherit DS Watts as HOLMES office manager. It meant that with his detective's forensic eye, nothing would be missed. He was also one of the good guys – respectful, easy to get on with, and reassuringly trustworthy. That's exactly what I needed right now, to be surrounded by people like DS Watts, because I was still suffering from the emotional aftermath of a protracted discipline inquiry into allegations of sexual discrimination brought by two female sergeants.

A DCC from another force was called in to investigate my alleged conduct and, after many months, he'd concluded that I'd done nothing wrong. The problem was that I didn't know how to cope with the attack on my integrity. It'd taken a sledgehammer to my subconscious mind that caused me to believe that something bad was going to happen at any moment. It was a sharp intake of breath kind of feeling that made me anxious for no reason. Accordingly, I'd become more and more distant from everybody, including my family, and any interaction with a female caused my heart to race and my stomach to churn. I knew that it was no way to live, but my world had been blown apart and everything that I believed in, the values that my parents taught me, didn't seem to count for anything anymore. I was in a dark place. I'd seen it before in individuals who'd been treated shabbily by the force, a tear was never far from surfacing, moistening their eyes, and it was hard for me to admit that I now belonged to what I called the 'emotionally fucked-up', club. A tear was never far from my eyes, either. Definitely not a good look for a SIO, I thought, as I took a deep breath wondering what tomorrow would bring, and whether my nerve would hold in front of the assembled team of detectives.

TWO

'I think we're going to need a bigger car park'

It was around seven the next morning when I arrived at Courtland Road. The Force Training Centre used to be a school that had become surplus to requirements. Although the inside had undergone some refurbishment, the outside still resembled the shape of a giant box and, with the gigantic metal fencing they'd erected for security, it'd be hard to imagine a less welcoming sight.

I sat for a while in my car thinking about how far I'd come as a SIO since my first big case back in 1998. It was the murder and dismemberment of a working prostitute, Natalie Clubb, whose badly decomposed body was dumped in a local drain. The first briefing was memorable for the fact that I'd allowed my debilitating shyness to win. I'd panicked and mumbled incoherently like a gibbering idiot. It was embarrassing for me and for the expectant audience waiting to be briefed. I'd managed to overcome my shyness and fear of speaking in front of others to a degree, by simply doing it every day and by putting the whole thing into perspective - it wasn't life or death for God's sake. But the discipline investigation came not long after and all my confidence vanished. Public speaking, briefings, and meetings of any kind, filled me with dread and, as a consequence, I lived in a state of perpetual anxiety. I wondered what the daily rollercoaster adrenalin rush was doing to my body, when DCI Redmore pulled up alongside me.

We'd worked closely together since I'd arrived in Hull back in July 2001. If you didn't know DCI Redmore, you'd think that he wasn't interested in anything you had to say or anything that was going on around him. He gave off an air of being permanently bored. But you'd be wrong, he was just blessed with an inner calm and a quiet way about him, that's all. Although it'd taken me some time to realise this, the more time I spent in his company, the more I came to value his thoughtful, unassuming approach to everything he did. He was exactly the same some twenty years ago, when I was a young constable and he was an established detective. He'd helped me deal with a local prolific burglar and taught me how to do a thoroughly professional job working at his own measured pace. Over the past year, when we'd both led numerous murder investigations, he proved himself to be loyal towards me and that meant a great deal.

The incident room was already buzzing with energy. The beginning of a new case never failed to lift my spirits, and so not to be disappointed, I decided to reserve judgement when it came to who'd been seconded onto the investigation. DS Watts had done his best given the circumstances: there was no proper established process for resourcing major inquiries as there was prior to LPTs. He'd simply called detectives (community officers with detective skills) he knew would do a good job and asked them if they wanted to be part of the team. But as DS Watts briefed us both on staffing for the incident, he threw his hands in the air in frustration,

"I can't believe that some won't even bother to ask their sergeants whether they can be released, they're so pissed off and demoralised. Can't blame them I suppose."

I looked at the list of officers on the team and I hadn't worked with any of them before. I knew that it was unfair to judge their abilities based on the fact that I didn't know them, but given my inability to trust anyone, I'd have given anything to walk into a room full of people I was comfortable with and not have to worry about saying the wrong thing. This would be a new set of individuals to be exposed to, each with their own agenda, and I knew that they'd be forming their own impression of me.

"Trev, can you see if DS Weir's available?"

"Already done. He can come in a few days. He's just got something to finish and he'll be here. Says he can't wait."

That was brilliant news. DS Weir was one of the most capable and professional officers I've ever worked with. Things were looking up. I began to feel better knowing I'd be surrounded by DS Watts, DI Dorning, DCI Redmore and now, DS Weir. They were all loyal, old school detectives who, like me, were on the outside looking in. Time for my first briefing in the conference room.

There were two seats at the front for DCI Redmore and me, and it was no surprise to see that the detectives were sat in a semi-circle as if they were attending a training course. It was behaviour expected of them since the police service had moved away from being a disciplined organisation, when you were told what to do and you did it without question, to one that allowed officers to pretty much challenge everything that was asked of them.

It was around 1989, when I first noticed a significant change in attitude by newly qualified probationers fresh from training school. I was a uniformed sergeant at the time, and I walked into the parade room to find a young constable sat back in his chair with his feet on the table reading a newspaper. When he saw me, he simply carried on reading, stifled a yawn and muttered,

"Alright mate, how's it going?"

"Comfortable are we, can I get you anything? Tea, coffee?"

"No, I'm alright ta. Thanks for asking."

"Don't 'alright mate' me, get your feet off the table, get out onto the streets and do some bloody work. Move it."

The young probationer clearly hadn't come across me before because he then said exactly the wrong thing,

"Calm down sarge, just on my refs."

"Don't 'calm down sarge' me, you cheeky bugger. Your refs are over now get out."

At that moment, I sensed that the future for supervisory officers in the police would be a bleak one. The new regime for training probationers in the art of constantly reflecting on how colleagues made them 'feel', soon found its way into training courses introduced under the radar as 'political correctness' in the workplace. The force looked for a way of punishing those whose language or behaviour unwittingly or otherwise caused offence to their colleagues, and a grievance culture was born. It proved to be a culture that permeated every aspect of the organisation. Employees seized the opportunity to come up with their own interpretation of 'political correctness'. The champion of the grievance policy, Maggie Bloom, was a regular sight in police stations dotted across the force area, and whenever she pulled up in her bright orange car, officers ran for cover fearing the worst. I often wondered whether the public would believe what really went on behind the scenes. They'd shake their heads in disbelief and demand a rebate on their council tax. I hoped that the officers sat in front of me had come prepared to leave 'political correctness' to one side. The only thing that mattered was finding Rachel.

"Morning. I'm Detective Superintendent Davison. Some of you know me, others won't. And this is Detective Chief Inspector Redmore, deputy SIO. In a moment DI Dorning will bring you all up to speed on what action he's already taken to find Rachel. This won't be a long briefing because Rachel has been missing since the early hours of New Year's Day and there may be a slim chance that she's still alive. Every second counts."

I delivered my usual soapbox-type speech, warning them that I'm not an easy person to work for and I'd be demanding hard work, high standards and a forensic attention to detail. To be fair to them, I also made it crystal clear that I'd almost certainly offend them from time to time, but that they shouldn't take it personally, they'd just have to deal with it. When I announced that if they didn't wish to remain on the inquiry given my direct comments they should leave now, there was an uncomfortable silence, nervous glances exchanged, but nobody left. I needed to send a strong message to everyone from the beginning, that there'd be no room on my investigation for anything other than individuals being at the top of their game. I'd children of my own and heaven forbid, if any one of them went missing, I'd be demanding that the police moved heaven and earth to find them. I nodded to DI Dorning to begin.

"Sir, thank you. Rachel Louise Moran, born on the 17th of January 1981, which makes her 21. She's six-foot-tall, pale complexion, blue eyes, bleached blonde hair with dark roots. She was wearing a claret-or-plum-coloured dress, black suede jacket and white Nike trainers......"

My pulse began to slow as Alan talked, and I could feel my adrenalin levels subside. So far, so good. I'd managed to deliver a performance, one that probably intimidated those detectives who didn't know me. It wasn't my intention to be such a pain-in-the-arse, it was just my way of coping with the shyness and shattered self-confidence.

My first meeting after the briefing was with Lisa Fleming, the press officer assigned to the case. We'd worked together in the past and she'd proved to be extremely competent, trustworthy and loyal. The SIO's office was small with just enough room to fit two desks in. Mine was the one nearest the door and either DI Dorning or DCI Redmore, would be using the other one. Normally, I'd have an office to myself for privacy but it suited me to share with people I trusted.

Despite feeling comfortable with Lisa, I was nervous about being alone with females in meetings for fear of receiving another malicious complaint. For the most part, although slightly bemused, they complied with my request for another person to be present. Those that didn't, were disappointed. But I couldn't care less. I was sick of the complaint culture. At one time, the only complaints you had to worry about were from villains, who weren't impressed with the way that they'd been arrested, and that was fair enough, given that they usually had a strong case. But now everything you did and said at work had the potential to offend.

That got me thinking about PC Alfie Banks. Back in 1982, when I joined the force, probationers were given a two-week period double-crewed with a senior constable. I had the pleasure of spending my time with Alfie, a stockily built individual, who was a top-class rugby player in his day. When he spoke, every sentence was packed with the words, 'fucking' or 'fuck'. So, when he first laid eyes on me, it was 'who the fucking hell are you for fuck's sake'? He very reluctantly agreed to me being his partner, but he spent most of our first shift together complaining about why he had to show, 'fucking retarded probationers', around. He only spoke to me once that day, 'just do as I fucking do, got it'? And so, when we were called to attend a mass brawl in the centre of Hull, Alfie jumped out of the car, got hold of some random person involved in the fight and punched them hard in the stomach as they tried to resist arrest. They duly keeled over in pain as he expertly slapped the handcuffs on before throwing them into the back of a police van. I did as I was told and copied PC Banks. Before long, we were on our way back to the station to deal with our prisoners. In the custody suite, I was nervous because the custody sergeant was bound to ask if our prisoners had been injured as a result of their arrest. To my astonishment, both said that they hadn't been. I looked at Alfie and he just winked.

Alfie was definitely the most ill-tempered officer I've ever come across, permanently angry and aggressive. I don't think I ever saw him smile. He'd a unique view of the world which was that everybody in it was a 'fucking idiot', apart from him. Sadly, he resigned from the force and I missed him after he'd gone. It had something to do with him being a part of my life back then and I couldn't have cared less why he'd had to go. I smiled at what Alfie would've thought about internal complaints being made by colleagues. I reckon he'd have dealt with it himself by way of a punch to the stomach in some dark corner.

"Sir, are you OK?"

"Yes, sorry Lisa. I was miles away."

"I've got a feeling this is going to escalate quickly. The nationals are beginning to take notice. Local girl of good character gone missing is probably the angle for them."

Just as we were about to discuss the media campaign, DI Dorning burst through the door and said without a hint of irony,

"I think we're going to need a bigger car park."

I looked out of the window and he wasn't kidding. Whilst I was used to dealing with the local press on murder investigations, this was clearly going to be something else on a much bigger scale. I'd never seen so many vehicles from so many different and varied media organisations assembled in one place before: Sky News, BBC, ITV, Times, Guardian, Daily Mail, to name a few. It was a sight to behold. The car park was big, and there was normally plenty of room for police officers on training courses and detectives on major inquiries, but now it was bursting at the seams. Large trucks with satellite dishes perched on top covered every available spare inch, and I wondered what the reporters from the nationals thought about our prestigious training facility set in the grim heart of Orchard Park Estate.

"It must've been my press release late last night about a Detective Superintendent taking over the case. They'll be assuming the worst, I'm afraid. Looks like we're going to be busy. I'll put them all in the canteen to give us some time to think."

My message to the assembled press was one of hope that we'd find Rachel alive until I could prove otherwise. After all, we'd absolutely no idea what'd happened to Rachel. Although deep down it didn't look good, whenever I found myself tempted to make assumptions in police work, I thought about DCI Stewart. He was the SIO on a case that appeared from the scene, a blood-soaked kitchen, to be a domestic murder. The male had a history of violence towards his girlfriend, but the problem was that the couple in question had vanished without a trace. DCI Stewart confidently predicted though, that the body of the female would be discovered, and if it turned out that she hadn't been murdered, he'd show his bare arse in Burtons' window in the centre of Hull. About a year later, the couple turned up having spent a prolonged working holiday in Northern Ireland. DCI Stewart never did do what he'd promised but it was a valuable lesson to us all, and it was in the back of my mind as I thought about Rachel. Could there possibly be some innocent explanation for her disappearance?

Sergeant Wood and PC Holding both looked nervous as I invited them in to my postage stamp-sized office. They were the FLOs already assigned to the case by the FLO coordinator at HQ, soon after Rachel had disappeared. The problem was that I didn't know either of them, and my track record for reserving judgment on people I'd not worked with before, wasn't good. Based on first impressions, I liked Sergeant Wood more than his partner. PC Holding had one of those faces that didn't register emotion. Happy, sad, elated, angry – I'm not sure you'd have been able to tell. Maybe it was something he could do nothing about, I thought, and so I gave him the benefit of the doubt despite his one-word answers to my questions.

Sergeant Wood sensed my frustration and provided the information I wanted: the parents' home on Hall Road had been thoroughly searched, various items belonging to Rachel to give us her DNA and fingerprints recovered, and we'd a good description of the clothing she was wearing when she'd said goodbye to her mother, Wanda. At 0145hrs that morning, it was freezing cold and Rachel wasn't dressed properly, wearing only a flimsy purple-coloured dress with thin shoulder straps and a sloping hemline, and a black waist length jacket with fur trim on the collar and cuffs. Rachel put on her Nike Cortez trainers for the mile-long walk home. I wanted to know more but I knew it was going to be a long day, and there were a million other things I had to be getting on with. Before they left, I made it crystal clear what I expected from them both.

"You've done a good job. But I'll warn you now, I'm not an easy person to work for. I'm going to need to know every aspect of Rachel's life in double quick time. Leave no stone unturned. If you let me down, you'll be replaced. Good luck."

They must have wondered what they'd let themselves in for as they made a lightning quick exit from my office. I wouldn't have been surprised if they went straight to the FLO coordinator pleading to be taken off the case. I had some sympathy for their position, having to justify themselves to the detectives on the case, who'd be wary of their none-detective status, justify themselves to me, and be the face of the police to the obviously very respectable hard-working family. I'd have made a poor FLO, I thought. There'd have been no problem on the investigation side, but I was absolutely useless at talking to people in general. To do so effectively and compassionately, when a family is facing its darkest hour, takes a special skill and a special kind of person. I had to hope that Sergeant Wood and PC Holding would prove to be special individuals.

DCI Redmore breezed into the office at his usual measured pace and announced that it was time for lunch. It was a big canteen designed to accommodate the various training courses and major investigation team officers. It was pretty full most days and it was rare not to see someone you knew from the past, and today was no exception. I walked in and noticed one of the female sergeants who'd set me up back in early 2000. My heart started to race, adrenalin pumped through my veins. They say that a particular song can take you back to a certain time in your life but so could a bloody nasty grievance, believe me. The basic human instinct to seek revenge for what they'd done to me had been a powerful force from day one. It was overwhelming, all-consuming, with no outlet. The civilised society perspective of turning the other cheek always sounded like a load of bollocks to me, and I wondered whether those who preached forgiveness and that wanting revenge is corrosive and a waste of time, had ever been wronged.

"Davo, are you OK?"

"Yes, I'm OK. Just seen a ghost from the past that's all."

We sat with Alan and Trev and I suddenly felt better. The canteen was buzzing with conversation. Even though it was cold outside, the strong afternoon sun cut through the thick bars of the metal security fence that was so high, it seemed to disappear into the sky. If you didn't know any better, you'd think you were in a prison rather than a police training facility.

"Don't think I need to worry about delivering a high-profile media campaign based on this morning. I've told them we're keeping an open mind but deep down, what do you all think?"

"If Rachel's still alive, what plausible explanations could there be for her disappearance? Abduction and being held hostage? Maybe, but doesn't seem likely to me. Accident on the way back to her house? But she's not in any hospital. Started a new life somewhere else? Again, doesn't seem likely given that we've seen all her friends and she doesn't seem the type. There's been no activity on her phone, no transactions on her bank account, no messages to anyone. She was really close to her Mum and Dad. Doesn't look good to me. It was the right decision to scale the whole thing up to a murder investigation."

Both Alan and Trev agreed with Maly, and our thoughts turned towards the almost inevitable conclusion that Rachel was no longer alive and what might've happened to her.

"In my experience, the majority of murders are committed by somebody known to the victim. I've been doing some research and stranger murders are pretty rare in this country. Two, maybe three a year. Could be boyfriend. She was pissed off with him. What if she went to have it out with him when he was at the party on Bransholme. Could've got out of hand. He could've hidden the body and maybe we just haven't found it yet," said Trev.

"You really ought to see the video interview with Rachel's boyfriend Mark, boss. Can't make my mind up about him. He doesn't seem to be upset given that they've been living together for ages."

Of course, Alan was right to say what we were probably all thinking. I planned to watch the video later. Alan had done a good job deciding to video both Mark and Rachel's Mum, Wanda, rather than take written statements. I'd used videoing of witnesses extensively, notably on the Clubb investigation. It proved to be one of the best decisions I've ever made and it had a massive impact at the subsequent trial. The majority of the witnesses were prostitutes, pimps or drug dealers and their videos were recorded in police interview suites, warts and all. Most of them were high on heroin at the time, and it showed to the court that we'd been open and transparent in the way we'd handled challenging and dishonest witnesses.

My detectives had heaved a sigh of relief when they realised that they'd be sat in a nice warm video suite, as opposed to wondering what lay behind the door of their next witness. Drug dealers usually had vicious dogs to protect them and, as a detective constable, it was the one thing that I hated about making enquiries at homes of criminals. On one occasion, armed with just my notebook and pen, I knocked on the front door of a known villain. I could see that it wasn't closed. There was an eerie silence that seemed to last for ages. And then, the biggest bloody Rottweiler I'd ever seen poked its head through the gap and with a mighty shove of its mammoth neck, smashed the door against the wall. Glass everywhere. I froze as it tried to make up its mind whether to savage me or not. Fortunately, the villain's wife came to my rescue and said exactly what I expected her to say, 'oh don't worry he won't hurt you, he's a big softy at heart'. The owners of ferocious dogs always said the same thing.

After lunch, I settled down to watch Wanda's video. There would be no better way of finding out more about Rachel. Despite what she must be going through, Wanda conducted herself with absolute dignity from the beginning. Softly spoken, gentle and slightly nervous, she talked openly and in much detail about Rachel's childhood. Wanda didn't need to be asked any questions, the FLOs just listened as she gave as much information as she could, hoping that it might make a difference in finding her beloved Rachel still alive and well. I'd have done exactly the same, I thought, as Wanda reminisced about how Rachel came into their lives on 17 January 1981, the youngest of four children. Wanda's overwhelming pride at being the mother of Kerry, Vanda, John and Rachel was obvious. It was in every word she said and yet life hadn't been easy for the family. Ray spent much of his working life away as a deep-sea fisherman, leaving Wanda to raise the children on her own, and then the family

22

had to face the trauma of a diagnosis of type 1 diabetes for Vanda. The age difference between Rachel and her siblings meant that she spent most of her early years as a lone child. Finally, Ray secured work in Hull and, for the first time, he was able to be at home every day, which led to a strong bond being formed between father and daughter.

She explained how they were very protective parents, particularly towards Rachel as she was the youngest, and I formed the impression that this family, with its Catholic faith, wasn't the usual kind of family I came across in my line of work. It made a difference only because the more I listened to Wanda, even though DCI Stewart's experience was always at the back of my mind, I just couldn't see the family being involved in Rachel's disappearance.

Wanda talked lovingly about how she became very close to Rachel again between 2001 and 2003, following a brief period that lasted only a few months when they hadn't spoken. It was over Rachel moving out of the family home on Hall Road to live with Mark. Wanda told the FLOs that she returned one day to find Rachel packing her belongings and because Wanda disliked any kind of confrontation, she allowed Rachel to go. Ray was heartbroken and what made matters worse, was that Rachel moved in with Mark's mother in Preston, a small village many miles away to the east of Hull. Although Wanda understood that Rachel wanted to be with Mark all the time, months passed with no contact with Rachel. But the bond between mother and daughter proved too strong for this to continue, and Rachel and Mark moved into a council-owned maisonette on Saxcourt, only a mile away from the family home on Hall Road. Rachel secured a job working in a crèche at a school close by, which provided the opportunity for her and Wanda to rebuild their fractured relationship. It seemed to Wanda that it was as if Rachel left as a child and returned very much a grown woman, the equal of her mother in every sense.

When Wanda was asked to describe Rachel, what followed just made me feel really sad. She thought carefully before gently but nervously allowing a glimpse of her daughter through a mother's eyes: 'beautiful is how I'd describe Rachel to you or anyone I suppose. She has this innocence in a kind of child-like way because she always sees the good in everyone. Little kindnesses impress her. I remember when she first started seeing Mark. She came home really excited and showed us a Valentines card from Mark. He'd bought it with his bus fare and had to walk home to Preston many miles away. It touched her greatly that he would do this for her and this cemented the start of their love affair. From the day she was born, Rachel has been a blessing to us. As older parents, did we spoil her, maybe, but it was hard not to, she made us all feel better for just being in her company. Rachel told me often how happy and content she was living with Mark, her kittens and being so close to her Mum and Dad again'.

I stopped the video to get a coffee. Here was just a normal girl brimming with life and, according to her mother, in a very happy state of mind. And I couldn't detect anything in what her mother said that would support the theory of her moving away to begin a new life without telling anyone. But, then again, it was possible. I was pretty sure there was more to come before we had a full picture of not just Rachel the daughter, but Rachel the young woman, struggling to come to terms with being an adult. Rachel would be no different from the rest of us just trying to get by each day, hoping to find sanctuary from 'the hardness of this world that slowly grinds your dreams away', as Springsteen puts it so well in one of his songs.

The FLOs turned to the events of New Year's Eve. Wanda was precise in every detail. It was heartbreaking to watch her agonise over why she hadn't driven Rachel to Saxcourt. Not once did they ever allow her to walk home alone, even during the daytime. That's the kind of parents they were and it reminded me of my own parents, they'd have done exactly the same in those circumstances. But Wanda had been drinking, so had Ray and John and they were already in bed, and Rachel couldn't drive. Outside the family home on Hall Road, Wanda pleaded with Rachel not to go back to her own place. She even used Ray as a last resort, saying that he'd be mad at Wanda if he found out that she'd let Rachel walk home on her own. It made no difference. All Rachel was concerned about were her kittens, hungry and all alone in the dark. Wanda recalled that a stranger appeared as they argued and most probably overheard much of what was said. Out of pure desperation, for a moment, she thought about asking the young man to walk Rachel home, but then realised that it was unwise to do so as she watched him disappear in the direction Rachel would be heading. Wanda forced herself to stop worrying and reasoned that Rachel was nearly twenty-two, used to walking distances, her home was less than a mile away, the road was brightly lit, and the world would be happy and merry given that it was New Year's Eve. What harm could she possibly come to in the circumstances? And so, with a heavy heart and a huge amount of reluctance, she said goodbye to Rachel, whose last words to her mother were: 'I'll be OK, don't worry, I'll ring you as soon as I get home'. Rachel never did call her mother. Wanda waited for about twenty-five minutes, time enough for Rachel to get home, before calling on her landline. No answer, and then she tried Rachel's mobile, again, no answer. Wanda repeated this until about four-thirty when she finally went to bed, hoping that maybe Rachel had gone over to see Mark at the party on Bransholme.

I knew what was coming next. The awful realisation that Rachel had vanished. Wanda woke about ten on New Year's Day. She heard Ray on the telephone and so she dashed downstairs only to find that it was Vanda wishing them all a happy New Year. Ray was unaware of what'd happened and still believed Rachel was upstairs in bed. He was horrified and panic set in immediately. They managed to get hold of Mark on the landline but he could offer no comfort for them. He'd arrived home about seven, after riding back in the rain on Rachel's bike to find the flat in exactly the same state as he'd left it. The kittens hadn't been fed. The news from Mark was a hammer blow to Wanda, Ray and John. They called everyone they could think of connected to Rachel, including one of Wanda's relatives who lived locally and a couple of old school friends, with no luck.

Wanda decided that the only thing left to do was go to the police station. She went with her son, John because Ray was falling apart with worry. It was a good job I was on my own

26

because as much as I tried, I couldn't stop the tears from falling. I was actually watching a mother living through a parents' worst nightmare. I couldn't imagine a worse set of circumstances, not knowing where her beautiful daughter was and if she'd come to any harm. My fucked-up emotional state left me vulnerable, a tear never far from surfacing, and the trigger could be the slightest injustice or tragedy, never mind something on this scale involving such humble, honest and decent people.

At Priory Road Police Station, although there was only a skeleton staff on duty, Wanda and John received a sympathetic and responsive service. A statement was taken and then two officers decided to go to Mark's flat and conduct a search. Wanda, John and Vanda arrived shortly afterwards to find the flat upside down and a very distressed Mark. According to Wanda, Mark initially thought they were jumping the gun by going to the police but now he realised the seriousness of the situation. They left the flat with Mark being supported by his mother, who'd driven from Preston to be with her son. Ray and John went out searching for Rachel far and wide with neither of them knowing where to look.

The next day, Wednesday 2 January, a detective arrived at the door and Wanda took to him instantly. It was DC Tony Bailey, someone I'd not yet worked with but came with an excellent reputation. He was responsible for the recovery of CCTV footage from all over the city, and he provided her with some much-needed reassurance that her daughter's disappearance would be given the highest priority.

The FLOs had done a good job but Wanda was a model

witness: articulate, intelligent, and given the horrendous circumstances, calm and gentle as she'd spoken about the day her life changed forever.

Time to watch Mark's video. I knew there'd be numerous decisions waiting for me in the incident room. Everything was moving fast. It had to, just in case there was still a slim chance that Rachel was alive. Mark would have to be considered as a possible suspect until I could prove otherwise, and this video I was about to watch, might provide some answers. It would be me that would have to make that decision and it was a decision that I wasn't going to get wrong. I might well be in a bad place emotionally, but I'd never let what happened to me lessen my absolute commitment to this investigation.

Before I started, I thought about what I was looking for. Was it possible that Rachel left her mother fully intending to walk back to Saxcourt to feed her kittens, but then changed her mind and walked the five miles or so to Bransholme to confront Mark at the party? Maybe they argued and it got out of hand. Maybe Mark pushed Rachel and she hit her head by accident. Maybe Mark panicked and hid her body somewhere to give him time to get away. There was a load of maybes in there but there had to be. I was pretty sure that Mark's mother and Rachel's family would be horrified at the thought that I was considering the possibility that Mark was involved. They were the kind of people who would normally never come into contact with the police, and I believed that's how it should be, but now I'd a feeling that Rachel's family and the investigation, were bound together for some considerable time to come.

Mark was the complete opposite of Wanda. The FLOs asked question after question and his answers were barely longer than one or two words. He was younger than Rachel, slightly built and timid, nervous and lacking in confidence, and there was no display of emotion given that his girlfriend had vanished. To be fair to him, I don't think he ever expected to be sat in a police video suite; it was as if the whole thing was so overwhelming that he could hardly speak. It was the lack of emotion that worried me more than anything, though. If he was upset at the time, he'd a remarkable gift for hiding it as he answered the FLO's questions in a casual, matter of fact way. Perhaps that's just the way that he is. Maybe he never shows emotion, over anything. But failing to ask any questions about how the search for Rachel was progressing, didn't seem natural to me, and I could see why Alan and Trev had their misgivings.

The incident room was very much alive, with banks of computer screens, telephones ringing constantly and detectives collecting their actions for the day. This was where I belonged. This was where I felt the most comfortable, but just as I felt out of my depth back in in my earlier days as an inexperienced SIO, I was beginning to feel the same way over Rachel's disappearance. 'I couldn't remember a case even remotely similar to this one.

Maly Redmore called in for a coffee and a catch up. He'd a wise and experienced head on his shoulders and I wanted to know what he thought about Mark.

"Don't know really. Something's not right. I think we should get him in for a chat and put some pressure on him. I've a feeling there's more to Mark. We need to find out about his relationship with Rachel and if he's got a violent side to him. I'll sort it if you like."

Maly briefed me on what'd been done so far.

"House to house enquiries complete for the route from fifty-six Hall Road to twenty-two Saxcourt. Most of the houses in Saxcourt have been done. The force helicopter flew over the area and videoed it. DC Bailey's looking at CCTV, he should have a result soon with the images from Jacksons Supermarket. The searches are going well. There's a huge amount of open land to cover to the west and north of Orchard Park Estate. Horse section is doing a first-class job and so is the underwater search unit. They're busy with Barmston Drain but it's a slow job. We're on with likely suspects who live in the area with convictions for sex offences, like you asked for this morning. I've created separate projects on Rachel and Mark to be done asap. The last thing to do is give the National Crime Faculty a call and that'll be all your lines of inquiry up and running."

I looked at a map showing the search parameters I'd set, highlighted with a yellow marker pen. I pored over my policy book decision to make sure I'd got it right,

'To search open land within ½ mile radius bounded by Orchard Park Road, Middle Dyke Lane, New Village Road, Hull Road and Endike Lane to include all drains. To extend search to one-mile radius thereafter bordered by Dunswell and North Moor Lane'.

"What do you think? Have I got it right?"

"Seems OK to me. Logical as I'd expect from you, Davo."

"What's the staffing like inside on HOLMES?"

"Trev Watts is office manager and receiver as you know. Then we've got Sergeant Welsh as statement reader, DS Dudill as action allocator, DC Tomlinson, indexer, PC Clarke, indexer, Sarah Young as index supervisor and PC Pauline Yates, indexer."

"Outside?"

"Big Alan's in charge of outside actions, then we've got DS Austin and DS Kemp, a mixture of ten DCs and PCs. DC Philips is exhibits and you already know Sergeant Wood and PC Holding are the FLOs."

By now, it was about seven on my first full day in charge. Everybody else was still hard at work. I looked out of my office door. I could see DS Watts with his 'must do' in tray as full as ever, deep in thought eyes fixed on his computer screen making sure that HOLMES was doing its job properly. HOLMES would be churning out numerous actions based on the main lines of inquiry I set earlier and information coming into the incident room from the public. Had I got them, right? It was a question that I'd been asking myself all day. As usual, the chattering voice of negativity reared its ugly head. I told it to fuck off and go pester someone else.

I shut the door and wrote on the white board the decisions I'd made to progress the investigation. I'd learned through experience to plan for a trial at Crown Court, from day one of a major inquiry. That meant making sure each decision would withstand rigorous scrutiny at some stage down the line by smart-arse defence barristers, who'd be searching for ways to undermine any prosecution case. I had to think like them, see things from their perspective, to keep me one step ahead. Easier said than done, I thought, when I was operating purely on instinct.

The search parameters I agreed with the POLSA seemed to be logical in the circumstances and they could always be reviewed if necessary. But did we have enough resources committed to the search of open ground and the drains? Pretty much all of the available force resources, including search trained officers, dogs, horses and underwater search teams, had been deployed from the day Rachel went missing.

The media campaign had taken on a life of its own. The story had captured the imagination of the world in just a few days and spread as far as Australia, New Zealand, and America. Lisa had already planned another press conference with the family. We badly needed confirmed sightings of Rachel but if we widened the appeal to include the possibility of Rachel walking to Bransholme to see Mark, then we ran the risk of being swamped with calls from the public that would take up valuable time and resources. The problem was, I couldn't rule out the possibility that Rachel did go to see Mark. Separate projects looking into every aspect of the movements and background of Rachel and Mark, would soon tell me everything I needed to know about them both, including their mobile phone records. Should I policy Mark as a suspect now, I wondered, based purely on his video I watched earlier, then I'd be able to put a force surveillance team on him to track his movements.

DC Bailey was wading through the mountain of CCTV footage already gathered, and he promised me that he'd have an answer as to whether Rachel reached Jacksons Supermarket as soon as possible. The supermarket was located midway between 56 Hall Road and Rachel's home, 22 Saxcourt.

Was the investigation heading in the right direction? What would another experienced SIO think if they were called in to review the case? Normally, I'd be absolutely confident in setting lines of inquiry for a murder to catch the killer but this case was different. I knew that I was going to need some help. The National Crime Faculty would be my first call in the morning. They'd access to every expert under the sun, and their job was to go around the country offering help and advice to SIOs, struggling to solve complicated cases.

It'd been a long day and I was tired. I shouted to everyone to go home and reluctantly one by one they left. Alan and Trev called in for a chat. They both looked shattered but I could tell that they didn't mind working so late. I kept a bottle of whisky in my cupboard for times like these. I poured three shots. Keeping a bottle of whisky always reminded me of a DCI in Scotland.

I went to see him with two trusted colleagues, DC Dave Causer and DS Col McVeigh, over a job we were doing to catch a criminal, who was travelling the country committing armed robberies at Building Societies. His MO was to hide a sawn-off shotgun up the sleeve of his long black leather coat, and produce it when he needed to threaten and terrorise anyone who tried to stop him from pulling off his latest heist. On one occasion, the local police had him surrounded inside a pub in Scotland. When the officers entered, he pulled up the sleeve of his overcoat, slowly, to reveal the shotgun, and told them that he'd count to ten before opening fire. Needless to say, the officers made a lightning exit and the villain calmly finished his pint.

When we arrived, the friendly DCI disappeared into a room adjoining his office. He came out holding a bottle of single malt whisky.

"Is this one OK? I've got some different ones if you'd prefer. Come and have a wee look."

Col, Dave and I, weren't prepared for what we were about to witness - a room filled wall to wall with whisky and beer. It made my single bottle of whisky that I kept hidden away seem like much less of an indulgence. Before we could say a word, he'd poured four very large whiskies from the bottle he was holding. He threw back his glass and gulped it down in one,

"Come on now, keep up there's plenty of drinking to do before tonight."

He shared the rest of the bottle between us before announcing that we were to follow him to his hotel, which he owned and where we'd be staying. He drove off like a bat out of hell and we followed as best we could, despite having just consumed a quarter bottle of whisky each in about five minutes. It brought a smile to my face because when we met some of his team that night for a drink, they told us how he always expected his room to be filled with whisky and beer as if by magic. Everybody just chipped in to replenish stocks when necessary. We don't know how he did it but the next morning, he was up at dawn and into the office by seven.

It felt good to relax with Alan and Trev. I could say what I wanted without fear of upsetting anyone. They had no hidden agendas, no looking for glory and I couldn't ever imagine either of them talking behind my back. We left having resisted a second shot of whisky.

THREE

'He must have asked himself a thousand times. Why us? Why our family

O n my way into work it was one of those days when, as I looked across the vast open fields that defined the East Riding of Yorkshire, I was struck by the beauty on my doorstep. It was the way the strong early morning sunshine lit up the deep covering of snow that had fallen over Christmas. It was truly a sight to behold and yet it wasn't enough to keep me from dwelling on the past.

I sat in my car again outside the station, just as I'd done yesterday, and no matter how hard I tried, my stomach just kept on churning at the thought of yet another briefing. I pulled out a small leather-bound notebook that I kept. It was meant to be a kind of diary to record how I felt each day but it'd turned into more than a diary, with page after page full of ways to boost my low self-esteem. The cover was worn at the edges. I scanned the pages, and the litany of inspirational quotes hit me like a wave of positivity as if I'd just been injected with a confidence drug. I felt better. Time to put on another performance to make it appear as though I was this strong leader, who knew exactly what he was doing. Maly pulled up alongside me with a big grin on his face.

"Now then, Davo, you spend a lot of time sitting in your car. Coming in?"

Alan was waiting for us in my office. He was smiling and couldn't wait to blurt out his good news.

"Boss, DC Bailey thinks he's got Rachel on Jacksons' CCTV at 0201hrs. He thinks it's her and so do I but we'll need to get the family to confirm. There's a male in front of her timed at 0159hrs. It could be the man Wanda spoke about. We'll need to trace him. We've also got a witness who knows Rachel called Betty Dale. She was at home with her daughter when she saw Rachel walk past her house at 140 Hall Road, just before Jacksons. She thinks it was around two or just after. She specifically mentions Rachel wearing trainers."

The CCTV footage of Rachel at Jacksons, although yet to be confirmed, and the image of a man walking ahead of her, was real progress, and so was the witness Betty Dale. I could see why Alan was grinning from ear to ear. It was just what the investigation needed, and Maly and I couldn't hide our admiration for DC Bailey's discovery. It was a significant breakthrough. DCS Johnson appeared in the doorway.

"Sir, good to see you. Are you coming to the briefing?"

"Hope you don't mind. Judging by the look on your faces, things must be going well."

"Do you want me to bring you up to speed?"

"No need. Where's the briefing?"

"Classroom 1."

Time for the briefing. I glanced around the room at the officers sat in a semi-circle, and I was pleased to see PC Pete

Clarke. He was on my old shift when I'd joined the force and he'd always been friendly towards me. It was good to see him, and I flashed a smile of welcome in his direction.

"Morning everyone and welcome to the new faces amongst us. We've a lot to get through today. But before I begin, I'd like to welcome DCS Johnson. It's not often we get a senior officer at a briefing so it's good to have him here."

I did actually mean what I said. It was important for the morale of the team for higher-ranking officers to show their faces from time to time.

"DI Dorning will bring us all up to speed with the CCTV footage at Jacksons and a witness Betty Dale. But it's important for you all to see this not as a missing persons inquiry but as a murder investigation. We've gone over time and time again the possibility that Rachel ran off to start a new life somewhere else but all the circumstances just don't support that theory. She only had £10 with her and none of her clothing is missing. We now know she did reach the junction of Hall Road and Inglemire Lane, but what happened to her after that? See Rachel as a victim who has more than likely been killed by either Mark the boyfriend, or someone she knew maybe a friend, relative, or a stranger. The absolute priority is finding Rachel's body."

For about the next twenty minutes, Mark was the main topic of conversation. DS Keith Austin had the project to look into Mark's movements on New Year's Eve and to find out everything there was to know about him. Statements had been taken from people who were at the party on Bransholme and, according to DC Porter who was part of

DS Austin's team, they were all putting him there from five-thirty in the evening on New Year's Eve until six in the morning on New Year's Day. An action was raised to recover CCTV footage of the likely route Rachel would've taken, if she went to see Mark at the party. DS Austin had made arrangements for Mark to attend Courtland Road voluntarily later this afternoon. It'd give me the chance to meet him face to face and monitor his reaction to some difficult questioning.

After the briefing, Lisa and I discussed the press conference she'd arranged with Rachel's family. The plan was for Wanda to read out a prepared statement. Ray would be there and so would Vanda. Before going to meet them in the canteen, I sat for a while wondering what they'd think of me. I was nervous because if I'd been in their position, I'd be hoping and praying that the SIO was worthy of leading the investigation into their daughter's disappearance. Would their first impression of me be a positive one? I hoped that it would be.

Ray stood and shook my hand with an iron grip. Thickset and upright, he looked shattered, his moistened eyes shielded behind his glasses, with a tear not far away. He must have asked himself a million times, why us? Why our family? Wanda did most of the talking. I could tell that she was nervous but she appeared to have an inner strength that wouldn't allow her to break down. Vanda sat quietly by her side and peered at me through the biggest blue eyes I've ever seen. Ray looked as though he'd never stopped crying from the minute Rachel disappeared and then it really hit me, they'd no choice but to put their faith in me to find Rachel.

The burden of responsibility was suddenly very real and tangible. Would I be up to the task? There was no time to dwell on my doubts as we made our way to the press conference.

The room was packed with just about every news agency represented. Cameras exploded into life. Flash, flash, flash. The atmosphere was electric. I'd hosted many conferences in the past but this one was different. This was an appeal from a family desperately hoping that their youngest daughter was still alive and that there was some innocent explanation for her sudden disappearance. The emotional strain was too much for Ray. He broke down and sobbed, with his right hand covering his face and shoulders trembling. Vanda composed herself in readiness to read out a prepared statement.

"Firstly, we would like to thank the police for their efforts in the continuing search for Rachel and the media for their ongoing coverage, help and support. We wish to thank the many members of the community who have come forward with information so far. As a family we are just about holding it together. We are trying to comfort each other and Rachel's boyfriend Mark as best we can but as you will appreciate, we are ALL very much distraught. It has now been more than a week since we last saw Rachel and coping with our distress is becoming harder by the hour. Rachel was in good spirits at the time of her disappearance and we are unaware of her having any problems. For her to be out of contact for this length of time is unprecedented and completely out of character. We are all now very fearful for her safety."

Vanda lifted her head and looked straight into the

cameras with her striking blue eyes. I knew that she was about to appeal directly to Rachel and I hoped that her composure would last. She cleared her throat but the tears fell. Unable to carry on, Wanda put her arm around her daughter and whispered something in her ear. There was silence in the room. I looked at the assembled horde of reporters waiting patiently for one of the family to speak, and I wondered what made them want to become reporters in the first place. I guessed that it was dramatic occasions like this that made it all worthwhile. I wouldn't have lasted long though, I wouldn't want to write about the disappearance of Rachel for a living, or be sat in their seats witnessing the very tangible distress of a respectable family torn apart by grief. But, then again, maybe they wouldn't want to change places with me, either.

It was Wanda who delivered the heartfelt appeal that only a mother could.

"Rachel, my precious Rachel, if you are watching this, we beg you to get in touch by whatever means you can if only to let us know that you are well."

When the questions came, Lisa stepped in.

"Whilst the family are grateful to everyone who has lent support, they would now appreciate a short period of rest and reflection during which any media attention will be dealt with by Mr Davison or me."

I accompanied Ray, Wanda and Vanda downstairs and into the car park. Alan was ready to drive them home. By now, Ray had composed himself and apologised for not being able to speak in the conference. It was an awkward moment because he'd nothing to apologise for. Before he left, he shook me by the hand and didn't let go until he looked me directly in the eye and pleaded with me to do everything within my power to find Rachel. He made me promise never to give up, no matter how long it might take. The family deserved to know that they could place their trust in the police. I tried to put myself in their position for a moment, and not to trust in the police would drive me mad wondering what they were doing and could they be doing more. I watched them disappear out of the car park, and I realised that I was bloody freezing. Time to return to face the hungry press.

Lisa was doing a first-class job in my absence - cool under pressure and confident in a reassuring way. Not surprisingly, the main question was, did we think that Rachel was still alive. My response was to maintain that this was still a missing person inquiry, although the significant amount of resources already assigned to the search for Rachel reflected our level of concern. But then I steered their attention to the possibility that Rachel had changed her mind and walked to Bransholme to see Mark at the party. I knew that this would be reported far and wide, probably generating false sightings that would need investigating. It would also point the finger of suspicion towards Mark.

DI Dorning and DS Austin brought Mark in for an informal chat around two. As expected, the press had been quick to act on the theory that Rachel walked to Bransholme in search of Mark - it'd been all over the radio and television within minutes of the press conference ending. In the video suite on the first floor, Keith was doing his best to explain to Mark why it was necessary.

"You're making it look like I've had something to do with Rachel going missing. Nothing to do with me. Will this take long? I'm off to karaoke tonight."

Mark was sat on the settee next to DS Austin.

"We just need to talk to you to see if there's anything you can help us with. It's possible that Rachel could've tried to meet up with you, isn't it?"

"No. She wouldn't have wanted to leave the kittens."

Mark had one of those faces that showed absolutely no expression or emotion. His video statement already showed that he wasn't a big talker. The FLOs had done a good job in the circumstances, faced with mostly one-dimensional answers to their questions. But I sensed that he could tell us much more about Rachel: her state of mind, whether she was happy, whether she had the capacity to plan a new life away from him, how annoyed she was over the kittens, and had she ever done anything like this before. Was he hiding something? Or was he just naturally shy and feeling nervous, given the fact that he was way out of his comfort zone, sat alone in a police station with three detectives for company?

"Alan, a word please. Keith, I'll leave you to talk to Mark."

In the next room there was a video monitor set up so we could watch and listen to Keith talking to Mark. I got straight to the point.

"What do you think? Is he capable of killing Rachel and concealing her body?"

"I just can't get my head round why he's not more upset. The so-called love of his life has been missing for over a week, vanished into thin air and he doesn't seem to be that

43

bothered. But let's suppose Rachel did walk to Bransholme to confront him at the party and killed her by some kind of accident. What did he do with her body? He hasn't got access to a car as far as we know. We've searched the house where the party was. Surely her body would've been discovered by now if it was in the open."

"I agree. Thinking back to the Clubb case they dismembered her body to get rid of it. It really isn't that easy to conceal a body. But we're going to have to put him in or out pretty quickly as a suspect. I need to read the statements from those who were at the party with Mark."

"I've read them. It was Dale Bottomley's party and there were about thirteen people there at different times during the night. It would appear that Mark was there between 5.30pm and 6am, apart from a couple of hours when he went with Danny Appleby and three females to a local pub. Seems to check out, although the statements aren't very detailed."

"What's the connection between Mark and Dale Bottomley?"

"There isn't one as far as I can tell. Mark's a big mate of Danny Appleby, wherever he goes Mark goes. No idea who Danny Appleby is, though."

"By the way, find out where the karaoke is and get two detectives there. See what he gets up to."

Back in my office, I settled down to read the statements of people who were at Dale Bottomley's party. Alan hadn't been kidding when he told me that the statements weren't very detailed. He was quickly becoming the master of the understatement. I knew that when I looked back in future years long after this case reached its conclusion, I'd remember his dry observations. The comment about needing a bigger car park delivered with such a deadpan expression had made me smile, once I'd recovered from the shock of seeing so many press vehicles assembled in one place.

My disappointment in the quality of the statements grew with each page. There was little detail, and they weren't good enough for me to make a judgment on whether or not Mark was present at the party all night. I'd have to be convinced beyond reasonable doubt, that he left the party around six in the morning to ride home on Rachel's bike in the rain as claimed by Dale Bottomley. It would be the missing detail that would convince me, nothing else. Apparently, everyone left the party by four, apart from Helen Franklin, Samantha Rogerson, and Mark Shepherd. When Franklin and Rogerson went to bed, Mark and Dale stayed up playing computer games. But the statements raised more questions than answers. Why had Mark remained after everyone left, including his big mate Appleby, leaving him with Dale who he hardly knew? What did they do all night? Did they watch TV and if so, which programmes? Did they listen to music? What were they drinking and how much?

I resisted the urge to explode in a fit of exasperation, even though the statements would have to be retaken. They would take time to be done properly, time that we didn't have. Maybe the detectives who took them, hadn't been taught how to take a statement to the standard required on a major inquiry, and that got me thinking about PC Paul Gorman, who'd helped me as a young constable.

He was in what they used to call the plainclothes department at the time. It was formed to deal with shoplifters, homosexual behaviour in public toilets, and pretty much anything else that uniform or CID didn't fancy dealing with, including coroners' files. I'd just got back to the station having attended my first sudden death. I'd absolutely no idea what to do or where to begin, which must have been obvious to everyone in the parade room to the delight of my old mentor, PC Archie Banks, who muttered something like, 'told you all he was a fucking retard. Fucking probationers'. For some reason, Paul leapt to my defence and told Archie that he was out of order, to which my old colleague replied, 'and you can fuck off as well. Twat'.

Paul spent hours guiding me through how to put together a coroners' file. He taught me something that I've never forgotten: how to write a polished and professional statement brimming with detail. After reading my first attempt covering only two sides of paper, he politely pointed out that it needed to be longer and contain much more information. I'd struggled to recall the layout of each room, whether the doors were open or closed, whether the lights were on or off, the smell in the house, the exact position of the elderly lady in the bath, what she was wearing and so on. My powers of observation were pedestrian at best but with Paul's invaluable help, the final product ran to more than twenty sides of paper. It'd achieved his aim of giving a sense of actually being there through my eyes, as if trying to compensate for not being able to record the events on video. I remember reading out my statement at the coroner's inquest into the sudden death and being complimented for the thoroughness of my evidence. Looking back, his guidance marked the beginning of my understanding of how to make the criminal justice system work to my advantage: through the power of words.

Given my own lack of competence as a probationer prior to Paul's intervention, I decided against giving the detectives responsible a rollicking. I asked Alan to come in and close the door.

"Before you say anything boss, I know the statements aren't good enough and I know they're going to need to be taken again. You're not going to like this but Dale Bottomley's already gone back to Portsmouth. He's in the Navy. The good news is he's not left the country yet so we've got a couple of weeks."

"For fuck's sake, Alan. More time lost. I'll leave it to you to brief the officers concerned but I want bloody brilliant statements, I want to know every detail about the party there is to know."

In fairness to Alan, he accepted my disappointment with good grace and any awkwardness between us quickly evaporated as Maly sauntered in with some news.

"Looks like we've got a new DCC. Not sure where he's from. Don't know why he'd want to come here. Promotion probably."

DS Trev Watts joined us to mull over the implications of Maly's news.

"I hope he'll get rid of bloody LPTs. If he does, he'll get my support."

An officer in uniform appeared in the doorway as if he realised that he was interrupting an important discussion and would be prepared to wait until we finished. We continued to chat for a while and just as I had the last word with,

"Anyway, I'm sure we'll meet the new DCC soon enough.

Hope he knows what he's letting himself in for."

Alan stood to attention and threw me a worried glance.

"Hello Sir, I'm DI Dorning. You must be our new DCC."

I looked over my shoulder and sure enough I could see by his epilates that he was indeed a DCC. I apologised for not recognising him. Maly, Trev and Alan left my office in record time, leaving me to squirm over my last comment.

"And what might I be letting myself in for Detective Superintendent?"

He spoke as if he was angry. He looked like he was angry. But then he broke into a smile and said that he was only kidding. Bloody hell, I thought, a chief officer with a sense of humour, what a refreshing change. We sat and talked for what seemed like ages. For some reason, I didn't feel intimidated by him. It had, I think, something to do with his demeanour. He appeared to have a degree of humility that I'd not seen before in a chief officer and so when he asked for my views on the force, I decided to resist the temptation to tell him what I really thought. It wouldn't have made any difference, and I was pretty sure that it wouldn't take him long to figure it out for himself. After he'd gone, I felt an overwhelming sense of calm, because it would've been the perfect opportunity to be critical and vent my anger and frustration over how I'd been treated by the force. But it would've also been the wrong thing to do.

I caught site of DS Shaun Weir in the incident room. It was good to see him. He was someone who I'd the very highest regard for, both as a detective and human being. Things were definitely looking up, I thought, with the new DCC leaving a favourable impression on me, and now the arrival of Shaun.

Most of the afternoon was spent in my office with Detective Sergeant Shirley Penman and Detective Inspector Dianne Taylor from the National Crime Faculty. DS Austin had already faxed them a report about Rachel's disappearance and so they were up to speed with what we'd done so far. I'd never met either of them before and I'd no idea what to expect: would they be credible individuals able to offer some practical help based on years of detective experience, or would they be the kind of officers who just fancied a secondment to the Faculty from their home force, just to boost their CVs? I needn't have worried. Within about thirty seconds, despite being females, I knew we'd be able to work together and I knew they'd be able to provide me with some much-needed support. I formed the opinion that political correctness wouldn't be an issue with the two confident detectives, and I felt at ease in their company. Alan and I briefed them in as much detail as possible.

From the beginning, it was obvious that they did this for a living, visiting forces across the country offering help to struggling SIOs. They agreed that we were right to treat the disappearance of Rachel as if it was a complex murder investigation and proceeded to offer some fifty or so practical suggestions to move the investigation forward. As Alan scribbled down copious notes to capture their impressive list of things for me to consider, a quote I'd read about planning came to mind: 'Planning is an unnatural process; it's much more fun to do something, and the nicest thing about not planning is that failure comes as a complete surprise rather than being preceded by a period of worry and depression'. The more they talked, the more I realised that this was indeed unfamiliar ground for me and judging by the look on Alan's face, it was the same for him too.

Their investigative plan included stuff we'd not even thought about. Installing a recording device on Wanda's landline telephone in readiness for Rachel's birthday, 17 January, and asking friends and relatives to turn off their mobile phones for the day, was a good example. If Rachel was alive, maybe she'd call on her birthday. I had to admit that it was a bloody good suggestion, and it was one of those uncomfortable moments when I realised that I wasn't as good as I thought I was. There was more to come as I put my dented pride to one side and listened.

Had we considered the possible significance of the taxi driver Francesco Dominic Penna? He'd come forward of his own volition. Based on his description of Rachel not wearing 'dressy' shoes, there was little doubt that he'd seen her walking briskly along Hall Road in the direction of Saxcourt and was probably one of the last people to have seen her alive. Could he be responsible for Rachel's disappearance? The detectives were right to remind us of the recent murders of Holly Wells and Jessica Chapman by Ian Huntley. He'd introduced himself to the inquiry claiming to have seen the girls shortly before they disappeared, and his home was searched routinely in order to eliminate him from the enquiry. Penna would have to be revisited and questioned in more depth.

Had we formulated a body recovery contingency plan at a national level? This would enable the force to retain the lead as evidence gatherers, should Rachel's body be found in another police area.

Had we placed Rachel's DNA on the National DNA database?

Had we considered the identification of other persons using mobile phones in the area at the time as potential witnesses, by securing data from cell sites?

Had we circulated a list of property belonging to Rachel nationally? Rachel's belongings could have been found and handed into the police in another force area.

To give Alan a rest from writing, I suggested a coffee in the canteen. I asked DS Watts to join us.

"I have to say I'm really impressed with you both. Some excellent practical suggestions we've not even considered."

They both looked a little uncomfortable at my comments. Maybe they weren't used to compliments from a higher-ranking officer.

"Based on what we've discussed, do you have a view on what could've happened to Rachel?"

"We never give an opinion, Sir. All we can do is offer help and support and give you the benefit of our experience. This is our day job. We get to do it all the time. But anything is possible. We're not the ones with the difficult decisions to make though."

I didn't press DI Taylor any further because I understood exactly what she meant. They wouldn't want to suggest one theory had more merit than another. But they did stress the importance of a coordinated search strategy to trace a possible abduction site, crime scene and likely places for body disposal.

"We'd recommend that you contact Chuck Burton. He's a

Detective Inspector. His official title is Behavioural Investigative Advisor. He's supported by the C.A.T.C.H.E.M. Team and they specialise in female murders and abduction."

"What does C.A.T.C.H.E.M. stand for?"

I had to ask because I'd never heard of it and I don't think Alan or Trev had, either.

"Not sure of the exact wording Sir, but it's basically a database that contains records of all child murders in England, Scotland and Wales since around 1960. I can't think of anyone who's got more experience and expertise than Chuck. He's very highly regarded nationally. Also, you might want to consider contacting a SIO in West Yorkshire, Detective Superintendent Chris Gregg. He investigated the murder of Leanne Tiernan and conducted a massive search of homes in an effort to find her. He was the first SIO to carry out a search of people's houses by consent."

"How do you mean by consent."

"He did it by asking residents if they'd allow the police to search their homes. If they refused, a Section 8 PACE warrant was applied for from the Magistrates to allow them to search."

"Did it work?"

"No, not exactly. The search covered houses within a certain area without success. But if they'd carried on, they'd have found her in a freezer a couple of streets away. I'm pretty sure he will be of some help though."

After they'd gone, I went for a walk. I needed time to think. Although the meeting with Dianne and Shirley was a source of inspiration, I recognised that all too familiar feeling of being way out of my comfort zone. By now, it was late afternoon and Orchard Park definitely looked even less welcoming in the dark, I thought, as I headed across the road towards Saxcourt to see Mark. The street lights were too dim to be of any reassurance to residents on the estate. Most of the houses were sat back from the main road arranged in about a thousand alleyways, and if you didn't know your way around, you could easily get lost.

I wanted to see 22 Saxcourt for myself and so I entered through the communal door that led into the building. The stairway up to the first floor was made of concrete and so were the landings. Graffiti decorated the dirty beige-coloured walls. As I climbed the stairs, my footsteps echoed amidst the sound of raised voices, loud music – boom, boom, boom - doors slamming, dogs barking and children crying. I knocked on number 22. I wasn't expecting Mark to answer the door but he did. He didn't look too happy to see me. I brushed past him without waiting to be invited into the small maisonette he shared with Rachel. I received a much warmer welcome from their two kittens.

"Mark, I was passing so I thought I'd call in. You look smart. Still going to karaoke?"

His hair was gelled neatly and his shirt looked like it'd just been ironed.

"Yes. Just on me way out. Getting picked up by taxi."

"Where's the karaoke night?"

"Club in Patrington."

"That's a long way from here. Why so far?"

"Grew up in Preston. Not far from there."

Mark really was a man of few words. I asked about the

kittens and their names. He told me they were called Speedy Tomato and Batman and that Rachel chose them. He seemed nervous and kept looking out of the window for the taxi. The small living room was clean and tidy and I tried to imagine what Rachel would be doing now if she'd made it home in the early hours of New Year's Day. Saying goodbye to Mark as he headed off to his club in Patrington maybe, before playing with her two kittens. Wanda told us that a domesticated life living with Mark on Orchard Park Estate was all that Rachel had wanted.

The modest surroundings reminded me of my own upbringing living on a council estate not far away. Our front room was smaller than the one I was standing in, so small that I could sit on the settee positioned on one side of the front room and rest my feet on the mantelpiece above the fireplace on the opposite wall. Life was much simpler back then. In the summer holidays, I played football with a local crowd of kids from the estate from dawn until dusk, only coming home for meals. The house was always filled with the sound of the latest Dylan, Hendrix or Beatles LP, despite my Dad's attempts to lift the needle from the turntable when he thought my brother and me weren't looking. In the end, he gave up and to my surprise, he came to enjoy Dylan and eventually we were woken every day to the sound of 'Gates of Eden'. It was a bloody fine way to start the day in readiness for my morning paper round.

The sound of the taxi horn broke the uncomfortable and awkward silence and then he was gone. I thought about Mark's apparent indifference to Rachel's disappearance. He'd just left in a taxi to go and sing karaoke at some club miles from anywhere way out to the east of Hull. It just didn't make any sense, and all the attention he was receiving seemed to irritate him as if it was an inconvenience. Could he be responsible for Rachel's disappearance? Should I policy him as a suspect based on this behaviour? I'd nothing to lose, although it might weaken our case at some future trial if I was wrong. Defence barristers always liked to point out that there were other suspects identified, apart from their own clients. It helped plant the seed of reasonable doubt in the juror's minds.

Back in my office, Alan and Maly were discussing the meeting with DI Taylor and DS Penman. Alan was talking about how impressed he was with them both and how it was a refreshing change to meet such positive individuals. Trev was busy attempting to make sense of Alan's notes so that he could feed their impressive list of ideas into HOLMES, all the time muttering something like, 'bloody hell, Alan, are you sure this is written in English?'

I told them about my visit to see Mark and none of us could offer an explanation for his apparent lack of concern for Rachel. Why wasn't he at home waiting for any news or walking the streets looking for her? The problem was that it'd be a few days before the statements from the party were retaken, hopefully to a much better standard, a standard that would give me the confidence to be able to policy Mark as a suspect or eliminate him completely. My gut instinct was to deploy the force surveillance team to follow Mark, but in order to comply with proper procedure, he'd have to be formally named as a suspect. The days of the end justifies the means culture when it came to following people, had long gone with the introduction of RIPA in 2000. Pre-planned covert surveillance of any kind on individuals now had to be authorised because to do so without permission, would be to 'infringe the right to a private life' under Article 8 of the European Convention on Human Rights.

I imagined what my old mentor PC Archie Banks would've thought about the concept of the right to a private life when it came to criminals. 'Private life, private fucking life, I'd stick their fucking private lives up their fucking arses. What about the rights of the poor fucking people who've had their houses burgled'? Of course, he'd be right, but I knew that there was only one way to protect the rights of Rachel and her family, and that was to make sure that every decision I made would withstand any amount of scrutiny at Crown Court. For today, I decided against making Mark an official suspect. After all, he told us he was going to Patrington and so we were well within our rights to go to the club where he was singing, and we'd be well within our rights to make sure that he got home safely afterwards.

By now, everyone had gone home, and although I should have started reading the mountain of statements assembled in my in-tray, I didn't feel like it. I needed to get out of my tiny office that lacked any sense of familiarity or intimacy. I needed a pint to take my mind off the voice of doom and gloom chattering away constantly in my head. I headed for a Tetley's pub, The New Inn, I used regularly when I was a DC. I knew that it'd bring back fond memories of a time spent with my old team comprised of Bernie Orr, Steve Ward, Cameron McMillan and Ken Miller. The CID used it as one of their preferred drinking establishments whilst on duty. It wasn't difficult to see why; it had a welcoming landlord and landlady, and although the locals eyed the police with suspicion and contempt, our presence was tolerated.

My entrance caused conversations to stop, only the music continued. The regulars glared in my direction. It was their way of letting you know that you were on their territory, but before long, I was soaking up the familiar atmosphere with a pint in my hand. I felt better as I imagined being surrounded by my old team, and I began to chuckle to myself thinking about the life I used to have with my trusted and colourful colleagues.

Bernie was my partner. Before I'd arrived, she'd preferred to work alone but we soon struck up a friendship that proved to stand the test of time. She was a proper female and didn't give a fuck about political correctness. Thank God. Steve Ward was the Welsh joker blessed with razor-sharp awareness to see an opportunity to take the piss, and there were so many opportunities. I felt sorry for Ken Miller in particular, because he provided the perfect target for Steve's unique blend of wit and sarcasm. Ken was definitely old school, and he was a serious individual who liked to do everything by the book. The conservative way he dressed and his cautious approach to life and the job, meant that Steve would find something every day to wind him up about.

On one Sunday morning on early shift, Bernie and me followed Steve and Ken to the docks on Hedon Road for breakfast at one of the cafes. Steve was driving and Ken was in the passenger seat. The docks were full of large containers waiting to be loaded onto ships. As we followed Steve, I could see that there was an empty container with a ramp leading up at an angle to the inside. Normally, I wouldn't have given it a second thought but with Steve around, anything was possible and sure enough, Bernie and me watched in amazement as Steve approached the ramp and proceeded to drive into the empty container. He then calmly parked the car as close as possible to the container wall so that Ken couldn't get out, locked the car and closed the container doors. Steve couldn't stop laughing as he walked off with Ken's radio.

"For fuck's sake Steve, you can't leave Ken in the container," I said.

"Oh, he'll be OK whilst we have breakfast. He'll see the funny side eventually. Come on give us a lift. I'm bloody starving," said Steve in his unmistakable Welsh accent.

Reluctantly, Bernie and me went along with the wind up on poor Ken. After all, what could possibly happen to him locked inside a container, we reasoned. The problem was that when we returned to let Ken out, the container had vanished. Then an urgent message came over the radio.

"Control to DC Ward."

"Go ahead."

"DC Miller's been rescued from inside a container on King George Dock. The container's been loaded onto a ship and he's asking that you come and find him. Oh, and the DI wants to see you when you get back."

Needless to say, we found Ken onboard a ship bound for Poland and due to sail within the hour. Fresh from his bollocking by the DI, Steve still couldn't stop laughing as Ken proceeded to sulk for what seemed like forever. There were so many similar episodes that came to mind, and as I sat alone wondering where those lost years had gone, I noticed a villain called Wayne Ford stood at the bar. I'd dealt with him before for house burglary and if I wasn't mistaken, he was currently wanted for escaping from prison. I had two choices: arrest him and take him to the station, or turn a blind eye, finish my pint and go home to a nice warm bed. I knew what I had to do and so I followed him into the next room. He recognised me instantly. With a 'you must be bloody joking', look in his eyes, I could tell that he was about to run.

"Now then Wayne. I wouldn't bother trying to make it to the door. You know I can't let you go. I've already got a load of coppers coming to lock you up."

The last comment seemed to do the trick and he settled resigned to his fate. I told him to finish his pint. It turned out that he'd escaped to see his newly born son for the first time. His girlfriend lived opposite the pub and so he asked if he could say goodbye to her and his baby. Against my better judgment, I agreed and within a few minutes, I was stood inside a tiny flat watching him say his farewells. I'm not sure that it was the way Wayne had wanted the night to end, me neither, but as I drove home, I was pleased that I'd treated him as I would have wanted to be treated, even though he was someone who broke into people's houses for a living, the lowest of the low in my book.

FOUR

'The photograph of a younger Rachel stared back at me'

It was now Thursday, 9 January. Nine days, nine long cold days since Wanda said goodbye to her daughter. Any slim hope of finding Rachel alive faded with each passing day, although the FLOs were under strict instructions to remain upbeat with the family. Everyone was working more than twelve hours a day. I'd pretty much swallowed up most of the force's specialist resources to search vast areas of open land and drains surrounding Orchard Park Estate. Every reported sighting of Rachel was being investigated. A close, forensic eye was being kept on Mark. Convicted sex offenders living in the area were being visited at their homes. The press coverage couldn't have been more high profile and widespread, and DI Taylor's investigative suggestions were being acted upon, including interviewing the taxi driver Penna again on video as a significant witness. What more could I do?

This was indeed unfamiliar territory for me. During a long career as a SIO, I'd managed to solve all of my cases with the help of some outstanding detectives. Solving a case and gaining a conviction, brought a kind of closure for everyone involved – family, police officers and villain. It restored the equilibrium in a way. It never occurred to me until now that one day I'd face a challenge that was beyond me, beyond the methodical problem-solving approach I'd relied upon throughout my career. Not because of arrogance or being high-minded, it was just that the approach seemed to work. But the mystery surrounding Rachel's disappearance was baffling. I was struggling for inspiration.

I knew that I'd have to move up a gear and think on a different level. The old familiar voice of negativity that was always ready and waiting to take centre stage, wasn't helping. 'Davo, you're not good enough, what if you've missed something, what if you never find Rachel, what if you're being conned by Mark, you're the SIO do something for fuck's sake'. The Davo of old would've shaken his head in disbelief at the person I'd become. He'd have been inspired by the challenge of a complex investigation and creativity would have followed. He wouldn't have been in a state of constant high alert over whether the personal agendas of others might bite him in the arse again. No, he'd be bold and wide in his thinking. He'd do what he thought was right, regardless of the consequences.

I pulled into the Force Training Centre car park. The adrenalin was flowing again and I was pumped up ready for action. Time to think wider. Time to be bolder. I began the briefing with a real sense of purpose.

"Morning everyone and welcome to the new members of the team. On the way into work, I had the unsettling feeling that the challenge of solving the mystery surrounding Rachel's disappearance might well be beyond me. This is unfamiliar ground for me and I'm pretty sure it'll be the same for you."

I could see Maly, Alan and Trev exchanging worried glances. They must be wondering what on earth I was doing or going to say next. Admitting that the challenge may well be beyond me was hardly the right way to build confidence, and I could almost hear Maly say 'what's he bloody playing at'. It certainly got people's attention.

"My gut feeling is that although we're only a few days into the investigation, we must assume that Rachel's dead. Time to plan for a trial at Crown Court and any subsequent appeal. We must, of course, find whoever is responsible for the death of Rachel but in many ways that will be the easy part. By far the bigger challenge will be to make sure they're convicted and that means convincing a jury beyond reasonable doubt of their guilt. Does everybody understand what I'm asking of you all?"

Shaun was the first to speak.

"Boss, it's about meticulous attention to detail in everything we do. Doing everything by the book, no corners cut. Making sure that the defence can't find fault with the investigation because that could cause a jury to have reasonable doubt."

"That's exactly it, Shaun. Exactly."

I wanted him to give an example to illustrate his point. I knew he'd be embarrassed and so I gave one on his behalf. I used the Natalie Clubb case and Shaun's interview plan that ran to over one hundred and twenty pages. It was so impressive that the defence didn't bother to cross-examine him at the trial. Shaun looked uncomfortable. I'd apologise to him later. I knew he wouldn't want me to tell everyone just how good he is but I couldn't think of a better example to give. On the plus side, everyone on the inquiry would be able to use Shaun as a kind of standard to aspire to and someone they could go to for advice. My plan was for Shaun's influence to spread throughout the team, for him to keep a watchful eye over the day-to-day conduct of less experienced detectives. He'd done the same thing on the Clubb case and it'd worked brilliantly.

"I said at the beginning that the case might well be beyond me only because I've not dealt with a set of circumstances remotely similar to these. Self-doubt comes with the job from time to time. If any of you become SIOs in the future, you'll know what I mean. We'll solve this case though, no matter how long it takes. But I've a feeling that we're going to have to make our own luck by thinking differently, more creatively, like your own life depended upon it. I want you to imagine two outcomes. One where we're all quietly celebrating the conviction of those responsible for Rachel's death. The other where we've failed to capture her killer or killers or failed to secure a conviction at Crown Court. I couldn't live with the second one. All I'm asking is for each and every one of you to go beyond what can be reasonably expected of you. Raise the bar for Rachel. Be bolder, think clearer and wider than you've ever done before."

I concluded the briefing with probably the most important message of all - the need to act at all times with a moral code of conduct, one that the public had every right to expect from us. Shaun had been spot-on to describe it as 'do everything by the book, no corners cut'. Amidst all of the shit

I'd endured over the last few years, apart from my family, it was all that I had left. It'd served me well throughout my life and it was something that I'd inherited from my late father.

As a kid, I couldn't escape his humble, unassuming influence. It was everywhere, from his total lack of vanity, to the absence of any self-interest in material possessions. All he needed to be happy was his family, a rolled-up cigarette and the Times newspaper each day. I imagined him sat in the briefing room and I wondered if he'd recognise the values he'd drummed into me. I'll never forget his parting words as I headed off to University full of 'I'm going to change the world', arrogance of youth. We were sat in our local pub the night before I was due to leave.

"Paul, I know you lack confidence. But all you need to do to be happy is to live a simple, honest life using the values I've taught you as a guide. Then, at the end of each day, as your head hits the pillow, you'll be able to sleep soundly safe in the knowledge that you've been kind, truthful and a credit to yourself. Nothing else matters. That's all you can do."

I've never forgotten those words and I'd lost count of the times when I thought about what he'd meant. He'd been right time and again.

Back in my office, I called a meeting with Maly, Alan, Shaun and Trev. I apologised to Shaun. He just smiled and went slightly red in the face. With a mischievous grin, Maly was the first to speak.

"Quite a speech in there. I'm having the soapbox dismantled as we speak."

"Well, I agree with what you said, boss. It's about time somebody tried to raise the doom and gloom around here.

Bloody LPTs have killed the force and I'm sick of it being OK to be mediocre. I'll make damned sure that my staff live up to your expectations."

It was a welcome show of support from Trev. Whatever I said in the briefing created a positive atmosphere. I could tell by the renewed enthusiasm for what they had planned for the day ahead. I might well have about a million flaws and if you asked those who'd worked with me before, they'd no doubt be able to name them, but they'd also have to admit that I could inspire people to raise their game. I'd been told before by detectives I trusted, including Shaun. Inspiring people to think differently though was one thing, but it couldn't hide the fact that all we had was Rachel captured on Jacksons' CCTV, just after two in the morning on New Year's Day, nothing else to show for nine long days of determined effort by everyone on the inquiry.

But as we prepared ourselves for another long day, there was a knock at the door. It was the Underwater Search Team Sergeant, Dave Scott, who was at the briefing earlier.

"Sorry to interrupt, boss. My lads have found some of Rachel's belongings in Barmston Drain, just near to Hall Road Bridge. There's her passport so there's no doubt I'm afraid."

Sergeant Scott delivered the news with his usual deadpan expression. It was one of those – fucking hell, a breakthrough at long last – moments, and we could be forgiven for almost leaping up and down with excitement, even though it surely confirmed that Rachel was dead. A sad, melancholy feeling replaced the brief moment of elation I'd experienced only a second ago.

I followed Sergeant Scott out of the car park and left onto Hall Road. The snow had started to melt to reveal the true greyness and gloom of the concrete estate. The morning sunshine was trying its best to brighten the maze of forgotten streets and alleyways, but it would take about a thousand suns to make any difference. There was a young female pushing an expensive-looking pram along the slush-covered pavements, partnered by a pale, gaunt-faced hooded youth. There was a little kid with them, who was maybe three or four. For no reason, the female started to batter the poor boy and he started crying. I slammed the car to a halt, lowered my window and shouted for them to stop.

"Fuck off. Mind your own fucking business. Grey-haired twat."

My instinct was to get out of the car and lock them both up for assault on the kid but I'd more pressing matters to attend to.

"I'll be round to see you both later."

"Fuck off. Bastard."

I stopped after about a mile, close to Hall Road Bridge. A sizeable part of the drain embankment was already cordoned off with police tape, and a young constable stood to attention at the entrance ready to note down our names. A crowd had gathered on the bridge and were amusing themselves by throwing whatever they could lay their hands on into the drain, including shopping trolleys from the local supermarket, which was located only a few hundred yards away. Maly arrived and ordered the removal of the crowd. We put on SOCO protective suits and rubber gloves, and carefully made our way over the stepping plates to where Sergeant Scott was stood. There were some items laid out neatly on a piece of black plastic sheeting on the drain bank.

"These were found inside that black nylon handbag. The handbag was inside that torn black refuse bag."

I carefully picked up the passport. Inside was the name Rachel Louise Moran, number 5092290. The photograph of a younger Rachel stared back at me. I inspected the rest of the belongings discovered in the handbag, and all I could think of was the likely impact on Rachel's family. They'd have to identify the items to confirm that they belonged to Rachel. It'd probably be Wanda who volunteered, and I wondered how she'd cope when confronted with her daughter's green Nokia mobile phone, broken sunglasses, thong bearing little red love hearts, Nicotinel tablets and various items of make-up.

"And these are the things we found inside the bin bag with the handbag."

He pointed to a second sheet of items that included a padded bra, white Nike trainer, right shoe size 7, that was undone and impregnated with mud, and a green kitchen scouring pad with red staining that looked like blood. Sergeant Scott stood patiently as we studied Rachel's belongings.

"How on earth did they find this stuff? Dave and his team have done a bloody fantastic job to find that bin bag amongst the rest."

Maly was right to be amazed. The drain was deep and wide, and it was obvious that the local residents used it as a kind of universal tip for bin bags full of rubbish, old bikes, carpets, microwaves and fridges. Visibility was almost nonexistent. One of the divers came up for air and stepped onto the drain bank, exhausted. He took his breathing apparatus off and said hello as he gasped for breath. It was PC Dave Robinson, one of our most experienced divers. Sergeant Scott made sure he was OK after his spell in the filthy, murky water. I spoke to them both at the same time. They could clearly sense our excitement and looked embarrassed because they knew what was coming, a big thank you from senior officers. I knew that they wouldn't be used to it but it had to be done. Their collective achievement was what I was looking for, to go way beyond what could be reasonably expected of them. Visibility was down to about an inch, the water must be freezing, and God knows what lurked beneath the surface that could easily cause injury. They'd been doing this every day though since Rachel went missing. Outstanding, bloody outstanding. I'd witnessed some inspired pieces of police work in my time but this was right up there with the very best.

"This is the first break we've had apart from the CCTV at Jacksons. I can't tell you what this means to the investigation. Brilliant piece of work."

"Still a long way to go, boss. We've done about a mile and we intend to carry on until we reach the River Hull. I assume we're looking for a body now?"

Sergeant Scott's response was exactly what I'd expected, respectful, but keen to avoid dealing with praise for just doing his job. I'd dealt with the Underwater Search Team many times before, particularly on the search for Natalie Clubb's dismembered body, and they were all professional and dedicated individuals. Their reward was simply the satisfaction of knowing that they'd done what was asked of them to the best of their ability. You could look forever, and you wouldn't find an ego to speak of, in any of the team. It was almost as if they'd no time for such nonsense. Being around them was refreshing, and I wondered if I'd done the right thing by constantly seeking promotion. Looking back, the happiest and most stress-free period of my career was as a humble detective. No politically correct officers to supervise, no boring meetings and no rubbing shoulders with chief officers, just you and your partner trying to put the local burglars away.

"Boss, are we looking for a body now?"

"Sorry, Dave. Miles away. Your guess is as good as mine. Can't rule out the possibility Rachel's been killed and her body weighed down with something heavy."

"I'm no expert, boss, but it could take days for a body weighed down to surface. I'll get hold of the Environmental Agency and get them to lower the water level in the drain. Shouldn't be a problem. I'll make sure we search upstream again though after what we've found today."

I wanted to thank him for just being someone that I knew I'd remember in years to come as one of the good guys, but I'm not sure he'd have understood. I'd countless questions, but no answers. Where had Rachel's handbag and passport been dumped in the drain and why? Where was Rachel? Would she surface in the days to come? Would the mobile phone be of any help? I told myself to calm down, take a deep breath and think logically. I'd designate this area of Barmston Drain as Scene 1, hold a briefing with the press once Rachel's belongings had been positively identified, have her phone examined by experts, and conduct house to house enquires around relevant parts of the drain. The problem was that Barmston Drain ran for mile after mile, and there were numerous places upstream where Rachel's belongings could have been dumped. Would an appeal for witnesses help?

It was a question I asked Maly as we both stood on the drain bank shivering in the biting January wind. We must have looked like a TV detective cliché, with Maly in a long grey tweed overcoat and me in a long black leather coat that was two sizes too big for me. But at least it kept me warm and the way I looked was the least of my problems.

"Not sure. Chucking rubbish into the drain will be a pretty familiar sight around here, particularly black bin bags."

I could see his point as we stood and looked at the sea of floating bags. Appealing for witnesses would be almost pointless, but I knew that it had to be done. If Rachel was in the drain, some kind of vehicle must have been used. I thought back to the murder of Natalie Clubb. She was dismembered prior to being thrown into a drain in plastic refuse bags. Instead of expecting to find a body weighed down, should we be looking for bags filled with body parts, I wondered. Is that why we'd not found her? I didn't want to consider the possibility, the sight of poor Natalie's rotting torso at her post-mortem was one of the most horrifying things I've ever seen, never to be forgotten. Recovering every bag from the entire length of Barmston Drain, though, would be virtually impossible. I tried to work out how it could be done because there was no way I'd give up without a fight. Anything was achievable and that was part of the reason I enjoyed being a SIO, it gave me the rank and the power to do whatever was necessary to solve a case. I knew it was an assumption that Rachel was killed and dumped in the drain, but until I could prove otherwise, it had to be one of the main lines of inquiry.

DS Tony Dickinson, the SOCO supervisor, was busy videoing the scene and taking numerous photographs of the items found, including Rachel's passport. I liked Tony, most people did. He was one of a number of drugs squad officers, who'd been suspended for three years following a malicious and false allegation of corruption made by an informant. He'd returned to work as if nothing had happened, no bitterness towards the organisation, no wrestling with being wronged. Maybe it was because he wasn't alone in being accused, or maybe it was because he had an inner strength and was tougher than me. Either way, Tony always seemed to be smiling and it was good to see him. He was also extremely competent at his job.

On one occasion, I'd been called out to a suspected stabbing. A man had appeared on the doorstep of a house on Sutton Road in Hull, bleeding from what looked like a knife wound. He'd died within minutes and everything pointed to foul play. When I arrived in the early hours of the morning, Tony had already solved the mystery. He showed me a trail of blood that led from a greenhouse situated in the back garden belonging to the witness who'd called the police. Tony was able to convince me that the male in question had gone into the back garden for a piss on his way home from the pub, and as he'd stood with his hand against the side of the greenhouse to steady himself, a glass panel had given way and a shard of glass pierced his heart. The dead male's fingerprint in blood was found on the shard of glass, confirming that it'd been a tragic accident.

By now, the press had arrived and a crowd had gathered on the bridge again overlooking the drain. I decided to speak to the reporters otherwise there'd be no way they'd leave. I told them that we'd found some items that may be relevant to the case, and a press statement would follow in due course. But they weren't satisfied with such a bland comment, and I was duly bombarded with question after question. I always cooperated with the press because it'd have been foolish not to. It was publicity for free, usually at peak viewing times. Normally, it'd be a struggle to keep the local reporters interested. It was as if the editors placed a moral judgment on the victim in order to determine whether or not the public wanted to hear or read about the latest murder. This case though, had already proved to be so very different, breathtaking in the way it'd captured the imagination of a watching world. Maybe it was because it was every parents' worst nightmare to wait helplessly for news of a missing son or daughter and the longer the wait, the stronger the impulse to gather your own children around you to keep them safe. I'd already started to call home more often than usual to check on my kids. And then I heard someone in the crowd shout,

"There's that grey-haired twat. Looks a right wanker to me. A fucking copper as well."

I looked up to the bridge and I could see the hooded youth I'd spoken to earlier. He was leaning over the wall, giving me a vigorous two-fingered salute.

"Maly, that low-life up there on the bridge, can you get a

uniform to get his name. He's beginning to annoy me."

"Will do. I expect you'll be paying him a call."

Driving back to the station, I felt a growing pressure inside to make a decision about whether to policy Mark as a suspect. His reaction when told of the discovery of Rachel's passport might help me decide, I thought, and so would the opinions of my team.

There was a buzz of excitement in the incident room. The inspirational find of Rachel's passport was like a jolt of electricity for everyone involved. Lisa had been inundated with calls from every conceivable form of media.

"Bloody exhausted if I'm honest. I won't forget this inquiry in a hurry. I've a sneaking feeling that you're not going to tell the press everything. Am I right?"

Lisa grinned because she'd worked with me before many times and knew that I never revealed everything to the press. I always withheld some details that only the killer or killers would know.

"I was thinking of keeping back the discovery of the right trainer."

"Sounds OK to me. Worked before on Clubb. Alright to let them know about her passport?"

"Absolutely. They'll recognise the significance and at least it'll keep them interested for longer than usual."

Everyone was assembled for a briefing. It was late, maybe eight, but nobody showed any interest in wanting to go home. The FLOs were back from showing photographs of the items recovered to Wanda, and she'd made a positive ID on them all. There was silence in the room as the FLOs recalled how she'd struggled to keep her inner dignity and strength. Wanda had opened the front door to them as she'd done so many times in the last few days. They'd regular times for visiting, usually after the morning briefing and before they went off duty. An unplanned visit would have unnerved her, and I couldn't begin to imagine what it was like for the family to know that bad news could come at any moment. Wanda hadn't wanted to look at the photographs, and Ray stayed in a separate room during the FLOs visit. She'd asked the officers what they thought about the discovery of Rachel's belongings in the drain. They told her that we were still keeping an open mind and that there was still hope. Despite seeing a photograph of Rachel's passport, Wanda still tried to find a reasonable explanation for its presence in the drain: had she walked down Hall Road intending to go to see Mark on Bransholme, and maybe stopped on the bridge to look at the water, accidentally dropping her handbag over the side. The FLOs just listened as she came up with theory after theory, anything to keep hope alive.

DS Austin's late entrance came as I thanked the FLOs for a job well done. He'd been to see Mark at his flat across the road to break the news about finding Rachel's passport and other belongings. Mark's mother had opened the door. She seemed flustered and nervous. DS Austin couldn't hide his frustration as he recalled how Mark came from the bathroom and sat down without looking at him. There was an uncomfortable silence as he gazed down at the floor. The officer let the silence continue fully expecting Mark to ask him why he'd come, but he didn't ask any questions. No questions about how the search for Rachel was progressing, no questions about whether we thought Rachel was still alive, nothing. Eventually, DS Austin told him that we'd found Rachel's passport and mobile phone in her handbag in Barmston Drain. He replied, 'where's that'? That's all he asked. Nothing else. His mother asked him if he was OK and he replied, 'I'm sick of this, I must know every copper now'. Staggered by Mark's strange behaviour, DS Austin allowed the tension in the room to build as he waited for him to show some interest, to say something, but the awkward silence continued for what seemed like forever. When Mark eventually spoke, it was only to announce that he had to get across to Welshpool Close on Bransholme to meet up with Danny Rogers. They were due to get a taxi to the Railway Inn in Patrington, where Rogers was due to perform. DS Austin wisely gave Mark no choice but to accept his offer of a lift. On the journey, Mark only spoke once to say, 'she hasn't run away, she wouldn't leave her kittens'.

"I've never met anybody like him before. In the car, it was as if he was just going out as normal. Didn't seem on edge, just keen to get to the gig in Patrington. I can't get my head round why he doesn't appear to be that bothered. He'd just been told about us finding Rachel's stuff in the drain and if it'd been me, I'd have been bloody devastated at the news."

DS Austin pretty much summed up the feeling of everyone in the room. DC Spain would be at the pub and I'd already asked him to call me later to report on Mark's behaviour. Although it was getting late, I wanted to concentrate on Mark and the likelihood of him being responsible for Rachel's murder. I'd already ruled out Rachel's close family and friends. They'd all been seen and eliminated from suspicion. That left Mark or a stranger. What else did we know about Mark? Had he stayed at Dale Bottomley's party until six in the morning? Does he have a violent nature? Who are his friends and associates?

Since I'd been out all day at Barmston Drain, I knew there'd be information in the incident room that I wouldn't be aware of. Major inquiries were like that and this one was no different. The response from the public was overwhelming. Countless alleged sightings of Rachel on Bransholme and just about everywhere else in the country. Anonymous letters from people claiming to know 'who done it', pointing the finger of suspicion mainly at Mark. And, a clairvoyant's vision of Rachel's dead body located in a house in Bradford. I needed more staff. The inquiry was creaking under the strain of following up every potential lead with hundreds of statements taken already and hundreds more yet to be taken. Decision made, I'd policy the inquiry as a Category B murder investigation, and the force would have no option but to give me more outside and inside staff.

I glanced at Trev and Shaun and I was about as grateful as I could be in that moment for their presence. Between them, they knew everything. Trev, because he was just Trev, you could ask him anything about the inquiry and he'd know without having to look at his computer screen for the answer. And Shaun, because he'd the ability to soak up information and store it in his memory like a giant database. I'd already told him he'd be interviewing whoever was responsible for killing Rachel and I knew he'd read every piece of paper generated by HOLMES, accordingly. Shaun was the first to say something of any significance.

"Boss, I've had it on good authority from a reliable source

that Mark knows Ian Armstrong and we both know what Armstrong's capable of from the Clubb case."

I'd arrested Armstrong in connection with the Natalie Clubb investigation. Unfortunately, there wasn't enough evidence to charge him with assisting the killer to dispose of her body, but I was sure that he'd been involved to some degree. Could it be that Mark killed Rachel and asked Armstrong for help to get rid of her body by dumping it in Barmston Drain? Armstrong would know that Natalie's killer had made a serious mistake in assuming that plastic bags containing her body parts wouldn't be found once they were dumped in a local drain on Bransholme. Would he have learned from that mistake and advised Mark to weigh down her body thinking that it'd never surface? Did they do it together? Armstrong would definitely have access to a car and he'd certainly have the nerve. He was a drug-dealing low-life criminal of the worst kind, and if it was true about Mark's association with him, then it suggested that Mark had an entirely different side to him we hadn't seen.

DS Austin gave an update on a witness he saw earlier called Adam Slater, who reinforced that view.

"I saw Adam Slater today. He was assaulted by Mark when they were both on a course run by Johnny Park at the Hull KR rugby club designed to give confidence to club singers. On one occasion, Slater was on stage doing a routine when, without warning, Mark leapt on the stage and punched him so hard it split his tongue down the middle. Mark then punched him and punched him. Completely out of control according to Slater. Slater couldn't fight back because he's got a paralysed arm. Mark received a caution for the attack, which Slater described as vicious and unprovoked."

So, in just a few minutes our perspective on Mark changed: an association with Armstrong, and a propensity for spontaneous violence, put him into an entirely different category. If Mark was responsible, the question was when did it happen? Although the officers sent down to Portsmouth to see Dale Bottomley again hadn't returned, they'd called Alan with an update - Bottomley couldn't be certain that Mark left the party at six in the morning, it could've been earlier, maybe closer to four. That made more sense because we couldn't understand why Mark apparently stayed at the party after everyone had left. Mark didn't know Bottomley and his big mate Appleby had already gone.

"Shaun, can you take somebody with you and pay our good friend Armstrong a visit. He won't be expecting us at this time of night. You know what you're looking for."

Shaun knew Armstrong from the Clubb investigation and I couldn't think of a better person to send. By now, it was around ten. I closed the briefing and thanked everyone for staying late. It felt like we'd made some progress at last.

Back in my office with Maly, Alan and Trev, we spent the next hour or so reviewing the strength of the case against Mark. All we had at the moment was a purely circumstantial case against Mark based on a few key factors: Rachel had been really angry and there was every likelihood that she was determined to see Mark; Mark probably had the opportunity after he left the party and might have got help from Armstrong to dump her body in the drain; all friends and family have been eliminated; Mark has a violent nature; and he was strangely unemotional when told of the discovery of

Rachel's passport. We all agreed though that it was too early to go for Mark. The idea that Rachel had been abducted and was still alive had long since passed and so I'd nothing to lose by making Mark officially a suspect. It'd give me more time. We'd be able to put him under surveillance to monitor his movements, continue the search for Rachel, and hope that we got another break like today's discovery at Barmston Drain.

I made the entry in my policy book: 'To nominate Mark Sheppard as suspect 1 for the murder of Rachel Moran'. I hoped that I wouldn't live to regret my decision in the months to come. I'd no idea where the investigation was heading and whether or not I'd have to policy other suspects. The more suspects, the more it'd undermine any future prosecution case at Crown Court. A call from DC Spain silenced the familiar voice of negativity trying to cast doubt in my mind.

"Boss, just calling to give you an update from the Railway Inn in Patrington. Mark was sat with a male, probably Danny Rogers. They were close to the stage. Mark was wearing a very large cream puffa jacket, Manchester United top, dark jeans and trainers with a white stripe. Mark was laughing and joking as if he hadn't a care in the world. He didn't make any phone calls. Rogers did his singing act, if you could call it that. Mark just watched him. They both left in a red Laguna taxi. The driver was in his forties, wearing glasses and a body warmer. He got dropped off at his flat on Saxcourt."

I tried to picture Mark sat in some pub in a village, miles from anywhere way out to the East of Hull, dressed in a bloody great puffa jacket listening to his mate murdering some perfectly decent songs. Given the circumstances, 'laughing and joking', just didn't seem right to me. If he was responsible, I thought, then wouldn't he try to make it look like he was heartbroken? And if he wasn't, why was he out enjoying himself whilst poor Rachel, the so-called love of his life, was out there somewhere, still missing. If she'd left him and he had no feelings for her, I could understand, but he'd only just been told that her passport had been recovered from a drain not a mile away from where they lived. Wouldn't he have wanted to at least go down to the drain to see for himself? Either way, it was time for home.

FIVE

'There was a darkness that
shouldn't have been there

I got up early the next morning around five. I couldn't sleep. How could I after yesterday's major break-through? I'd lain awake most of the night planning for the day ahead. The strain of the investigation was beginning to take its toll with no likelihood of a day off in the near future, but all I had to do was think about Wanda and Ray to be cured of any kind of self-interest or pity.

On the journey into work, I recalled yesterday's briefing when I'd spoken, with a fair degree of passion, about the need for us all to raise the bar for Rachel. It got me thinking about one of my favorite quotes: 'Do one thing, and aim to be the best in the world at it'. The clue was in the words 'aim to be'. Nothing was going to stop me from aiming to be the very best SIO that I could be, and the minute I arrived in my tiny office, I wrote the words 'THINK WIDER. THINK BOLDER', on my white board in bloody great letters for all to see. Whatever the outcome of this case, it wouldn't be determined by a lack of positive thinking and bold actions on my part. As I stood back contemplating what those words meant for the day, I turned to see my old friend, DI Tony Burke, stood in the doorway.

"Now then, Davo. Living in a cupboard these days. Are

chief officers trying to tell you something?"

It was good to hear his thick scouse accent again. Tony had been my very capable deputy on the murder of Natalie Clubb, and he'd since managed to get himself back into the surveillance squad after a brief spell of 'career development' in uniform.

"It's good to see you, my friend. I see you're back doing what you do best and you've escaped LPTs."

It really was good to see him though because we'd come through some difficult times together, when he'd proved himself to be trustworthy and a diamond of a human being. Tony was also bloody excellent at surveillance, and I couldn't think of anyone else I'd rather have following Mark than my trusted colleague. It was a surprisingly positive start to the day, to see him again and be reminded of the life I used to know before I was promoted to Superintendent.

There were some new faces at the briefing - two more DSs and six more DCs. Would it be enough, I wondered, as I looked at the new arrivals? I knew some of them, including DC Stan Tate, who was about as hard as they come. He was a good rugby player in his time, and his stockily built frame and broken nose, gave him a kind of 'don't fuck with me', air about him. He did, of course, have a heart of gold but not towards villains. I remember, as a young probationer, being in the charge room trying to cope with a violent muscle-bound prisoner I'd arrested for attempting to kill a policeman. DC Tate was in the Drugs Squad at the time and happened to be in the charge room dealing with a case of his own. Unfortunately, the villain said the wrong thing to DC Tate along the lines of 'and you can go fuck yourself, twatface', before spitting at Stan and attempting to blind him by ramming his thumb in his eye. Within a split second, the detective delivered a knockout blow to the cocky prisoner in front of an audience that included the shift Inspector, who made a lightning exit out of the charge room as if it hadn't happened. Stan broke his watch as a result of rendering the prisoner unconscious. All he said was 'fucking bastard broke my watch', before leaving. I hadn't been in the job long and I looked for guidance from the charge room sergeant. It came in the form of 'well get him some smelling salts lad and clean up the blood and broken teeth. Quickly now'.

For the first time on the investigation, it felt like the assembled detectives were showing signs of bonding as a team - more smiles, more banter, more piss taking. Maybe it was a natural consequence of yesterday's events, or maybe there was a realisation that this was a unique opportunity for them to be part of such a complex inquiry. Whatever the reason, there was a collective feeling of optimism that we'd find Rachel's body in the drain, maybe today or within the next few days, and the surveillance on Mark might provide sufficient grounds to arrest him for her murder.

Back in my office, that was beginning to feel more like a second home, Maly summarised what was agreed at the briefing to make sure we'd not missed anything.

"Tony will do a good job following Mark. Pity Shaun couldn't track down Armstrong last night though. Everyone's got the message about the trainer and not telling anyone about it. Underwater search team are going further downstream and going back over what they've already done upstream. Press release has gone out. Mobile phone's on its way for analysis. Tony Dickinson's body recovery plan looks good. The planned reconstruction's arranged for Rachel's birthday. I've found a female police officer, who bears a striking resemblance to Rachel, to walk the route along Hall Road to Saxcourt. Over six-foot, slim, blonde hair. I've briefed DS Austin on his role with Mark. Think you've got all the right plates spinning. I can't think of anything else. I just need to set up the trace on Wanda's landline."

The FLOs had been withdrawn from supporting Mark now that he was officially a suspect. The plan was for DS Austin to befriend and support Mark no matter how long it might take, and if he was responsible or knew more than he'd told us already, then maybe he'd talk, eventually. I knew that I'd given Keith a difficult task. It was a technique Tony and me had used before to great effect on the Clubb case, but it'd taken months in some cases for my officers to gain the trust of witnesses, most of whom were drug-addicted prostitutes, pimps or drug dealers.

"Unless we find Rachel soon and make an arrest, we're going to get another SIO coming in to review the case. Do you think we'll be OK?"

"If you're asking me, have we done everything that could be reasonably expected and more, then I'd say so. You've had the Crime Faculty in to help. You've got Chuck Burton coming tomorrow, who's supposed to be the best when it comes to female abductions and murders. Let's see what he's got to say."

Maly was calm and measured in his analysis of the progress we'd made. He wasn't a big talker by any means but what he did say was always worth listening to. I was looking forward to meeting Chuck Burton. Even though he'd a well-earned reputation, I knew that I'd reserve judgement until I could make up my own mind.

Time to go and visit Ray and Wanda. My in tray full of statements to read would have to wait until later. I called first to make sure they were in. Wanda answered. I could hardly hear her voice, it was barely more than a whisper. Their house was only a mile or so away and so I decided to walk, a decision I regretted the minute I left the station, as the savage January wind almost froze my cheeks. It reminded me of when I used to live in Toronto, where the winter wind chill was cold like I'd never experienced cold before. But at least my leather coat gave me some protection as I headed along Hall Road. I had it in my mind that maybe walking the route Rachel would've taken might give me some inspiration, but all it did was make me dwell on the visit to Rachel's Mum and Dad. No matter how many times I'd done the same thing in the past, being a virtual stranger trying my best to communicate with a victim's family in the most unnatural and tragic circumstances imaginable, was the hardest part of my job as a SIO. They could never have believed in their wildest dreams that they'd be sharing a cup of tea with some tall, grey-haired, unfashionably dressed, nervous policeman, who'd come to discuss the disappearance of their youngest daughter. They'd no choice in the matter, they'd got me, and I had to balance my lack of self-belief, with a show of confidence to reassure them that I'd do everything possible to find Rachel. At least that's what I told myself as Wanda answered the door.

I went to the back door. I don't know why, it was just something that had stayed with me from being a kid brought up on a council estate. Nobody ever knocked on the front door of our house. It was as if the front door could only be used for special occasions, and of course, there weren't any to speak of. Wanda didn't seem surprised though as she welcomed me into their home. The back door opened into the kitchen that was long and narrow. The house was semi-detached and had a solid, respectable feel about it. A pleasant smell of fresh lavender hit me as I wiped my feet, took a deep breath and shook a pale and gaunt-looking Wanda by the hand. The moment I entered, I couldn't escape the familiar feeling of being an unwanted guest in their home, invading their privacy. How on earth could I even begin to understand how they were feeling?

Ray appeared quietly and shook my hand as Wanda made me a cup of tea. The days of grief and worry had clearly taken their toll. He looked older than when I saw him only a few days earlier at the press conference. We sat together in their living room at the back of the house. It was neat, tidy and comfortably furnished, with photographs of their children proudly mounted on the walls. There was a darkness that shouldn't have been there, given the bright winter sunshine that streamed through the patio doors.

Wanda talked without a pause. Maybe she couldn't bear any silence in their home, or maybe it helped in some small way to ease her pain. It was heartbreaking to listen to though, as she relived the moment a young man had walked past them as she'd pleaded with Rachel not to go.

"If only I'd driven her back, if only I'd walked back with

her, if only I'd persuaded her not to go, if only Mark had stayed in as he was supposed to do."

I just listened as Ray wandered in and out of the room. Eventually, he got straight to the point and asked what I thought about the discovery of Rachel's passport and mobile phone in the drain. I knew that what he was really asking was, did I believe that Rachel was still alive. I'd gone over in my mind countless times thinking what to say. Should I be brutally honest with him and tell him that I feared the worst, or should I be upbeat to keep hope alive? Ray sat quietly waiting for my answer, Wanda just kept on talking as if she didn't want to hear what my reply was going to be. I didn't know what to do. I'd never been in this position before. My instinct was to avoid answering Ray's question, it just didn't seem right, a stranger passing judgement on whether their youngest daughter was still alive. It should've been me asking the question, not Ray, for they would surely know better than I, if Rachel was still alive. After all, I was only the SIO, they were her parents.

I decided to talk about progress with the investigation instead. Ray listened, stiff with attention to what I was saying. His eyes were moist as they'd been the last time I saw him. I went through in some detail about all the practical stuff that was being done, apart from Mark being a suspect of course. I could see that the trace on their landline planned for Rachel's birthday, was something positive, something for them to cling onto. But the reconstruction was a different thing entirely. They didn't want anything to do with it, although they understood why it was being done. Maybe the mere thought of a reconstruction signaled the end of their belief that Rachel was alive and well, but I was only guessing and I didn't ask why.

Wanda continued to chat about Rachel as a child and how she'd grown into a wonderful young woman, who they looked forward to seeing every day. That was something I could understand, and for her to have been there one day and gone the next without any warning, made me think of my Dad and how he'd died suddenly of a heart attack. We'd argued the night before he passed away and I never had the chance to say that I was sorry. I should've told him that I loved him, but I never did. I should've told him just what a brilliant Dad he was, but I never did. It was something that haunted my every waking moment. But at least my Dad went before me and that's what he'd have wanted. Ray and Wanda were facing the likelihood that they'd have to bury their youngest daughter.

I left with a promise that they'd be kept up to date with progress, and I told them that they could ring me any time about anything. Walking back on my own was bloody awful. I thought about my kids to make me feel better. Sam, Jack and Cal, had all inherited my love of football. I watched them play every Sunday, work permitting, and sense of pride that I felt, was hard to describe. At least I had them to go home to, I thought, as I made myself promise to tell them all that I loved them when I got home.

Back at the station, Maly had some good news for me.

"The divers have done it again. They've found what looks like Rachel's diary, a black handled knife and the other trainer half-a-mile downstream from Milestone Bridge. I've been to the scene and its part of the drain they'd already searched.

Didn't want to bother you whilst you were with Rachel's Mum and Dad. The FLOs are on their way to show photos for ID."

"Fancy a drive to the scene?"

We stood on Milestone Bridge looking downstream. I could see Hall Road Bridge in the distance and the police divers carefully and methodically wading through all the garbage and slurry. The Environmental Agency had been true to their word and managed to reduce the water level in the drain. But their success in doing so only served to magnify the scale of the task ahead - so many more bags full of rubbish that were hidden beneath the surface of Barmston Drain. They'd all have to be recovered and searched. It'll take forever, I thought, as the traffic thundered past. It was one of the busiest roads out of Hull, and it didn't seem likely to me that Rachel's belongings had been thrown from the bridge, but anything was possible.

Barmston Drain was surrounded by a vast wilderness of open fields that over the years had turned an ugly shade of brown. It'd be hard to imagine a more depressing sight, with high-rise flats that should have been demolished years ago dominating the skyline, and a multitude of burnt out cars abandoned by local villains. It was as if the sun had failed to ever shine on this part of the world. The open fields provided easy access to the drain anywhere between the two bridges. The questions in my mind came thick and fast: if a car or van was used, why not take Rachel's belongings to the countryside and bury them or burn them? Why not dump them in the River Humber that flows into the North Sea? It didn't make any sense unless they'd no access to a vehicle.

But I was seeing things through my eyes and not those of a criminal. In my experience, most villains were fairly dim and did very little planning before committing a crime. There were, of course, exceptions. One criminal in particular sprang to mind, Neil Pattison, an articulate and intelligent drug dealer with an extraordinary propensity for inflicting gratuitous and unnecessary violence on anyone he didn't like. What set him apart from the usual Hull criminal, was his degree of preparation before carrying out his favourite crime, armed robbery, that made it difficult to catch him. The problem was that if Mark wasn't responsible, I'd no idea whether I was dealing with someone of Pattison's calibre, or some random stranger, who killed Rachel for no reason on impulse. Someone like Pattison would be several steps ahead and assume that the police would search the drain, discover Rachel's belongings thereby making it look like she was killed locally, whilst her body could be hundreds of miles away.

We couldn't hear each other trying to second-guess how Rachel's property had found its way into the drain, due to the noise from the passing traffic, and so we went back to the station for a coffee. Although the two discoveries in the drain were highly significant in terms of confirming what we already feared, without her body, all we had was Rachel on Jacksons' CCTV, and the image of a male passing that location just before. The male hadn't been identified, despite numerous press appeals.

"I've been to see Rachel's Mum and Dad, and Wanda talked in some detail again about how she tried to persuade Rachel not to go and how a young male had been passing at the time. She almost called after him to ask if he'd walk her back to Saxcourt. Where are we with CCTV after Jacksons?"

Maly told me that DC Bailey was doing a brilliant job wading through the mountain of CCTV tapes recovered. But it was proving to be a mammoth task and a difficult one, given that it was dark at the time, and much of the footage was of very poor quality. We all knew only too well the significance of knowing whether or not Rachel reached home. If she did, and Mark arrived home after the party, he had the opportunity to kill her, dump her body and belongings in the drain with the help of someone with a car, maybe Armstrong. If she didn't, had she been abducted and killed prior to reaching her flat by a stranger?

We spent the next couple of hours exploring every angle, every possible scenario. The feeling of frustration was growing by the second, and if I needed reminding that the eyes of the world were watching our every move, Lisa appeared at the door armed with all the latest press releases. She'd methodically and thoughtfully put together a portfolio of cuttings for me to read.

The nationals had smaller articles than the local Hull Daily Mail. With being so busy, I'd failed to realise just how much coverage the paper was giving to the story, particularly their crime reporter, Rick Lyon. There was page after page of headlines, with in-depth analysis of progress to date, including maps of areas searched, colour-coded to illustrate the scale of the operation and location of the first discovery. And photographs of the divers wading through bin bags, rusty bikes, discarded fridges and shopping trolleys. I'd never seen anything like it in all my time as a SIO. Whereas it'd been an uphill struggle to keep the press interested in the murder and dismemberment of poor Natalie Clubb, as I read some of the coverage by the HDM, there'd definitely be no such problem with this case.

'DIVERS HUNT INCH BY INCH – In the murky depths of Barmston Drain, police divers are searching for any clue which might explain what has happened to missing 21-year-old Rachel Moran'.

'If there's some visibility we look, but most of the time you can't see anything so I close my eyes. With nil visibility everything we do is by touch. During yesterday's search we formed a line across the width of the drain and did a line search. It's difficult work searching through the obstacles and debris. There's everything in there, including hypodermic needles, branches, fridges, trolleys and cars'. PC Ian Claxton

'Residents change their habits. The disappearance of Rachel Moran has changed the way people in Orchard Park live their day-to-day lives. Some parents are refusing to let their children walk home alone and women are more cautious about walking alone. They are also having to get used to living with the nation's media camped on their doorsteps as interest in the hunt for Rachel intensifies'.

'Mrs Moran has told the Mail she has been blocking thoughts that the worst could have happened and has been hoping Rachel is staying with unknown friends – scared to come home because of the attention her disappearance has attracted. And even after the discovery of Rachel's belongings, they are still keeping an open mind and clinging to the hope she may have discarded them herself for some reason'.

Reading Father Michael White's interview gave a different

perspective on how Rachel's family were coping.

'Priest tells of how parents refuse to give up hope for Rachel. Their faith keeps them strong. Their strength of character during their darkest hour has been praised by the parish priest who is helping to support them through their agonising wait for news about their missing daughter. They would come to Church every Sunday without fail – father, mother, Rachel and her brother John. That's how I became close to them. I prepared Rachel for her first communion and her confirmation. She was a beautiful child and she was quite coy and shy, which is an endearing quality in a child'.

It hadn't occurred to me that they'd such a strong Catholic faith. Although I'd no idea what it was like to believe in God because I didn't, I wondered if it would've been of any comfort to me at times when I'd felt lost and desperate. I remember as a kid reciting the Lord's Prayer each night knelt down by my bedside. It was something that my parents encouraged me to do. I believed back then that if I forgot for some reason, then something bad would happen to me. Gradually, as I grew older and stopped the nightly ritual, I realised that it made no difference. But I understood why people wanted to believe that there was a higher purpose beyond this life that could make sense of Rachel's disappearance. Non-believers would be quick to point out that if God did exist, then why had he allowed it to happen, but I knew it wasn't as simple as that.

Lisa interrupted my train of thought with a smile, a nervous kind of smile, as if she was about to tell me something I wouldn't want to hear.

"I think you'd better get ready for the next headline.

Front page today. Hull Daily Mail."

A huge picture of Mark sat with his head in his hands looking lost and bewildered, filled most of the front page.

'Boyfriend finds investigation into missing Rachel hard to cope with. With his voice barely a whisper he said, 'the pressure has been terrible...pressure from the police and press. It's difficult with the police finding things all the time. They've even questioned me about it but they've no reason to suspect me. I've been unable to eat or sleep properly since Rachel disappeared'.

"How's Rick Lyon got Mark to open up to him?"

"You know Rick, he can be very persuasive. This is a massive story for them."

The article did nothing to make any of us believe that Mark shouldn't be our number one suspect. What did he mean by saying that, 'it's difficult with the police finding things all the time'? Why did he say that he was unable to eat or sleep, when he'd spent most of his evenings since Rachel's disappearance enjoying himself at some karaoke club in Patrington? If anything, it made us even more suspicious. I just hoped that Tony's surveillance of Mark would provide some answers.

It had happened again, the day had gone by in a flash. I looked out of the window at the familiar sight of the media circus camped outside. It was snowing, which meant another tortuous journey home later. As I watched the snowflakes falling, Chief Superintendent Steel appeared unexpectedly at the door asking for me to bring him up to speed with the investigation. He was my boss and he'd never done anything to undermine me as far as I could tell, but whenever I saw him it always reminded me of the time when my world had come crashing down with a vengeance. The DCC had just told me that I was going to be investigated by an outside force, and removed from my job whilst it was being conducted. In the corridor outside his office, I'd crumpled in a heap, sobbing like a child. Mr Steel happened to be walking past and asked me if I was OK. Although he showed some sympathy and promised to keep in touch, he never did. And neither did any of my colleagues. Despite being a senior officer, I was treated like an outcast, with nowhere to sit, no office to work from, other than the station canteen. Eventually, though, after weeks of aimlessly wandering the corridors of HQ, I got a call from Inspector Merv Bishop, who used to be one of my sergeants. I'll never forget what he said,

"Now then, my old friend, I understand you're in a spot of trouble. You're more than welcome to share my office."

At one of the lowest points of my life and career, it was exactly what I'd needed to hear. I'm not sure that he understood the significance of his call. It was as if I'd been shivering in the freezing cold and he'd provided a warm blanket for comfort. His act of kindness, and continued support during the long months of the investigation, proved to be the perfect remedy to numb the pain caused by the cruel world of police discipline.

I wondered what Mr Steel was really thinking as we sat chatting together in my tiny office. Was he struggling to cope with being in charge of Hull, with crime levels at an all-time high? Had he come just because he thought he should, or was he genuinely interested? After all, Rachel was missing in his Division and he was accountable to his boss the ACC, who reported ultimately to the Chief. Accordingly, they all had a vested interest in the outcome of my investigation. The last thing the force needed was for such a high-profile enquiry to go wrong. I knew that the reputation of the force was at stake, given its relatively poor performance compared to other similar forces. Mr Steel was a man of integrity and seemed to work all hours in an effort to cut crime in the city, but the structure of LPTs was the problem. It was like trying to run a marathon on one leg – you might finish the course but you'd come last, and everyone would be wondering why you'd handicapped yourself in the first place.

After he'd gone, I almost felt sorry for him because he was chasing shadows in his quest to keep a lid on crime. I, on the other hand, knew exactly what I had to do: find Rachel, catch her killer or killers and secure a watertight conviction. Easier said than done, I thought, as I'd no idea what had happened to Rachel. Chuck Burton would be here in the morning, and I was banking on him being able to offer a fresh perspective based on his many years of experience.

I called Tony for an update on Mark's movements. He'd done nothing out of the ordinary, nothing, just shopping and staying in during the day on his own with the curtains closed. In the evenings, however, he still frequented his favourite karaoke club in Patrington.

"Boss, its early days my friend. It'll come if it's him. He'll make contact with Armstrong if they're in it together. And he's bound to tell somebody if he really has killed her. Human nature as you once told me."

Tony was right. If Mark was responsible, then it'd be

unlikely that he'd be able to keep it to himself. DS Austin's mission was to get close to Mark, to spend as much time as possible with him in the hope that he'd give himself away. Gone ten already. Home time.

SIX

'I'd trust your judgement and your instinct, that's all you can do. Good luck'

On the way into work, I got a call from Shaun, "Boss, I managed to get hold of Armstrong last night. He just bloody well grinned at me and told me to fuck off. Problem is he's got a cast iron alibi for the time Rachel disappeared. He was in prison. I've checked and he's not lying. He wouldn't say whether or not he knows Mark."

It was disappointing news. In my mind, I pictured Armstrong helping Mark. I knew that it was possible but not now. Could someone else have assisted him instead? Of course they could, I thought, but who?

"Look, what's your gut feeling, Mark or a stranger?"

"Boss, I really don't know. Everything points to Rachel being in the drain. I wouldn't be surprised if it was Mark and I wouldn't be surprised if it was a stranger. We need to be able to track her movements after Jacksons with CCTV. The witnesses aren't of much help apart from the taxi driver Penna. At the briefing, there'll be a load of stuff about Rachel. Trev knows more than I do but it looks like she's been pregnant twice. One ended with a termination. Not sure about the other one. Oh, and she has two credit cards both up to the limit. She had to take out a loan to repay them."

In every case, it always took time and a great deal of effort to form a true picture of the victim. They liked to call it victimology. I looked up the definition once and it came back as: 'the study of the ways in which the behaviour of crime victims may have led to or contributed to their victimisation'. From what I knew about Rachel and her family though, it didn't seem likely that Rachel would have contributed to her own downfall. Every aspect of Rachel's life would soon be revealed, either by my investigation or the media. It had to be done. But it's the last thing that Wanda and Ray would want, their precious daughter's life pored over by detectives, reporters and an unforgiving public. Any mention of a terminated pregnancy would, more than likely, tarnish the image of Rachel, young, slender, beautiful and in a stable relationship with Mark.

Thinking about Armstrong though reminded me of the Clubb case, and how the offer of immunity from prosecution for anyone with information about the killer or killers, had worked. It had to be worth a try. Bob Marshall, the head of the CPS, had agreed to the policy and so I called him. I told him that I would be sorry to see him go as he was leaving soon on promotion. After a brief conversation, he agreed with my request to offer immunity, and even agreed to go as far as extend the immunity to anyone who may have assisted the killer or killers. I'd get Lisa to put out a carefully worded press release later, one that wouldn't cause Wanda and Ray further distress.

I slowed down as I approached Milestone Bridge. I wondered, just as I did every morning, whether today would be the day when Rachel's body would be recovered from the drain. The voice of negativity reminded me again that I might never find her. All it did was to heighten my anxiety that something bad was going to happen. This constant battle to banish negative, energy-sapping thoughts was driving me bloody crazy. The answer was out there somewhere. There had to be a logical explanation, I told myself, as I caught sight of an unfamiliar figure getting out of his car in the station car park. It must be Chuck Burton. The permanently resident reporters showed some mild interest in his arrival.

"Is it Chuck Burton by any chance? I'm Detective Super-intendent Paul Davison."

He approached me in a no-nonsense, ready to do business, kind of way that was reassuring. I liked him already. Solidly built, with hair as grey as mine and a friendly smile, he replied,

"Yes, it is. Good to meet you, Sir. Sorry I'm early. Stayed here overnight. Wanted to walk the route Rachel would've taken."

We sat and chatted for a while in my office and he seemed to be impressed with all the stuff scribbled on the white boards covering the walls. He asked what, 'Think wider. Think bolder' meant. I wanted to tell him that it was my way of my way of staying focused, my way of challenging myself to be a better SIO. I didn't, because I wanted today to be about how he could help us find Rachel and not about my own fucked-up emotional problems.

Maly joined us and provided details about some new information received from witnesses, who'd come forward following the discovery of Rachel's belongings in the drain.

"We've got some tyre tracks leading from Thorpe Park Drive towards the drain bank. Need to be checked out but they could support the theory that a vehicle was used to dump her belongings and maybe her body in the drain. And a male was heard shouting, a woman screaming, and then the sound of a gunshot between 0230 and 0300hrs on New Year's Day, in the area near to where Rachel's passport was found."

Chuck sat and listened before offering his initial thoughts on the case.

"Finding Rachel's personal belongings in the drain suggests to me that the killer's thinking about his own protection and water is a very easy way to conceal and destroy evidence. Whoever's responsible will most likely to do the same with Rachel's body. This means that all the water within the immediate area will need searching. I say this because of the local knowledge factor, which I believe is very strong in this case."

Chuck spoke with a voice that was reassuringly confident and precise. The manner in which he was able to articulate what he wanted to say with a high degree of competence, made you want to listen. Even though I'd only just met him, I had the feeling that he was one of those rare individuals, who might just turn out to be as impressive as I hoped he'd be. His rugged, weather-beaten exterior, was probably a culmination of spending most of his career as a Detective Inspector, working at the coalface on numerous murder cases.

At the briefing, I read out Chuck's impressive CV to his obvious embarrassment. But I wanted the team to know that he'd come to offer his undoubted expertise in the abduction and murder of children and young persons, particularly females. And I wanted them to know that he was a behavioural profiler and that he'd be able to help us to determine the probable characteristics of Rachel's killer or killers, using the C.A.T.C.H.E.M database. Chuck explained what that actually meant in practical terms.

"It uses previous cases to provide the first meaningful approach to artificial intelligence. It's the distillation of facts from a comprehensive study of a particular crime and the persons who have committed it over the past forty years. The end product of the whole process is statistical modeling, designed to predict the probable characteristics of an unknown offender based on the analysis of historical crime data."

Alan was the first to speak. It didn't surprise me because he was a scientist and wanted to know the reasoning and logic behind artificial intelligence.

"How do you think your approach will help us in this case?"

"If it turns out that Mark isn't responsible, then I believe that Rachel was probably abducted and murdered as she walked home. I've come to this conclusion based on the circumstances of this case, the timescales involved and the fact that there's no evidence to indicate that Rachel reached home. The first piece of advice I always give is to 'clear the ground from under your feet'. In other words, investigate thoroughly family, friends, previous acquaintances and boyfriends, before considering that a stranger may be responsible."

"But we have done. Searched the homes of all her friends and family. Searched Penna's house. House to house has been done. Search of open fields. Search of the drain, which is still ongoing. Recovered Rachel's personal belongings. Visited all known sex offenders in the area and searched their homes. I could go on."

Chuck had obviously been in this position before, faced with a bunch of inquisitive detectives he hadn't met before. He had to strike the right balance between providing me with advice and support, without appearing to question what had already been done prior to his arrival, and he did.

"Can I say that I'm up to speed with what you've achieved so far in such a short time and you are to be commended. Think of the C.A.T.C.H.E.M database as a means of providing some direction and support to the SIO, Mr Davison. For example, in almost all the cases on the database, if the missing female isn't found within three days and there's no evidence of a planned stay away from the home address, these cases usually involve the sexual murder of young girls. Ninety-six per cent of all murdered victims are killed and disposed of in the first twenty-four hours. Twenty-six per cent of murdered victims have been found in the homes of the offenders. In seventy-six per cent of cases, the victim was murdered by someone known to them prior to the murder."

Chuck paused for breath and looked to me with a 'should I carry on', expression.

"Chuck, I think it would be a good time for you to give us the results of your analysis."

"I've searched the database and there are two cases

worthy of mention, the murders of Victoria Hall and Leanne Tiernan."

My assembled team of detectives sat and listened, spellbound as Chuck revealed the circumstances of how both girls died. Victoria Hall, who was eighteen at the time, left a nightclub in Suffolk in the early hours of the morning intending to walk home. She never did reach her home, she was abducted off the street, a short distance from where she lived. Her naked body was found in a shallow river three weeks later, some twenty-four miles from the location of the last sighting. She'd been strangled but not sexually assaulted. Chuck delivered the part that we'd all been waiting for with,

"The case is three years old and I'm sorry to say that her killer or killers haven't been found."

You could hear a pin drop in the room as he told us that her killer or killers hadn't been brought to justice. It was the last thing we wanted to hear. Twenty-four miles meant that whoever was responsible used some form of transportation.

Leanne Tiernan was a sixteen-year-old schoolgirl, who lived in West Yorkshire. She disappeared on her way home as she walked along an unlit pathway. The SIO conducted a massive search by consent extending to all houses within a one-and-a-half-mile radius of where they believed she was abducted. They didn't find her, but as DI Taylor had already told us, if they'd continued the search into the next street, they'd have discovered her body hidden in a freezer. She was eventually found in a shallow grave some sixteen miles from her home. She'd been sexually assaulted and strangled. Leanne's killer, John Taylor, was subsequently convicted by matching hair trapped in a scarf found around Leanne's neck, with Taylor's. The mood in the room changed from one of hopeful anticipation, to one of how the fuck is this going to help us find Rachel? Chuck seemed to sense the very tangible feeling of disappointment and continued on a more positive note.

"I know that in both the two cases I've mentioned, some form of transportation must have been used. But I believe that in this case, you should begin with the theory that Rachel was abducted before she managed to reach home. I know that Mark is a suspect but if it's not him, then I believe you should be looking for a male, most likely to be single, aged between sixteen and thirty-five with previous convictions for sexual assault and violence. He'll probably have an appetite for watching pornography and be inadequate in his relationships with females. He'll most likely live within five miles of where Rachel was abducted, or from where her personal belongings were found in the drain. I believe that you should keep an open mind about whether the killer had access to a vehicle. I'd investigate the theory that they didn't first."

Chuck was bombarded with questions from an audience of fact-hungry detectives that were clearly impressed with his almost encyclopedic knowledge of the C.A.T.C.H.E.M database. By the end of the briefing, they were fascinated, hypnotised almost, by his elaborate recall of other stranger murder cases that were mostly solved by inspired detective work. They could have listened to him for hours and so could I, but I wanted to show him the drain where Rachel's personal belongings were found and take a look at the tyre tracks off Thorpe Park drive.

We both decided to walk the mile or so to Hall Road Bridge to give us time to talk, and maybe going over the most likely scenarios for Rachel's disappearance, would trigger some kind of eureka moment in me. I knew that being a real life SIO wasn't like that. The arctic-like wind that blew into our faces as we headed along Hall Road, was about as real as you could get though, and so was the fact that I was no closer to finding Rachel than the day I got the call from Alan to say that she'd vanished.

"I know it's probably not what you want to hear, Sir, but if you don't find Rachel's body there are examples on the database of successful convictions for no-body murders."

Chuck offered this without warning. The consequences of failing to find Rachel appeared before me, like I could actually see the future. I didn't like what I saw. The chances of securing a conviction on purely circumstantial evidence would be slim at best. The absence of a body meant no forensic evidence and no cause of death. To build a case I'd have to rely on the killer or killers telling someone. If Mark was responsible, would he eventually crack under the pressure of living each day knowing what he'd done? If it was a stranger, how the hell was I going to find them?

"Thinking of the implications of not finding Rachel?"

"How did you guess?"

"I'd be doing exactly the same thing in your shoes. All I can do is give you the worst-case scenario."

I showed Chuck where Rachel's passport and mobile phone were recovered. The divers were still busy searching the drain. The water level was much lower now and there was still a huge amount of work to be done to complete the search. Chuck must have seen some things in his time, but even he appeared to be shocked at the grimness of scene 1 as rats roamed freely amongst the garbage, careful to avoid the team of dedicated divers and their motorised rubber dinghies.

We walked north up Thorpe Park Drive to where the tyre tracks had been reported. The area was still taped off as a possible scene. The tracks led onto the drain bank and judging by their width, the vehicle had probably been a large van of some description. We both agreed that it was possible that Rachel's belongings could've been thrown into the drain from where we were standing and so could Rachel's body. House to house enquiries with surrounding houses and flats though, had proved negative. Maybe the tyre tracks had nothing to do with anything other than a member of the public dumping rubbish. We both came to the conclusion that I'd just have to keep an open mind, until any further information came to light.

Back in my office that was quickly becoming my second home, I stood in front of the large white board, felt tip pen in hand, looking for inspiration from my assembled audience consisting of Maly, Chuck, Shaun, Alan and Trev. By the time we'd finished, it was filled with every possible scenario based on the assumption that Rachel had been murdered. The list of likely suspects began with Mark, but inevitably widened considerably to include old boyfriends, family acquaintances, or a random stranger with or without a vehicle. All were possible. The only real conclusion we came to after about three hours of discussion, was that we needed to find Rachel's body. Obvious to anyone, I thought, but she had to be somewhere - building, vehicle, buried in a shallow or deep grave, drain or river. The discovery of Rachel's belongings in the drain had led us to assume that we'd find her body there too, it was only a matter of time. Each day began with a high degree of anticipation that Rachel would be discovered either in the drain or some park or wood. But each day ended with nothing, despite the mammoth search operation that had taken on a life of its own with help from public-spirited volunteers from the estate. The search of open land for a shallow grave would have to be widened beyond the parameters I'd set. Chuck suggested contacting JARIC. They were able to fly over large areas of land and use thermal imaging cameras to detect changes in ground temperatures. It was a long shot but I'd nothing to lose. If Rachel was buried somewhere, JARIC might just be able to find her. Alan disappeared to make the call.

It'd been an extraordinary, exhausting day. Chuck was everything I'd hoped he'd be and was another example of how the very best police officers seemed to remain in the lower ranks of the service. He'd have made a fantastic Detective Superintendent, I thought, but I wasn't sure that he'd have passed the required promotion boards, or have wanted to, for that matter. He seemed perfectly happy going from force to force as the guardian of C.A.T.C.H.E.M. Before he left, I asked him if he'd any last observations and he responded with a question of his own.

"Can I ask what approach has brought you success as a SIO in the past, Sir?"

I thought about his question for a while trying to think of how success had come in my other cases. I told him that I relied heavily on my scientific background to solve cases, with an approach based on, every problem has a solution. I tried to sum it up as,

"Methodical, evidence-based, trust in my detectives, mixed with a dose of luck, common sense and gut feeling."

"I see no reason why you should change now, Sir. I'd trust your judgement and your instinct, that's all you can do. Good luck."

Why had he asked the question, I wondered? Maybe he wasn't allowed to say what he'd do in the circumstances of a particular case, or maybe it was because he was junior in rank. Either way, I knew that his words would stay with me because I hoped that they were meant as a kind of compliment. I wrote his words, 'Trust your judgement and your instinct' on the white board beneath, 'Think wider. Think bolder'. I tried to imagine him visiting other forces in the future and referring to my case as part of the C.A.T.C.H.E.M database, just as he'd done with the Victoria Hall and Leanne Tiernan cases. I'd want him to be able to say that we'd found Rachel by inspired police work and that her killer was safely locked away in prison for life. What I wouldn't want him to say, is that my investigation had turned out to be a no-body murder case, with Rachel's killer still on the loose. Rachel had to be found for her family, but she also had to be found for my professional credibility and that of my detectives. Chuck's visit made me more determined than ever to make things happen, make my own luck, widen my perspective and to 'trust my judgement and my instinct'.

The peace in my office was shattered by a knock at the door. It was Detective Superintendent Colin Andrews.

"Now then, buddy."

He called everybody 'buddy'. It was good to see a friendly face. We chatted for a while about what was going on in the force. Colin always had stories to tell that he'd embellish for effect, and he liked nothing better than to recall his latest battle with chief officers. He couldn't care less what people thought of him, he said whatever he wanted to with little regard for diplomacy. Some of us believed that, having been orphaned at a young age, it was his way of coping.

"Detective Chief Superintendent Johnson wants me to review your investigation. I know it's only been a couple of weeks and we'd normally do it after twenty-eight days, but he thought it might help."

We had a coffee together and I tried to find out the reason for the early review. Colin seemed surprised by my blunt and direct questions.

"Look buddy, I'd tell you if there was some ulterior motive behind all this but there isn't. If anything, they think you're doing a good job. Not sure if any of them would fancy being in your shoes. We've never had one like this."

On the long drive home, the voice of negativity returned. What was the real reason for the early review? Would I be replaced as the SIO? It'd happened to me before on the Clubb case. I knew that my reaction was a direct consequence of the way I'd been treated by the force. That's what I lived with every day now, I automatically saw the worst in everything and everybody.

SEVEN

'Another throw of the dice
by the police'

Over the next few days leading up to Rachel's birthday on 17 January, Colin conducted his review of my investigation. Rachel's birthday came and went without a call to her parents' landline. The FLOs spent the day with Wanda and Ray, and told me that it was heartbreaking to be by their side when what shred of hope they harboured for their daughter's safe return, had all but slipped away. The reconstruction on the same day attracted widespread media coverage, but it only served to generate more sightings of a female matching Rachel's description walking in the Bransholme area, in the early hours of New Year's Day.

On Wednesday, 22 January, Colin presented his findings to Maly, Alan and me in my office. I'd already read his report to chief officers and there were no surprises. He supported my decision to treat Mark as a suspect and was complimentary about my team and me. That meant that I'd probably be left alone to get on with finding Rachel. I lingered over his last paragraph, 'Finally, I commend the hard work of Detective Superintendent Davison and his team and I am confident that they will draw this matter to a successful conclusion be that the safe locating of Rachel or the apprehending of her murderer'.

"Colin, thanks for the last paragraph. How come you're so confident?"

"I don't think you've missed anything and it'll come. I know you and I know you'll keep going with the same methodical approach. That's all you can do."

"That's pretty much what Chuck Burton said, trust my judgement and instinct. I need a break through and I need it soon."

Colin left with words of encouragement. I was glad that he'd done the review. Whatever people thought of him, he was an experienced SIO and if he couldn't find anything that we'd missed, I doubt anyone else would. I got the impression from Colin that everyone was watching my investigation. It'd captured the imagination of uniformed officers, detectives, civilians and just about anyone else who worked for the organisation, just as it'd already done with the public, on a global scale. Lisa briefed me every day on the latest media coverage and today was no different. She breezed into my office as cheerful and upbeat as ever.

"Hull Daily Mail has loads in again. Rick Lyon has really taken an interest. They're leading with your amnesty decision. Look."

'Crime amnesty offer as police chief makes appeal. Someone knows where Rachel is'.

It was a good headline followed by page after page of coverage.

'The man leading the search for Rachel is certain someone out there knows what has happened to the missing 22-year-old. His concern is that whoever does hold the vital information in what is becoming an increasingly desperate investigation has something to hide themselves. That is why Detective Superintendent Paul Davison has taken the unusual step of promising to overlook crimes if it means people coming forward with information about Rachel's whereabouts. The push is now to appeal to the criminal fraternity who may have information about what has happened to Rachel but who may be not be comfortable in coming forward…..The appeal to Hull's criminal population is no reflection on Rachel's background or current circle of friends, but simply another throw of the dice by the police….It's about us all pulling together as a community to find Rachel'.

I liked the phrase, 'another throw of the dice by the police'. I added it to the other stuff I'd written on the white board. It got me thinking about what Chuck had said about Rachel being abducted before she reached home, and the obvious similarities with the two cases he'd discussed from the database. Up until now, we'd expected to find Rachel dumped in the drain together with her personal belongings, but what if she wasn't in the drain? She had to be somewhere else. Waiting for information from the public, waiting for Rachel's body to be found, waiting for Mark to put a foot wrong - there was far too much bloody waiting for my liking.

I needed a plan to be more proactive. I called Detective Superintendent Chris Gregg over in West Yorkshire, to find out more about his decision to search seven hundred homes by consent. When I came off the phone with him, even though they didn't find Leanne's body, it'd been a bold move on his part. I had to admire him for what Rick Lyon would no doubt describe as a 'throw of the dice by the police', and a bloody big throw by any definition of the word. I'd no idea how he came up with the idea in the first place because to enter and search a person's home, a search warrant would be needed. But that was exactly how he'd managed it if homeowners refused to allow his officers to enter and search, by persuading reluctant Magistrates to issue warrants under Section 8 of PACE. Apparently, there hadn't been any criticism of his decision to utilise so many force resources with no end product, because it was viewed by chief officers as a logical thing to do in the circumstances.

I sat for a while trying to get my head around the concept of knocking on somebody's front door and asking them if it was OK to search their home from top to bottom. I thought about the implications of doing a similar operation on Orchard Park Estate. Where would the officers come from to search so many houses? How long would it take? What if Rachel's body wasn't found? The force was struggling to cope with rising levels of crime and an avalanche of calls from the public, and an operation of this scale would place a massive strain on the organisation.

But then I looked up at the words on the white board. 'THINK WIDER. THINK BOLDER'. 'TRUST YOUR JUDGEMENT AND INSTINCT'. 'ANOTHER THROW OF THE DICE BY THE POLICE'. I knew exactly what I was going to do - search every house on Orchard Park Estate for Rachel's body. The urge to tell the team was overwhelming but I needed time to think it through. It was a massive decision to make, and I recalled the way I'd set myself up for a fall on the Clubb case by doing things differently. I'd pissed off the other SIOs and chief officers. I thought about the repercussions if the decision backfired on me - they'd be significant and far-reaching. I couldn't underestimate what it might do to my fragile confidence, but something in me said, 'fuck the consequences'. The Davo of old would've made the decision in a heartbeat, and be full of positive energy to get the job done, not sat worried about what people would think. That got me angry and more determined than ever to go my own way. So, what if it did all backfire on me, I thought, there'd be no happy ending for any of us anyway. But at least I'd be able to sleep at night knowing I'd done the right thing, and knowing that my Dad would've been proud of me.

I pulled out my policy book and carefully recorded my decision to search all houses and flats within a mile-and-a-half radius of the last sighting of Rachel. It was there in black and white. My instinct was not to share the decision with anyone else for the time being, I wanted to get used to the idea. I also wanted a bit more time to see if we could capture Rachel on CCTV after Jacksons and closer to home. I called Maly anyway. His response wasn't what I expected.

"I think it's a great idea. I'll come across and we can talk it through. I'm on my way."

Even though it was late January, the afternoon sun streamed through the window making my office seem brighter and bigger than it actually was. The residents of Orchard Park Estate had no idea what was being planned and neither did my team. It felt like the old Davo had returned as we explored in elaborate detail the enormity of the decision. But after our initial excitement at the thought of conducting such a massive operation subsided, Maly said something that brought me back down to earth with a bang.

"Of course, this'll only work if the residents cooperate. Otherwise, we'll be applying for hundreds of Section 8 warrants."

He was right. I formed a mental picture in my mind of residents refusing to allow officers to enter and search their homes. Maybe there was a way of appealing to Orchard Park Estate as a community, if such a thing existed, because I knew that I wouldn't change my mind now. If we had to apply for hundreds of warrants then so be it, Magistrates would just have to work a bit of overtime as we both laughed at the thought. The worst outcome would be not to find Rachel but then at least I'd know that her body was somewhere else and not close by. The best I could hope for if her body was being concealed, would be for it to be dumped during the operation. We both agreed that this was going to take some careful planning and that we'd announce the decision at tomorrow's briefing.

After Maly had gone, I started to think about that little kid I'd seen being beaten up the other day by a female and some hooded low-life on Hall Road. Uniformed officers had managed to get their names and address after issuing them with a public order warning for shouting obscenities from Hall Road Bridge. As it turned out, they lived in some high-rise flats not far from the station. The male was a drug dealer called Carl Freeman, affectionately known to everyone as, 'be free-man'. The good news was that he'd already been caught dealing drugs to undercover police officers and he was due to be arrested, along with numerous other dealers, and he most definitely wouldn't be a free man for a very long time to come.

I gave my old CID partner, Detective Inspector Bernie Orr, who was now in child protection, a call. I asked her to come with me to pay Carl Freeman a visit to check on the welfare of the little kid. It was good to see her again. If you didn't know her, you'd think that she was miserable for the sake of being miserable. She definitely wasn't miserable, she just liked to make people think that she was so they'd leave her alone and it worked, most of the time. When I'd first been posted into the CID, they put me on the group with Cameron, Steve, Ken and Bernie. Bernie had pretty much ignored me from the beginning, I was told not to take it personally, it was just that she didn't like many people and chose to work alone. To everyone's surprise, she asked if she could partner me one day and that was the start of a long-lasting friendship. It took what seemed like forever to get to know her properly but it was worth it in the end. Bernie turned out to be the sister I never had.

I'm not sure why she'd wanted to be my partner though. Maybe she judged me on what I did, as opposed to my reputation for being somebody with a load of degrees, just passing through the CID on my way up the promotion ladder. I do know that she was grateful to me for showing her how to study. She'd failed her sergeant's exam on numerous occasions and seemed destined to remain a constable for the rest of her service. With a bit of guidance from me and much hard work from Bernie, to her sheer delight, she passed both sergeants and inspectors exams in quick succession. It was probably the only time I ever saw her smile.

It felt like old times as we made our way up to the seventh floor by the stairwell. We didn't fancy venturing through the graffiti-covered lift doors and facing the sickly, unmistakable aroma of piss that would be waiting on the other side. The landing on the seventh floor was dark, cold and unwelcoming. Dogs barked, kids screamed and music pounded loudly, making the concrete floor vibrate to the competing sounds being blasted from behind closed, and probably reinforced, doors. As expected, the flat we wanted had a drug dealers' door. Bernie swung into action and knocked politely.

"Hello. It's Social Services. We've had a call about your little boy, Tommy. Just need to come in to see if he's OK."

A female replied.

"Fuck off."

"Look it'll only take five minutes, Donna. It is Donna, isn't it? Just need to see Tommy."

"Which fucking nosey bastard called you lot?"

"You know I can't tell you that. Come on Donna, it's freezing out here."

Then the door opened and Bernie pushed her way in leaving the door ajar for me to enter. When Donna saw me, she recognised me immediately.

"You're that fucking grey-haired copper. Get the fuck out of my flat."

Then the little boy appeared from behind the settee. He'd bruising to his face and arms.

"How's he got those bruises?"

"Nothing to do with you. Nosey twat."

"I won't ask you again."

"Go fuck yourself."

"Right Bernie, lock her up on suspicion of assault."

Donna definitely didn't want to be arrested and she flew towards Bernie, fist clenched ready to deliver a blow to my trusted friend and colleague. Bernie almost stifled a yawn as she expertly wrestled Donna to the ground before slapping handcuffs on our aggressive prisoner. Just as we radioed control to arrange transport to take Donna to the station, Carl burst through doorway. He recognised me instantly.

"Grey-haired black bastard. Leave my fucking girlfriend alone."

He came at me like a man possessed, and so I did what I always used to do as a uniformed constable on the streets of Hull when faced with an aggressive male, deliver a sharp blow to the throat with the side of my hand. It stopped Carl in his tracks and gave me a split second to get my right arm around his neck and to wrestle him to the floor. Back at the station, as I put Carl in a cell, I told him that I'd do everything in my power to put Tommy into care and that if they ever laid a finger on the little boy again, I'd find him and there'd be serious consequences, starting with a kick in the bollocks.

We agreed to finish the evening with a pint in the New Inn for old times' sake. I told her about arresting Wayne Ford the last time I was in and all she said was,

"Should be a warm welcome then."

I expected her to suggest going to a different pub in the circumstances but she didn't. It wouldn't have been the same, and we both knew that it might well be a long time before we'd be able to do this again. When I opened the door of the pub and the regulars saw me, everything fell silent. It was definitely not a warm welcome and for a moment I considered turning around and leaving. But then as we ventured further towards the bar, something totally unexpected happened. I heard somebody shout,

"I'll buy him a pint."

As the landlady pulled me a pint, she must have read my mind.

"I bet you weren't expecting that. They all know what you did, letting Wayne see his kid and girlfriend before taking him in. Even coppers have hearts. What's the world coming to."

We sat for a while and Bernie asked how I was coping. She knew better than anyone how the grievance had taken its toll on my life. We'd worked closely together on some new force policy for vulnerable witnesses, and she'd witnessed at first-hand how much I'd changed from the person she knew when we'd worked together as detective constables.

"I'd go back to those days if I could. They were better days working with you, Steve, Ken and Cameron. Probably the happiest time of my career."

"You'll have me crying next. Don't be soft."

We both went our separate ways, and I thought about just how indebted I was to Bernie for looking after me during that time.

EIGHT

'Do you believe it's Rachel?
Yes, I do boss'

Maly was already in my office when I got to work. He was sat with Alan having a coffee. I could sense that he had something to tell me.

"There's some CCTV we want you to take a look at. DC Bailey's been working all hours and he thinks he's found something. Come on."

I followed them both to the office where DC Bailey was working. It was in darkness, the only light coming from a bank of video screens. As respectful as ever, DC Bailey sprang to his feet in a nervous kind of way.

"Morning boss, I'd like you to take a look at these images. Timed at 0220hrs on New Year's Day. CCTV footage from just across the road from the station. That's the underpass leading to Saxcourt. Watch."

I looked at the screen and the quality of the image was poor due to the dim street lighting. I could just make out a figure move across the screen from right to left followed a few seconds later by another figure. DC Bailey looked at me expecting some kind of reaction, but I hadn't a clue what I was looking at so I asked him to play it again. I was still none the wiser.

"Sorry boys. Not sure what I'm looking at."

"Boss, the first figure, there, looks to me like a female with light hair wearing a dress. And the second figure, I'm not sure about but looks like a male to me."

He talked me through the footage again, but I still wasn't convinced. All I could make out was a figure moving that appeared to be a female but I was by no means sure.

"You must have better eyesight than me, Tony. All I can make out as I look at the figure is light for the head and hair, dark for the clothing and light for the legs."

"Boss, I've got used to looking at poor quality images. I've been doing it for days. My instinct tells me that what you're looking at is Rachel. I've already been out and walked from Jacksons to the underpass and it took me about twenty minutes. The times would fit with Rachel captured on their CCTV at 0201hrs."

Maly and Alan looked at me.

"What do you both think?"

"We agree with Tony but it isn't clear by any means. I doubt whether Wanda, Ray or anybody who knows Rachel, would be able to identify her from the footage and there's no way of enhancing the quality I'm afraid. Tony's already checked," said Alan.

If it was Rachel, then in just a few hundred yards she'd have reached the safety of her home and without saying anything, we all knew that the second figure could well be her killer. In terms of the search of homes, this would change everything. The mile-and-a-half radius would have to start from the point of the last sighting. It was a massive decision to make, either to use Jacksons as the last confirmed sighting of Rachel, or use the one I was looking at now, heartbreakingly close to Saxcourt. Maly knew what I was thinking because I'd already told him about the search by consent, but Alan and DC Bailey had no idea. DC Bailey certainly had no idea about the significance of my next question to him.

"Do you believe it's Rachel?"

Without a moment's hesitation, he replied.

"Yes, I do boss."

"That's good enough for me."

I patted Tony on the back in a kind of awkward show of gratitude. It was one of those things that you wished you'd not done in the first place, but shaking his hand would have been too formal. He was definitely embarrassed and so was I, but if he was right, then he'd made a startling discovery.

Back in my office we pulled out a map of Orchard Park Estate. There was a significant distance between Jacksons and the sighting near the underpass I'd just seen. We drew a radius of one-and-a-half miles from both locations. Alan asked why. When I told him about my decision, he slumped back in his chair from a standing position as if he'd just been hit by a freight train. I could see that he was turning over in his mind the implications of what I'd just said and, as expected, the 'how on earth are we going to do that by consent', question came, followed by numerous others about the logistics of conducting such an operation. You could almost see the steam coming out of his ears as his brain went into meltdown. Alan knew me well enough to know that I was deadly serious and that I wouldn't change my mind.

"The question is, from where do we begin the search? Jacksons or the underpass near to Rachel's home?"

They didn't answer, because they knew that it was my decision. If I got it wrong, it was my responsibility and that's how it should be as the SIO. Looking at the map, it became clear that the question I'd asked was potentially going to be the most important of the investigation so far. My thoughts turned to the Leanne Tiernan case and for all their efforts, the police missed her by one street. I had to get it right. Was it Rachel on the underpass? It could be anyone given the poor quality of the images. But the timings were about right given the distance from Jacksons, and then there was the shadowy figure of what looked like a male following a few seconds later. I thought about what Chuck said about trusting my instinct, and Rick Lyon's use of throw of the dice. Searching homes by consent was already a massive gamble, deciding on where to begin the searches though, was on a much bigger scale. I looked at the map again, although there was a degree of overlap, they covered different areas and mostly different homes. Decision time.

I walked into the briefing not knowing what the reaction would be from my team. I felt strangely confident in what I was about to say. I'd nothing to fear and I knew that I'd be able to argue passionately why I'd made the decision in the first place.

"Morning everyone. I wanted the whole team to be here because I've made a decision to conduct an operation that hasn't been done before in this force and only once in all of the other forces in England and Wales. We're going to search every house within a mile-and-a-half radius of the last sighting of Rachel. DC Bailey believes he's found Rachel on CCTV walking not far from Saxcourt, followed by what looks like a male. Timed about 0220hrs. There's no way to positively ID the image so it's a judgement call. I'm satisfied that it's Rachel and so we're going to begin the searches from that location. It'll take some time to get your head around what I've just said. Is it a gamble? Yes, I believe it is. And yes, it probably is the biggest decision I've made as a SIO, but it's not a decision I've taken lightly. We've searched open land, drains and outbuildings, so why not people's homes? The only difference is that we're going to need the consent of the homeowner to enter and search. That's all. That's the bit that's different and goes against everything you've been taught as a police officer. Thinking in those terms seems to make the idea much more logical. It does to me anyway. For the search to succeed though, I'm going to need your full support and the help of officers from right across the force. I've no idea how we're going to do that, given the problems facing the force."

There was an awkward silence in the room as people thought about the implications of what I'd just said. I went on to explain in some detail how I thought it could be done referring to the Leanne Tiernan case. And then I made Alan almost fall off his chair when I announced that I wanted the searches to begin on Tuesday, 28 January, only four days from now and that he'd be responsible for planning the operation. Trev was the first to comment.

"Well, I agree. It's a positive move. We need to make our own luck. It'll create a buzz around the force for a change. I'll help in any way I can. We're going to need a shed load of coppers for the searches though."

I could tell that most of the team didn't know what to say. I wouldn't have either. It was a lot to take in. Normally, I'd have asked everyone to keep the decision to within the team for fear of the press finding out and alerting everyone on Orchard Park Estate of our intention. But there'd be no point. News of a massive operation on this scale would spread across the force in the blink of an eye, and I just hoped that it wouldn't be leaked to the worlds' hungry media. There was no turning back now. I'd just formally announced that we were going to potentially, search hundreds of houses by asking people to let us into their homes and turn them upside down looking for Rachel's body. There was much to do and so I concluded the briefing. I walked confidently to the door, leaving a slightly bemused and shell-shocked team behind.

Back in my office, Alan looked at me and all he said was,

"Does it have to be Tuesday?"

"Can be sooner if you'd like."

"Now you're taking the piss Sir, with all due respect."

Alan was right, I was taking the piss. I just felt good about the whole thing, like I was in control of the investigation for the first time, instead of it being the other way around. The feeling of elation though, was short lived as we discussed the operation. It became clear that I hadn't given much thought to the logistics of conducting such a huge search. Alan calculated how many officers we'd need each day to complete it within a reasonable timescale of about four weeks, the time it'd taken West Yorkshire Police to search for Leanne Tiernan. It would be over a hundred. Maybe I'd underestimated the enormity of the task but I knew that somehow, we'd begin the search on Tuesday.

From that moment on, my office became the heartbeat of the operation. It was as if the whole team had moved up a gear. I called Chief Superintendent Steel to tell him about my decision. As the commander in charge of Hull, I needed his authority to release staff for the search. I also asked him to let the ACC and DCS Johnson know. The chain of command had to be respected. To be fair to Mr Steel, he seemed genuinely interested in my reasons for making such a resource-hungry decision and said that he'd support it in any way that he could. It wasn't long before DCS Johnson called, again offering to help. I knew that within minutes every senior officer would know about the operation. Now, there really was no turning back. I felt more alive and at peace with the world than I had done for a very long time.

By the end of the day, Alan briefed me on the progress he'd made. I could tell that he was under pressure. I'd given him an enormous task to achieve in just a few days. Looking back, I couldn't think of an occasion when I'd demanded more from an individual. His plan was first-class and much better than anything I could've come up with. It was all there, Lisa to brief the world's press at 0800hrs on Tuesday, 28 January, and arrange for Wanda and Ray to appeal to the residents of Orchard Park Estate to open their homes to the police; search to be led and coordinated by force POLSAs; search teams to consist of three constables with uniform, detective and search trained, skills; force solicitor, Stephen Hodgson, prepared and ready to apply for Section 8 warrants; SOCO supervisor and SOCO teams on standby to secure and preserve evidence; and Maly and me, to deliver briefings to the search teams. There was more of course, much more and, as Alan talked, I couldn't have agreed more with whoever it was that'd come up with the quote about how planning is an unnatural process. But it wasn't just unnatural, it was bloody difficult and challenging. I knew that the next few days would be filled with a fair degree of 'worry and depression' before the big day arrived, and I'd have to guard against my old friend, the voice of negativity driving me mad. 'What if you don't find Rachel? What if you're searching in the wrong area? What if the officers think you're a lunatic and miss her body because they don't believe in searching by consent, or because they can't be bothered? You'll look a right twat then'.

"What are we going to do if this gets leaked to the press?"

It was a question that I knew would cause a considerable degree of tension between now and next Tuesday.

"Already thought of that, Sir. If you'll OK the overtime, I've already arranged for extra patrols in the area to stop anything that moves, anything that looks suspicious. It's part of the plan anyway. When the searches begin, we'll be doing the same thing, searching vehicles just in case somebody tries to get rid of Rachel's body in the boot of a car or back of a van. Superintendent Hardy's happy to authorise the stop and search of all vehicles."

"Bloody hell Alan, is there anything you haven't thought of."

"I'm sure there'll be something."

We were all exhausted by the mental challenge of the day. It was a day that I'd never forget, because it was another reminder that the force was blessed with some outstanding detectives. I had the overwhelming urge to tell them so. The entire team had pretty much assembled in the incident room ready for home.

"I won't keep you long. The search of Orchard Park Estate will be the biggest ever undertaken by the force. When the press finds out, it'll be in all the papers and on every TV screen. The search for Rachel has captured the imagination of the public the like of which I've never seen before. The only reason I've made the decision is to find Rachel. It's a gamble that could backfire on the force and me, but I believe it's the right thing to do. This is our opportunity to show the world just how professional we can be. This is also an opportunity to show that you're proud to be detectives. Before you go, I want to thank you for your support over this decision and for the long hours you've put in. I told you on the first day that I wouldn't be the easiest person to work for, and many of you I'm sure, will already have judged that to be a gross underestimation. But it doesn't matter what you think of me, the question is, do you trust me to lead the investigation? I believe that I've the answer to that question by the way you've all responded today. Thank you again."

After everyone had gone home with just my thoughts for company, I was still coming to terms with the fact that I'd made a decision that would almost certainly set me apart yet again from the mainstream. Would anybody else have made the decision, I wondered? Probably not, and I knew that I'd have to prepare myself for the inevitable unforgiving fallout that could only happen in the police, should Rachel not be found.

NINE

'That's the police culture right there in a nutshell. Always ready to think the worst'

It seemed like the forthcoming search operation was the only topic of conversation across the force. Wherever I went, people were curious to know why I'd made the decision in the first place. Did I know where Rachel was and was the search some kind of elaborate smokescreen? It was a question that had been posed by a senior officer in the canteen. Alan had overheard the conversation and reported it to me, although he wouldn't tell me who the officer was.

"You don't seem as upset as I'd thought you'd be, boss."

"His comments are not worth getting upset over. They don't surprise me, either. That's the police culture right there in a nutshell. That's everything that's wrong with the police. Always ready to think the worst. They'll be hoping that I crash and burn over this. If you ever feel like telling me who it was, I'll do an Archie Banks on them."

Alan looked puzzled.

"Doesn't matter Alan, it's a long story from the past."

Why on earth would I conduct such a massive search operation if I knew where Rachel was? I shook my head in disbelief at what Alan had just told me. I wished more than anything that I did know where Rachel was and I'd order a dawn raid with armed officers in a heartbeat.

"Can we discuss the operation boss? I'm afraid I'm struggling for officers even though the four Div. Commanders have been really supportive. I can see it being a real problem if the searches go on for any length of time. We're not a big force like West Yorkshire. All I can think of doing is appealing to everyone across the force, even if they've got to come on their rest days or they work in a force department."

"How many have you got so far?"

"About thirty that's all. It's nowhere near enough although we're OK for specialist search-trained officers. The problem is detectives and uniforms. We're going to need at least a hundred, as you know, to do it properly and that'll be for every day we do it."

We agreed that Alan should put out a general appeal for help. We'd nothing to lose. It would be an appeal for the force to pull together as a kind of community with a common aim to find Rachel, just as we'd be asking residents on the estate to open their homes for the greater good. Maybe the force would surprise me. It didn't seem likely, given that morale amongst the rank and file was about as low as you could get. Alan had suggested delaying the start of the operation, but he didn't say it with any conviction, he knew that I wouldn't change my mind.

By now, it was Saturday, 25 January. My stomach churned every time I thought about Tuesday and I thought about Tuesday all the time. The pressure was building. You could feel the tension in the team. They were just as a much a part of the investigation as I was and their professional reputations were at stake.

DS Austin came to see me to discuss Mark. He was still a suspect but during Tony's surveillance operation on him, he'd done nothing out of the ordinary. In fact, he'd pretty much done nothing, apart from stay in his flat watching DVDs or shopping locally.

"Boss, I've got quite close to him as you asked. He's beginning to open up to me but all he talks about is Rachel, how much he misses her and how much he feels for her. He maintains that the argument they had wasn't really an argument. She'd been annoyed with him for leaving the kittens but not enough to walk over to Bransholme in the freezing cold. And it's looking more likely that he left the party around six, although I can't be certain."

"What do you think? Could he have killed Rachel?"

He thought for a while before answering. I didn't know him that well, certainly not as well as Shaun or Trev. Maybe he was nervous, given the fairly unfriendly and cool behaviour I showed towards most people. I'd have been nervous too, given what he was about to say.

"Boss, I'm going to stick my neck out. I don't think Mark killed Rachel. I don't think he's capable. I can't see any motive now I've got to know him better. I don't think he's got the bottle to have gone through with it and then hidden her body. It's more a gut feeling than anything else."

I couldn't fault him for basing his judgement on 'gut feeling'. I'd done the same thing over my decision to search Orchard Park Estate, and it got to thinking about how, as police officers, we used gut feeling or instinct, pretty much all of the time in trying to guess whether or not a villain was telling the truth. 'I swear on my baby's life it wasn't me', would be in the top ten pleas of innocence and so would, 'I swear on my mother's grave'. I was conned a few times as a young probationer. It happened to most officers to begin with, although it was still a shock to discover just how good people were at lying. Villains were experts.

I remembered as a uniform constable chasing a Mini with a stolen microwave sticking out of its boot. Unfortunately, despite my best efforts, the Mini managed to escape. When I went to see the registered keeper, of course they'd already reported it stolen. It was an eighteen-year old male, who did a convincing job of lying and so did his devoted family. I arrested him anyway, and he later admitted his guilt after he was unable to explain why glass fragments from the shop window he'd driven into in order to steal the microwave, were found on his clothing. It'd been a valuable lesson to learn.

I spent the rest of the weekend shut away in my office wondering how I was going to cope with the planned events for Tuesday. It filled me with dread. I'd have to command attention from the world's press as I described the circumstances surrounding the search of Orchard Park Estate. I'd have to brief the officers who'd be conducting the searches. They'd all be assembled in the canteen waiting for me to enter and deliver an inspirational briefing. Each and every one of them would be looking at me and I'd have no idea what they'd be thinking. Maybe all the females would be listening to what I said to determine whether there'd be any grounds to complain about me. Maybe the first question would be to do with breaching the human rights of residents by insisting on entering their homes. What if some of the officers refused to take part on those grounds? How I longed not to have such negative thoughts, but the malicious complaint against me had sprung from a speech I'd given that was about as inspirational as you could get. And, if you'd asked any of the audience, apart from the two female sergeants, for their opinion, then based on the positive feedback I'd received afterwards, it was a huge success. As Neighbourhood Watch Coordinators, my detailed plan for reducing crime and anti-social behaviour within their neighbourhoods, was what they'd wanted to hear. I'm pretty sure that if you'd asked them what the chances would be of a complaint being lodged against me for publicly humiliating the sergeants, they'd have said less than zero. Was I being paranoid now to automatically assume that every interaction with another member of the organisation, had the potential to end up at some trumped up industrial tribunal? When you've been kicked in the bollocks without warning and for no reason, you could be forgiven for being in a state of high alert at the prospect of it happening again. As I wondered why the service had changed so dramatically over the years, Maly came in for a chat.

"Thought you could do with some company. You've been locked away in here for most of the weekend, are you OK?"

"Did I ever tell you about a Superintendent in another force. He was head of personnel. Anyway, he had a board on the wall in his office with a list of names of officers who were on sick leave. He drew a smiley face against those who were due to come back to work and a glum face for those who were on long term sick. Unfortunately, a female officer on long term sick came in to see the Superintendent for a welfare chat and saw the glum face. The next thing the Superintendent knew was that he'd received a complaint against him from the officer. The force ended up disciplining the poor Superintendent on the grounds of sexual discrimination and it even went to an industrial tribunal. He resigned over it because it caused him to have a nervous breakdown."

Maly just shook his head. He must have guessed what I'd been thinking about.

"You've got to let it go. We've had these conversations before and I can see that it must be hard to get over but we've a big day on Tuesday and you're going to have to be at the top of your game. The service has changed. This force has changed. You were just in the wrong place at the wrong time. I'd say it was a kind of perfect storm. You're a big character, you speak your mind, you don't suffer fools. I'd say you were an easy target, wouldn't you? But isn't what we're about to do on Tuesday more important?"

He was right of course and I told him so. I believe that he was trying to tell me that there were far worse injustices going on in the world than what'd happened to me. He left with words of encouragement and a warm, if awkward, handshake.

It was late Sunday evening and the place was deserted. With only my office for company, and Maly's wise words still fresh in my mind, I pulled out Arthur Ashe's memoir, Days of Grace from my briefcase. I'd read it about ten times, and it

135

always reminded me of just how insignificant my problems were when compared to what'd happened to the once great tennis player. He was given a blood transfusion contaminated with HIV that subsequently caused his premature death from AIDS at the age of fifty. The book had a profound effect on me because it captured perfectly just how proud he was of his reputation: 'If one's reputation is a possession, then of all my possessions, my reputation means the most to me. Nothing even comes close to it in importance. Now and then, I have wondered whether my reputation matters too much to me; but I can no more easily renounce my concern with what other people think of me than I can will myself to stop breathing. No matter what I do, or where or when I do it, I feel the eyes of others on me, judging'. I felt exactly the same way. With my hard-earned reputation in the eyes of the force fractured beyond repair, I knew that I was in a dark place, a place I thought I'd never be or even knew existed.

Looking back, I believe that I suffered some kind of nervous breakdown. It wasn't like having a broken arm that would mend and be as strong as it was before the break, it was worse, much worse, and I understood the meaning of depression for the first time. What I'd not bargained for though was that the emotional damage would be far harder to fix, with little chance of a return to the innocent and carefree life I used to know and took for granted. Although some officers were given access to counselling, they were perceived to be weak within a macho culture. Everyone seemed to know who they were and they became fair game for the organisations' piss-takers. Eventually, I'd had to accept that I couldn't heal on my own and so I plucked up the courage to make the call to occupational health, knowing that it'd probably affect my career.

The counselling consisted of looking at a computer screen with a load of flashing lights moving frantically from side to side. The idea was to think about all the bad stuff that had happened to me, whilst gazing at the screen. It was supposed to somehow erase it from your memory but it didn't work for me. Talking about how I felt with the counsellor though, was of some help but not in a positive way. I've never forgotten his parting words to me at the conclusion of our last session,

"I'm afraid to say that the ordeal may well have shortened your life."

On the journey home, it took me a while for his depressing news to sink in because his reasoning made sense. High levels of stress can cause serious health issues. I had to smile at the irony of it all. I'd gone to a counsellor seeking help with my mental health, and now I had the added worry of wondering how long I had left to live.

TEN

'I've absolutely no idea'

On Monday, 27 January, the day before the massive search operation was due to begin, I arrived at work to a glum and nervous-looking Alan. He'd worked tirelessly on planning the search of Orchard Park Estate ever since I'd made the decision a few days earlier. It was an excellent plan, and I told him so, but I knew that he'd take it personally if things didn't go well tomorrow.

"Still only got about thirty or so officers, maybe a few more, but not enough to do it properly. Sorry boss."

"Look Alan, you've nothing to be sorry for. You've done a great job. We'll just have to go with what we've got. It'll just take a little longer that's all."

He didn't look altogether convinced at my shrug of the shoulders attitude because he knew that wasn't me, he knew I'd be disappointed. I took him for a coffee in the canteen so that we could go over the plan one last time. The canteen was busy as usual with officers attending numerous training courses and, as we entered, there was a strange atmosphere as if everyone was talking about the search. I asked Alan if he'd heard what people were saying about my decision and as diplomatic as ever, all he said was,

"The general opinion is that it's certainly different,

138

unexpected, maybe a bit off the wall."

That's all he was prepared to say and I didn't press him further. It would have made him feel uncomfortable because he definitely didn't like or agree with gossip. I never once heard him say anything about anybody that he wasn't prepared to say to his or her face. It was an endearing quality that was hard to find in the police and I admired him for it. Lisa joined us and managed to lighten the mood with her usual wide-eyed, upbeat nature. I could tell from the very beginning of the investigation that she was determined to grab the opportunity to work on such a high-profile case with both hands. And, although the intensity of the media spotlight had taken her by surprise, she'd risen to the challenge with calm authority and a commendable degree of skill. As she glanced around the canteen, she said something that I wasn't expecting.

"Everybody's talking about your decision in the press office. They think it's a really bold move. They're really envious of me although some of them find you a bit scary. Don't worry, I've told them you're not scary at all. You just demand a lot from people that's all. You just have really high standards."

Back in my office, the day took an unexpected turn for the better when Alan checked his e-mails.

"My inbox is full with offers of help from all over the force. There's even a Chief Inspector who's willing to come out from some department or other. There's support staff, officers from squads I never knew existed, officers on their rest days. Blimey, we'll have more than enough at this rate."

Alan heaved a massive sigh of relief. I'd obviously not

fully realised the extent of the pressure I'd put him under to deliver the perfect plan for me. He slumped back in his chair and all he kept repeating was,

"Can't bloody believe it, can't bloody believe it."

His sigh of relief though was nothing compared to mine. I was careful not to show him just how relieved I was at the sudden turn of events, but inside, I was really punching the air with joy and elation. It appeared as though the force had come together in a way that I'd not thought possible. Maybe it was human kindness that caused people to offer to sacrifice their time for the greater good, or maybe it was simply the desire to be part of something different and uplifting. Whatever the reason, I was bloody grateful and I shook his hand in a rare show of gratitude. Alan bolted out of my office to tell the rest of the team. My normally laid back, cautious and dependable colleague, couldn't hide his emotions as he delivered the news to a shell-shocked audience. Trev looked more surprised than anyone.

"Hang on, so what you're saying is that people from all over the force are willing to come out on their days off and work for nothing. And office bound officers are offering to come out in the cold to help. How did you manage that?"

"I've absolutely no idea."

In all my time in the police, I'd never come across anything like this happening before, and judging by the looks of amazement, neither had any of my team. Before long, Alan announced that there would be over a hundred officers for tomorrow's operation. He'd arranged for two briefings. Maly to deliver the first at 0800hrs, whilst I'd be busy talking to the press with Lisa, and me to do the second at 0900hrs.

More good news from Lisa as well, it appeared that there'd been no leaks to the press. They'd no idea what was about to happen, although they'd received a press release from Lisa to say that an important announcement would be made at 0800hrs tomorrow. I spent the rest of the day going over and over the plan with Alan and Maly. This was really happening, too late to stop now. We couldn't think of anything we'd missed and so I told Alan and Maly to go home early and get some well-earned rest.

As the afternoon sun faded, I sat alone in my office wondering what tomorrow would bring. In just a few days, my idea to conduct such a massive search of Orchard Park Estate had been turned into reality by my outstanding team of detectives, who'd given life to the words I'd written in my policy book. But now came the fear of facing the world's press and convincing an audience of officers to take the search operation seriously. My stomach churned at the thought of being stood there alone, riddled with self-doubt. I opened my leather-bound notebook full of quotes, and flicked through the pages searching for one about how to deal with fear. Eventually, I found one by Mark Twain. 'Courage is resistance to fear, mastery of fear, not absence of fear'. It made sense, and I couldn't argue with the wisdom contained within his words. But how was I going to find the courage to master my fears before tomorrow?

ELEVEN

'Go with that gut instinct and see where it takes you.'

It was Tuesday, 28 January, the first day of the massive search operation. I couldn't remember the journey into work because from the minute I'd woken, my mind had gone into meltdown over the plan to invade the privacy of the residents of Orchard Park Estate. With Mark Twain's quote still on my mind, I'd lain awake most of the night wondering where I was going to find the courage to be the SIO everybody would be expecting me to be. It felt like I was stood on the edge of a bloody great cliff, alone, and one more negative thought would cause me to stumble and fall.

It was still dark as I strode purposely across the ice-covered car park. The press had already gathered in unusually high numbers. Although it was still only around seven, the station was bustling with officers making their way into the canteen. I pushed the door open to take a look and I was met with a sight that I'd never seen before. The canteen was full to bursting. Normally, I wouldn't have ventured in because I knew that all eyes would turn to me and I'd feel uncomfortable and self-conscious. I tried to stay positive, wouldn't it be a good thing to see the SIO in charge of such a massive operation, I told myself. And so, I just clenched my fists, took a deep breath, and did something that was totally out of character, I sat down at a table with a group of constables that I hadn't seen before.

"Mind if I join you?"

I didn't wait for a reply and I sat next to a young, slightly nervous male officer.

"Here for the search?"

"Yes, Sir."

"For those of you who don't know me, I'm the SIO. Can I ask where you're all based?"

They looked at each other in an awkward kind of way. They were probably wishing that I'd bugger off and leave them to finish their breakfasts, but I wanted to determine their level of understanding of what would be expected of them during the search. The young officer next to me replied in a respectful voice.

"Grimsby, Sir."

"How come they've been able to send five of you across to help out?"

They exchanged glances as if they couldn't think of what to say and then he said.

"We're all on rest day. It was Amy's idea."

He nodded in the direction of a female officer sat opposite me. Her friendly face lit up as she spoke.

"Sir, we've all been following progress with the case from the beginning. It was something my Dad said as he watched the news about it being a parents' worst nightmare. He just looked at me and gave me a big hug. I knew what he was thinking. That's it really. I asked everyone here if they'd volunteer and they agreed. We all just want to help to find

Rachel."

What she said and the way she said it, didn't belong in a police station canteen, a place more used to piss-taking and banter. The way she talked about her Dad had been gentle, moving and surprising. Maybe there was hope for the force after all. Five young officers had given up their well-earned rest day to travel a considerable distance to join the search for Rachel. It wasn't what I expected. The act of human kindness almost brought a tear to my eye and I struggled to thank them properly before leaving. I missed the opportunity to probe them as I'd intended. Time was pressing, and I needed to collect my thoughts before the press conference.

The atmosphere in the incident room was electric. Trev was sat in his usual place squinting at his bank of computer screens. Although he'd not had a day off since Rachel's disappearance, he looked remarkably fresh.

"We're ready. I've got enough staff to cope with any calls. At least I hope I have. I can't believe how many people have offered to help. Bloody miracle if you ask me."

He wasn't kidding. The incident room was full to overflowing with unfamiliar faces. There was a collective sense of optimism that I didn't recognise and it took me completely by surprise. In my office, Alan was busy poring over his plan. He looked tired and anxious and this was only the first day of the search. But I understood why, he'd probably drained his reserves of nervous energy worrying over whether or not his plan was going to work. Maly, on the other hand, was cool, calm and collected, as he nursed a cup of coffee.

"Alan, you've done a brilliant job. Canteen's full of

officers and I've never seen so many staff in an incident room before. Well done."

We chatted for a while as if today was just another day and then Maly was gone. It was nearly eight, and he was due to deliver the first briefing to his half of the officers assembled in the canteen. I made my way up to the first floor where the press would be waiting for me in one of the bigger classrooms. I climbed the stairs slowly, thinking about what I was going to say. Would I succumb to crippling self-doubt when I walked into the room in just a few moments time? Would I be unable to speak as if I was experiencing a kind of panic attack? It'd happened so many times before, it was almost part of my DNA now.

I entered the classroom as if I was the most confident person in the world. So far so good. Most of the reporters knew me by now and, according to Lisa, I'd managed to convince them that I was this aloof, arrogant and distant individual. I wondered what they'd think if they knew that I was quivering inside desperately hoping that I'd be able to keep my composure. Knowing that I'd an important announcement to make though, gave me the upper hand. They'd no idea what was coming.

"Morning. I'll get straight to the point because I've a feeling that today will be a long day. As we speak, DCI Redmore is briefing about fifty officers. I'll be doing the same immediately after we've finished here. They will begin a search of all houses and flats within a one-and-a-half-mile radius of the last sighting of Rachel Moran. Following some outstanding work by one of my detectives, we believe that Rachel may have almost reached her home. There is some

CCTV footage that I'll be releasing. It shows a figure that we think is Rachel, followed closely by another person, possibly a male. I'd like you all to put out an appeal for that person to come forward. The reason for all the secrecy surrounding the operation is because we'll be searching by the consent of the homeowners. I'm aware that this approach has been used only once before and that was in the case of Leanne Tiernan in West Yorkshire."

Questions from the bemused gathering of reporters came thick and fast once they realised the significance of what I'd just said. What are you hoping to find? How long will it take? What if the homeowner refuses to allow your officers to enter? Have you told the family? Rick Lyon from the Hull Daily Mail had asked the last question.

"I'll answer the question about the family first. Yes, they are being told now by the Family Liaison Officers. I'm hoping that they'll agree to make a personal appeal to the residents of Orchard Park Estate to help in the search for Rachel by allowing my officers into their homes. But if they don't allow entry, then I'm prepared to apply to the Magistrates for warrants under Section 8 of PACE. I'm hoping that won't be necessary but we'll search every house no matter how long it takes. We'll be looking for Rachel. It's been twenty-eight days since she disappeared and my degree of concern for her wellbeing is reflected in the level of resources being deployed. We've searched every inch of open ground, searched mile after mile of local drains with no sign of Rachel apart from some of her belongings. The next logical step is to search homes and garages. I don't want to say anymore at this stage other than you're all welcome to come along and observe the operation."

I stood abruptly and left, leaving Lisa to deal with the aftermath of the bombshell I'd just delivered. As I walked down the stairs, I looked out the window. It was indeed a sight to behold as hordes of smartly dressed officers in full uniform streamed out of the station ready to begin the searches. Even the gathering clouds couldn't dim the spectacle as their waterproof yellow reflective jackets, cut through the early morning gloom. Mothers taking their children to school stopped and watched. They'd obviously never seen so many officers gathered in one place. It wasn't something you saw every day, and it reminded me of the miners' strike back in 1984.

Forces would meet at a predetermined place before being deployed to various picket lines. It was usually somewhere that had the capacity to feed hundreds of officers. I remembered watching one bus arrive full of Nottinghamshire constables, all over six feet tall. They looked impressive and menacing at the same time. I wondered how today's politically correct police forces would view Nottinghamshire's recruitment policy back then, that only allowed male officers over six feet tall to join. There was simply no height restriction now, and that got me thinking about a young female probationer barely five feet tall, who'd knocked on the door of a house on the Bransholme estate in Hull. I was her sergeant and I'd asked her to attend a domestic dispute between two local nutcases. Many had tried and failed to resolve their differences but the outcome was always the same, battered female and the male arrested for assault. Time for a softly-softly approach, I'd thought. I observed from the comfort of the patrol car as the huge male had literally filled the doorway, but he failed to notice the tiny figure in uniform and closed the door on the hapless officer. Undeterred, she knocked again but this time, when the door opened, she shouted and waived her arms around to get his attention. Startled is the only word to describe the expression on his face as he looked down. He'd probably never seen a police officer so short in stature before. It did the trick though, the gorilla of a man took a shine to the young officer, and before long, she'd calmed the warring couple and left them cuddling on the sofa. There had definitely been a 'I don't know what all the fuss is about', smile on her face as she'd climbed back into the patrol car.

I carried on walking down the stairs pleased with the way I'd handled the press. The bigger test was still to come, how to stand tall and proud in front of more than fifty officers and win their hearts and minds so that they believed in what I was doing. This was no time to worry about what they thought of me. This was no time to think about whether or not I'd offend anyone. This was the time to be positive. All that mattered was finding Rachel.

But as I stood ready to begin, I could feel my power slipping away. I'd been in this position so many times before, and I knew what was a split second away - dry mouth, pounding heart and an inability to string two words together. There was an awkward silence that was interrupted by Maly as he entered the canteen and stood a little behind me. I wondered why he'd come but it was good to see him anyway. Maybe he knew that I was apprehensive about talking in front of so many officers and wanted to offer his support, or maybe he knew there'd be some difficult questions about human rights. I thought about what the Davo of old would make of my performance. 'For fuck's sake, why can't you for once step up to the mark and just get on with it. It's about finding Rachel, not your fucked-up emotional problems'. That was enough for me to regain my composure, to the obvious relief of the expectant audience.

"Thank you all for coming out on a very cold and windy January day. I know that many of you have come on your rest days. I'm overwhelmed by the response from the far corners of the force. I also want to say thank you on behalf of Rachel's Mum and Dad. I'm not sure how today will go. I'm not sure what you all think about my decision to search Orchard Park Estate either. But I made the decision following some outstanding work by one of my detectives. There's some CCTV footage that we think shows that Rachel very nearly reached her home in the early hours of New Year's Day. I believe that she was probably abducted shortly afterwards. If she was, and it was someone on foot, then houses on the estate need to be searched as a priority. What you are all about to do today, is the first step in determining whether or not Rachel's body is concealed locally in a house, garden, garage or vehicle. You should all have a copy of the operational order prepared by DI Dorning. Are there any questions?"

Talking about why I'd made the decision in the first place helped to settle my nerves, and I could feel my power returning. I just hoped that it wouldn't desert me when the questions came.

"Sir, can I ask what power we've got to enter people's

homes? I know that a lot of us are thinking the same thing."

I caught sight of the male officer who'd asked the question. I didn't recognise him. It didn't really matter who asked the question though, because I sensed that they were all thinking the same thing.

"I'm glad you asked the question. We don't have any power to enter and search. I'm hoping that householders will let you in with their consent."

"With all due respect, Sir, what are we supposed to do then if they refuse?"

"If they refuse, record the fact that you've been refused entry. And then the householder will be visited again and again, and if they still refuse then we'll apply for a PACE Section 8 warrant. That's how they managed it on the Leanne Tiernan case in West Yorkshire. Anyway, we need to move on. Time's pressing."

It was obvious that they were having difficulty coming to terms with the concept of searching by consent. I would've been too, if I were in their position. It didn't get any easier when I described in some detail what was expected of them.

"You'll be working in teams of three. A uniform with a detective and a search-trained officer. The operation will be coordinated by a number of POLSAs. They'll make themselves known to you after the briefing. Make no mistake this isn't a PR exercise. You'll be looking for Rachel's body. In the Leanne Tiernan case, although they didn't find her, she was actually hidden in a freezer. You'll need to conduct a thorough search of any house you're given permission to enter. This hasn't been done before in this force and so you're going to have to make it up as you go along. I needn't remind you of the consequences if Rachel is subsequently found in a house you've already searched. I don't for one-minute underestimate just how difficult this will be. You'll need to search lofts, under floorboards if necessary, freezers, cupboards, wardrobes, vehicles, rubbish bins, garages, outhouses. I could go on."

There was silence in the canteen. My audience looked bewildered and shell-shocked. Was I right to warn them of the consequences of failing to conduct thorough searches, I wondered?

"With all due respect, Sir, are you saying that we could get disciplined for not doing the searches properly."

"That's not what I'm saying. I made a promise to Rachel's Dad, Ray, to do everything in my power to find his daughter and to never stop looking. That's all I'm trying to do. I have to place my trust in each and every one of you today. I can't be with you when you knock on every door. You'll be the ones making the tough decisions about what you think of the householder, how thorough to search, where to search. I could go on. But policing isn't an exact science. You may become suspicious for no other reason than gut instinct. Go with that gut instinct and see where it takes you. As you leave each house, ask yourself the question, what would Rachel's Mum and Dad think of the search? I believe that you all understand what it is that I'm asking of you. When you leave the station, be outstanding, be proud to be a police officer, show the world what you can do."

I could've continued the briefing and talked forever, but I learned a long time ago that in police work things rarely turned out as planned. Reality was always different and I'd no idea what to expect.

Lisa was waiting for me in my office. She'd just returned from breaking the news of the operation to Ray and Wanda. They'd agreed to make a televised appeal to the residents of the estate for them to open their homes to the police, and a press release had already gone out to that effect. We left the station together and walked across Hall Road. Dark clouds full of rain hung over the estate, and there was a gale force wind blowing as we headed to where the press had gathered waiting for our arrival. I stopped for a moment and looked around me. I could see officers knocking on doors. No answer, no answer, no answer. At that moment, I wondered why on earth I'd made the decision in the first place. If people weren't at home or they couldn't be bothered to answer the door, the operation would be a failure. And then it started pouring down with rain, with a vengeance. Within seconds we were soaked. The reporters were huddled around the entrance to Mulcourt. I'd agreed to live coverage of me knocking on a door and the search of a house. It had to be done at 0930hrs precisely, and so there was no time to wait for the rain to stop. Tina Gelder from ITV had somehow positioned herself into pole position ready to get close to whoever opened the door. She flashed a nervous smile in my direction as I chose number 9, Mulcourt.

The miniature front garden was neat and tidy and the door looked as though it'd been recently painted. I felt the eyes of the world bearing down on the back of my neck. After all, this was live and a no-answer wouldn't make for good TV. I knocked on the door with a fair degree of force. It seemed to take an age for the door to open. But open it did, slowly. I wasn't prepared for what happened next as an elderly lady appeared reluctantly in the doorway. She was shabbily dressed and must have been over ninety years of age. Her face looked like it'd never smiled, and there was little joy in what she had to say as her frail, tiny frame stiffened at the sight of so many reporters.

"What the fuck do you want and what are you lot fucking staring at?"

"Hello, I'm Detective Superintendent Davison. We're searching all houses on the estate looking for Rachel Moran who's been missing since New Year's Day. We'd like to come in a have a look around if that's OK."

"Rachel who? Never heard of her. I don't give a fuck who you are, you're not coming in here, now fuck off and leave me alone. Grey-haired twat."

She slammed the door in my face. To say that it wasn't what I was hoping for would be a massive understatement. There was an awkward silence. Millions of people would be watching as an elderly lady had just slammed the door in my face and told me to fuck off. The day had taken a depressing turn for the worse as the rain continued to pour down on this God-forsaken place. I must have heard the phrase 'and now I'll hand you back to the studio', about a thousand times before the press ran for cover. Lisa and me were stood alone, soaked to the skin. From the height of exhilaration that I'd felt at making the positive decision to search the estate for Rachel, to the depths of despair at having a door slammed in my face.

"Lisa, could this day get any fucking worse. I'm bloody soaked. I'm bloody freezing and the operation looks like being the worst decision I've ever made."

"You weren't to know the old lady would be so obnoxious. Not your fault. Just bad luck."

Lisa was trying her best to stay positive and I didn't expect anything less from her. We sheltered from the rain in the entrance to a building that was boarded entirely by ugly metal shutters. I soon discovered that it was in fact the local supermarket as the shop door opened outwards with such force that it almost knocked me over. Lisa began to laugh and it wasn't long before I joined in. There was nothing else to do in the circumstances. It was the worst start to the operation that I could've imagined and it didn't get any better when I got back to the station. Maly was waiting for me in my office. He had a broad grin on his face.

"Sorry about the old lady. Watched it on the news. Bet you weren't expecting her to tell you to fuck off."

"I bet I looked a right twat. Felt like a right twat. Any feedback from the searches?"

Maly's demeanour changed instantly, I sensed that it wasn't going to be good news.

"Some of the houses haven't been searched thoroughly. I've given the officers concerned a bollocking. Don't worry. They've been told to go back and do them again."

I sat on the radiator to dry my clothes as the rain lashed my office window. I began to laugh again as I told him the story about the local supermarket with its boarded-up metal shutters. We sat together over a coffee wondering how it'd come to this. The TV screen in the incident room seemed to be showing nothing else but coverage of the old lady slamming the door in my face. I had to admit though, that I'd have found it amusing if it'd been another SIO. Pretty soon it'd be the talk of the force and that was something I could do without.

By now, it was lunchtime and Maly had to go and tend to his other cases. His news had been the last thing I'd wanted to hear, and he understood that I probably needed some time on my own. I wouldn't have wanted to be around me either, given the mood I was in. I wasn't surprised that some officers didn't appear to be doing what was asked of them, pissed off maybe, but not surprised. They were being asked to do something that they'd never done before to the standard that I expected and demanded. I'd been told a long time ago that I asked too much of people. Maybe I did but I couldn't see the point in doing anything in a half-hearted way. Didn't make any sense to me. As my mind turned over what lay ahead in the coming days and weeks, there was a knock at the door. It was one of the incident room staff.

"Sir, sorry to disturb you but there's a DC Darren Key on the phone and he's quite upset."

My heart sank. Why would a detective be upset for God's sake? It was the first question that entered my head. Didn't he agree with the principle of searching by consent? Did he think that it was a breach of people's human rights? Had I said something at my briefing that had caused offence sufficient to attract another grievance? If I thought that I'd made progress over the past few days, this corrosive, stomach churning feeling, left me feeling helpless once again.

"Put him through."

I picked up the phone in anger more than anything, I was in no mood to listen to what I thought I was going to hear. I couldn't have been more wrong.

"Boss, it's DC Key…."

He was sobbing, and finding it difficult to speak.

"Darren, take your time. What is it, what have you got to tell me?"

"We've found a body…in a cupboard…she's dead… we've got two in custody for murder."

"Where are you?"

"19 Nashcourt."

"OK. I'm on my way. Don't do anything. Just stay put."

Although I couldn't be certain, I knew in my heart that it was Rachel. My brain went into overdrive thinking about what needed to be done and then the significance of the phone call began to sink in. My plan had worked and, for a moment, I felt a surge of relief and professional pride but that was all it was, a moment. A wave of sadness hit me. Sadness for Rachel's family. I knew that Ray and Wanda had clung onto the hope that their precious daughter would return safely and that there'd be an innocent explanation for her disappearance. But not now. I called Sergeant Wood, who was already with them, and told him to break the news of the grim discovery. They had a right to know even though the body hadn't been formally identified. His voice cracked, all he said was,

"Oh no, thank you. I'll tell them now."

I tried to imagine what he'd say and how Ray and Wanda would react. I couldn't bear to think about it now, there was so much to do. I opened my office door into the incident room. Everyone stopped and looked up from their computer screens, they'd obviously guessed that the phone call had been important.

"That was DC Key on the phone. I'm both relieved and very sorry to have to tell you that a body of a female has been found at 19 Nashcourt. Two males are in custody for murder. That's all I know until I get down there. Rachel's Mum and Dad have been told."

I'd seen it many times before when a team of dedicated police officers who'd worked tirelessly on a murder case achieved a breakthrough. There was a real sense of achievement that you could almost touch. To me, it was just human nature and had nothing to do with being in any way insensitive towards the victim or victim's family. But I could tell by their reaction that today was different. There was no sense of achievement, no sense of elation, just silence as they tried to digest what I'd said. Trev was the first to react.

"Better get a move on then. Loads to do. This is just the beginning. Anything you want me to do boss?"

"Can you get Alan for me. He's gone for his lunch and get hold of Tony Dickinson. Tell him I'll meet him at the scene."

Alan rushed back from his half-eaten lunch. We didn't say much as we walked the short distance to Nashcourt. I just said well-done but he didn't reply. I could see a large group of reporters, and a police officer struggling against the wind and rain to attach some crime scene tape around the communal entrance to the building. Suddenly, his helmet flew off and one of the reporters managed to grab it as it headed off towards Hall Road.

Lisa arrived to deal with the press as we entered by the front door that led into a dimly lit foyer. Tony had somehow managed to get there before us and he was stood at the top of the stairwell. He'd already changed into his SOCO suit, and as we put on ours, he described the layout of the first floor. I could see the front door to number 18 and an adjoining door at right angles.

"That door opens into a small utility cupboard used to store rubbish. It's part of the flat but separate if you know what I mean. We've already moved the occupants out. A single mother, a small child and a dog that won't stop barking so we've got full control of both flats."

I looked to my right and I could see an officer in uniform stood to attention.

"I'm PC Hague, Sir. I searched the store cupboard belonging to number 19 and found the body. DC Key and PC Dennison are inside the flat with two males, Marc Fuller and Michael Little. They're under arrest."

As he talked, he kept pointing towards the cupboard door that was closed. I could see rubbish piled high on the landing - plastic bags that were full to bursting, old pieces of carpet and filthy cardboard boxes.

"That's the rubbish that was on top of the body Sir, when I eventually managed to open the door."

The front door to the flat was closed. The two suspects would be taken out of the flat to different police stations but before I did anything else, I wanted to see the body in situ. Tony and Alan stood waiting for me to make the first move. It wasn't something I was looking forward to because I knew deep down that it was Rachel, and if she'd been killed soon after her abduction, then there'd be a fair degree of decomposition. Although council flats usually had a familiar smell - damp, cold, musty and depressing - there was something else in the air. It was sickly, nauseous and sinister, the kind of smell you'd never forget.

I opened the cupboard door. Inside it was small, maybe only three feet square. Looking down, I saw a leg that was partially exposed, the skin was smooth, pale and delicate. It didn't look real and so I touched it. It was so cold and there were clear signs of decomposition. The body appeared to be in a fetal position wrapped in an old curtain and a blue-coloured bed sheet. Although Tony and Alan, like me, had pretty much seen everything in their careers, they'd not been ready for the horror of witnessing the brutal aftermath caused by her killer or killers. We just stood, not talking. Inside, I was screaming with rage. Fucking bastards, fucking cowards, fucking low-life scum. But losing control wouldn't undo what'd already been done; a human being or beings had made a decision to end a young life before it'd barely begun.

"Right, we've a job to do. If it's Rachel and I don't think there's much doubt, then all we can do for her and her family is to move heaven and earth to convict those responsible for her murder. And that's exactly what we're going to do."

I knew that this was just the beginning of a long road ahead that would lead to Crown Court many months from now. Although we'd found the body and there were two in custody, there could be no room for complacency. Every action taken from now on would be open to scrutiny by some smart-arsed defence barrister. I'd have to be on top form and I'd have to make sure that everyone involved with the case would be on top from as well.

"I've already called the pathologist. It's Professor Milroy. I knew you'd want him here before we moved the body. And

159

I've got a forensic scientist coming too."

"Thanks, Tony."

I called DC Key to get more information about what was happening inside.

"We're OK, Sir. I'm sat with Fuller and PC Dennison's with Little. Looks like Little's the one who's responsible. He admitted it straight away. Fuller claims he knew nothing about what's in the cupboard. Went mad when he was arrested."

"I want you to bring Fuller out first. He'll be taken to Tower Grange by other officers. Well done."

The door opened slowly. DC Key emerged with Marc Fuller in handcuffs. His appearance didn't surprise me. I'd have instantly picked him out of any crowd as Hull born and bred with his gaunt, thin face and clammy, pale complexion. The streets of Hull were lined with males who looked just like him. He was sweating, heart pounding and restless as the detective ushered him forward.

"Why you arresting me? It's that sick bastard in there what done it. I know fuck all about anything."

He spat out the words in a typical local Hull accent. We waited for a while until Fuller had been safely escorted away from the expectant group of reporters. I looked out of the small window on the landing. A crowd was gathering despite the torrential rain. Normally, residents of the estate wouldn't show any interest in police activity; they'd be used to the sight of some local burglar being carted off. But this was different, people had got behind the search for Rachel - apart from the elderly lady who'd slammed the door in my face - and there were some worried and concerned faces looking up at me. I called PC Dennison, who was alone in the flat with Little.

"Sir, I'm OK. Says he's responsible and that he's wanted to tell somebody. Tried to make notes of what he's said."

The young officer's voice was barely a whisper. Alan had already told me that PC Dennison was still in his probation and yet here he was having already arrested two males for murder. He seemed calm but I needed to get him out of the flat as soon as possible; if Little had committed murder, then he was capable of anything, including harming PC Dennison.

"Just try to remember everything he says. Keep him calm. Sounds like you're doing a great job. I want you to bring him out when you're ready. Other officers will take him to Queens Gardens. Be careful."

PC Dennison emerged first leading Little by his handcuffed wrists. Little looked straight at me as if he recognised me. Maybe he'd been watching the TV that morning before the searches began, or maybe he'd been following the almost 24/7 news coverage of Rachel's disappearance. He didn't say anything as he disappeared down the stairs to a waiting police van. I knew that I'd never forget his eyes, it was the first thing I noticed about him. They were black as hell and they didn't fit his round, chubby face with his receding hair, goatee beard and moustache. I tried to imagine just how he'd managed to entice Rachel, if it were she, into his flat. With his slightly hunch-backed, flabby upper body dressed in filthy clothes, and the overwhelming stench of cigarettes and urine coming through the open doorway, there'd be no way that she'd have gone willingly. Nobody would. Tony must have read my mind because he was scouring the stairwell with his usual keen eye for detail. He called me down to take a look.

"Can't be certain but looks like blood spattering on the wall to me. I'll get it tested. If he abducted her off the street this could be her blood. Just an assumption but can't see how he'd have got her into his flat unless he used force, maybe a knife would be my guess."

The unmistakable voice of Professor Milroy shattered the sombre atmosphere as he entered the building talking to one of Tony's SOCOs. He was a big character blessed with an upbeat personality, and he commanded his surroundings with an air of confidence and self-belief. I'd seen it many times before as he automatically became the centre of attention, everyone else just listened as he spoke. He'd a habit of verbalising his thoughts. It was strangely off putting because you never knew if he was thinking aloud or actually talking to someone wanting an answer. But he was bloody good at his job and that's all I cared about right now. He moved forward to open the door to the store cupboard. A bead of sweat ran down his forehead. His mood turned, and his friendly chatter turned to an eerie silence as he carefully examined the inside.

"Better recover the body carefully still wrapped in the curtain and blanket. She's been dead for some time I'm afraid judging by the degree of decomposition on her skin. There's a small wound on her chest and a trickle of blood."

I took another look. He'd moved the body slightly and part of the curtain to expose her chest and more of her legs. She was wearing a dark dress that covered her breasts. Just above the neckline, there was a small wound and a trail of dried blood. Both the curtain and blue sheet that she was wrapped in looked like they were heavily soaked in blood. Her knees must have been forced against her chest to make her fit into the tiny space and then rubbish piled high on top of her. The Professor leant against the wall for a moment and, if I wasn't mistaken, even though he must have been to countless horrific scenes, this had clearly affected him.

"Poor girl. Very sad."

Tony, assisted by one of his SOCOs, DC Chapman, placed a sheet of plastic on the cold, red tiled floor, and carefully lifted the body out of the cupboard still wrapped in the curtain and sheet. I tried not to look at her, I didn't want to look at her. The killer or killers had not only stolen her life but also her dignity, and left her in a tiny cupboard that might well have been her grave if she'd not been found. At least now, even though there'd be post-mortems, her family would be able to lay her to rest. I had to close my mind to the horror and concentrate on what needed to be done. I knew it'd be the only way I'd be able to get through today. Tony and his team wrapped her body in the plastic sheet and then placed it into a body bag in readiness for the journey to the mortuary. It was agreed to conduct the post-mortem at 6pm, leaving me plenty of time to go inside Little's flat.

The Forensic Scientist, Dr. Warner, a specialist in blood distribution, arrived. I'd worked with her before some time ago on a case involving the anal rape of a ninety-two-year-old lady. She'd impressed me with her enthusiasm and I hadn't forgotten just how likeable she'd been. It was good to see her again because I knew that she was extremely competent and would do a first-class job.

There was no natural daylight and so Dr. Warner led the

way into Little's flat with a powerful torch. Immediately beyond the front door was a small entrance hall, maybe only five or six feet square. The warm, claustrophobic stench of stale cigarettes and urine hit me again like a wall of filth. We both recoiled for a moment.

"I can't be certain but I'd say that this could be where she was attacked. I'd say somebody has tried to clean blood from the floor. They've not done a very good job fortunately. A palm print in blood on that door jamb looks promising."

There was barely room for the both of us never mind Tony, who was videoing the proceedings. I looked down at the beige-coloured vinyl tiles. There was a piece of soiled green carpet, a basketball, tins of paint and a pair of black adidas tracksuit bottoms. We moved to our left into the bathroom. The walls were a kind of orange-mustard colour and the green checked curtains were closed. A black mountain bike was leant against the bath that was covered with a thick layer of grime. The sink and toilet were filthy and disgusting and so was the floor.

The bedroom was to the right of the bathroom. The first thing I noticed was the window. The curtains didn't match. I was pretty sure that the one on the left was the same pattern as the one that had been used to cover her body. There were two beds: one was a single adjacent to the window, and the other was a double on the opposite side of the room. An old TV positioned at the foot of the double bed, gave out a flicker of light. We had to tread carefully because the floor was littered with all kinds of junk - pornographic magazines, overflowing ash-trays, polystyrene takeaway containers and empty coke bottles. The walls were covered with pin-ups of nude females, apart from a flag of England and another that I didn't recognise. It had a gold cross set against a black background.

"I'm really not looking forward to testing the bedding."

I knew exactly what Dr. Warner was thinking and I had some sympathy for her. The heavily stained sheets made my skin crawl. Although I'd had the misfortune of witnessing the worst squalor imaginable during my career, this was on a whole new level. As I stood knee deep in garbage, I knew that there was no way that anyone would enter Little's flat willingly. I'd already made the decision in my mind, the flat would have to be kept until the trial for the jury to see at first hand. It was something I'd done before on other murder cases. If I were a juror being asked to make such a big decision about somebody else's life, then I'd want to see for myself. Definitely. Photographs and videos had their uses but they were no substitute for the real thing. A moment inside Little's flat would have more impact than a thousand photographs.

The next room along from the bedroom was the living room. There was at least some light coming from the window that had the same patterned curtains as the one found wrapped around the body. They were drawn revealing a single net curtain that was probably white at one time but no longer, cigarette smoke had clearly taken its toll. I walked across to the window, careful not to make contact with a settee and matching single chair. I'd a clear view onto Nashcourt. The crowd had grown and it was still raining heavily. Opposite the settee, there was a gas fire with a wooden surround. I could see some photographs of Little and other males drinking together, arm in arm, on top of the mantelpiece. Looked like some kind of party, or night out on the town.

The kitchen led directly off the living room. The curtains were closed. Rotting food and dirty plates, covered every available surface - in the sink, on top of the fridge and all over the floor. And then I saw something that looked out of place, a set of knives arranged neatly in a purpose made wooden stand. There was a box alongside showing a picture of the set of Gruntik Imperial kitchen knives of different blade lengths. Dr. Warner shone her flashlight and carefully picked out the longest knife from the block.

"Looks like this one has been cleaned. The others are filthy and greasy. This one isn't. Smells funny as well. I'd say it's been bleached."

Could this be the knife that was used to kill Rachel? Dr. Warner was keeping an open mind until it could be tested, but if it had been bleached, then any traces of blood would be destroyed.

It was time for the post-mortem. I left the forensic examination of the flat in the very capable hands of Dr. Warner, Tony and his SOCOs, a task that I knew would take days to complete. I escaped via the rear entrance careful to avoid the crowd of onlookers and the press. It was still pouring down as I walked the few hundred yards back to the station. I thought about going into the incident room but I didn't feel like talking about what I'd just seen. There'd be time enough for that tomorrow at the briefing when I'd be in a position to give my team the results of the post-mortem. I drove past 56 Hall Road and headed into the city. The FLOs were still with Ray and Wanda. How on earth would they be coping right now? Would they be clinging on to the remote possibility that it might not be Rachel? Should I stop and talk to them? I'd be of no comfort to them, I thought, and I didn't want to be late and so I carried on.

The mortuary was becoming like a second home for me. I'd been so many times over the past couple of years, I'd become almost immune to the experience of watching a body being taken apart. But I knew that this time would be different, it felt like I'd come to know Rachel. In the mortuary car park, I smothered my arms in aftershave; it always helped to block out the unforgettable smell of death. I was the last to arrive. Tony was sat listening to Professor Milroy talking about some of his recent cases.

"Back again. Can't keep away from the place. Coffee as usual."

Mike, the mortuary attendant, smiled as he greeted me. His overly long moustache still looked ridiculous, particularly with his pointed nose and thin face. But I liked him. He was working at the mortuary when I'd begun as a probationer back in 1982, and he'd been part of the usual initiation procedure for raw recruits. I'd fallen hook, line, and sinker for the dead body that suddenly came alive at three in the morning routine. It'd frightened me to death but fair play to him, he'd a sense of humour that probably helped to keep him sane working in such a bleak place for so many years. DC Chapman was busy preparing for the post-mortem, and DC Philips, the exhibits officer, immediately stood up and shook me by the hand. I think it was in recognition that the operation had been successful but he didn't speak. It didn't seem appropriate in the circumstances. I acknowledged Professor Milroy and opened my notebook. I was ready to document everything, I was ready to stand by his shoulder and listen to his every word. I was ready to ask question after question.

Professor Milroy began his investigation into the cause of death. He'd a way of working that I'd seen many times before. It was brisk and efficient, and to the independent observer, it might seem to lack empathy. I'm not sure that I'd be any different though, given the number of post-mortems he carried out every year. How could he be as involved emotionally as me? He'd probably have another case tomorrow and the next day and so on. But I wanted him to care because I knew that it was Rachel. I wanted him to somehow show me that he'd remember this one above all others.

The body lay on the cold, metal mortuary table, still wrapped in the curtain and bed sheet, still curled in a fetal position. The Professor began by gently straightening the body and uncovering her face. There was no doubt in my mind that it was Rachel. There was a degree of decomposition, particularly to her eyes that would be heartbreaking for Ray and Wanda to see. She'd have to be identified by other means, maybe DNA or dental records. I was pretty sure that the Coroner wouldn't want to put the family through such an ordeal. The Professor continued.

"External examination. Body of a white female. Height 181cm. Estimated weight 60kg of thin build. Hair dyed blonde and quite long in length. Eyes have undergone decomposition. Own natural teeth present. Toenails painted pink. Mud present on the front of the left lower leg and also running across the left thigh. Three bruises on lower left leg, one to her right ankle. Wearing red dress, knickers and a black jacket."

There could be only two explanations for the presence of mud on her left leg: either she'd fallen down, maybe trying to get away from her attacker, or she'd been dragged along the ground against her will. It didn't seem likely that she'd just lost her footing for no reason, and the bruises supported my theory that Rachel fought her attacker. I imagined her struggling on the concrete stairs leading to 19 Nashcourt and bruising her legs on the edges of the steps in a desperate attempt to break free.

Professor Milroy expertly removed her clothing to reveal the full horror of the brutal assault on her body - frenzied, without mercy and unbelievably cruel. Poor Rachel's upper back, neck and head were littered with stab wounds that looked deep and wide. She'd been attacked from behind, most probably in the tiny entrance hall of Little's flat. He held up her black jacket to the light.

"Seventeen stab defects in the back and multiple stab defects on the collar. I'd say a knife was used with a blade width of three centimeters or so. Single sharp edge."

Her dress was sleeveless with two thin shoulder straps that were still intact. They'd not been severed by the knife slicing through the jacket.

"Professor, if she'd been wearing the dress at the time of the attack, can you explain why the straps haven't been cut?"

"No. Sorry. Can't explain. Does seem odd though."

It seemed odd to me and it seemed odd to Tony as well.

Either the knife had simply missed the thin straps, or the straps must have fallen from her shoulders during the attack. The question that was preying most heavily on my mind though, was whether or not she'd been sexually assaulted. It was the most likely motive, and yet the Professor announced with a degree of certainty that he didn't think she had. What other motive could there have been? Was the eminent Professor, right? How could he know without waiting for the intimate samples to be examined? Maybe the detective in me wanted a semen profile to be found. DNA evidence might well prove to be the only direct evidence to present to a jury. I was determined to keep an open mind. I was pretty sure that it would be one of the first questions Ray and Wanda would ask, and I was already turning over in my mind what I'd say when the time came. I'd have to tell them that it could be weeks before the results would be known.

The post-mortem finally came to an end some four hours later. Professor Milroy delivered his conclusions, and I wrote down every word that he said.

"Death was due to multiple stab wounds of the neck and chest. The principle fatal stab wounds were to the chest, which have penetrated from the back to the front causing damage to the lungs and other structures including the aorta. The stab wounds would have caused hemorrhaging, both into the chest and externally. Blood would have entered the airway and could have been coughed out. The stab wound defect on the back of the chest, number 22, was a large defect with evidence of the knife having been withdrawn and re-entered through the wound. It penetrated the full width of the chest, with the tip of the knife passing through the skin of the front of the chest, causing wound, number 27. There were no defence injuries. There were no obvious marks of restraint."

The small wound I saw on Rachel's chest had been caused by a knife being thrust so forcefully into her back that it passed right through her body. Why had her killer used so much force on such a fragile young woman? Why so many stab wounds? Why such a frenzied attack? I thought about how to convey to a jury the brutality and savagery of her murder. They wouldn't be shown photographs of Rachel's twenty-seven wounds - it'd be far too prejudicial and probably leave them mentally and emotionally scarred for life. Although they'd be able to see the location of the wounds on a simple outline drawing of a body produced by Professor Milroy, I'd need to find a way of assisting the jury to better understand the context of what he'd just said.

"If it's of any consolation to her parents, I believe that she died very quickly from any one of the principle stab wounds to her back, although I can't say for certain. I believe that she was dead when the wounds on her head and neck were inflicted. It'll be a while for the toxicology and swab results to come through I'm afraid. I'd look at identification through dental records. But there's little doubt that it is the body of Rachel Louise Moran. And in my opinion, the degree of decomposition would lead me to conclude that she probably died in the early hours of New Year's Day. Her body would still have been warm when she was put into the cupboard before rigor mortis had set in."

It was late, maybe eleven. We all went our separate ways. There was nothing else to say. It'd been a long and exhausting day, and I'd experienced just about every emotion there was to experience given the circumstances. I took a different route home. As I drove west out of the city, I could see the familiar, imposing and majestic outline of the Humber Bridge in the distance, bathed in light, against the black sky. For a city better known for high levels of crime and deprivation, it was something to be proud of. I parked down by the foreshore, almost directly beneath the bridge. It was a quiet place frequented mostly by dog walkers, couples in cars with steamed up windows, and police officers on nights catching up on their sleep.

I stood on the bank of the enormous river as it thundered past on its long journey to the North Sea. I was hoping that the gale-force wind would clear my head but all I could think of was the many post-mortems I'd been to over the years. I could see their faces as they appeared before me in the darkness: little George Lofty kept in a cardboard box from birth and slowly starved by his mother until he no longer had the strength to live; Natalie Clubb, a prostitute, murdered and her body butchered and thrown into a drain; a local alcoholic who lived on the streets and was kicked to death by a man for no reason; and now Rachel. There were many more, of course. Perhaps I'd reached my limit of coping with so much death.

I felt the pull of the mighty river. It'd be so easy to jump in and be done with the struggle of living with all that living had come to mean to me now. I'd give anything to go back to how I used to be. But I couldn't find my way back, no matter how hard I tried. It was the mental exhaustion that made me feel like I was being buried alive. It was the mental exhaustion that gave me no peace. I understood now why people felt like they'd no option but to end their lives, and if there was a top-ten list of favourite ways to go in Hull, then jumping off the Humber Bridge had to be right up there. As a uniformed constable, I'd been called many times to try and stop some poor soul from taking their final leap. Some I managed to talk down, some I didn't. Back then, I'd no idea just how they were suffering, but I'd a good idea now.

I thought about what the Davo of old would say to me, 'are you seriously thinking about ending it all? What about your family, your wife, your children? Get a grip for God's sake, selfish bastard'. He wouldn't have entertained such dark thoughts and I felt ashamed of myself for even contemplating suicide. No matter how low I felt, I knew that I'd an important job to do and that was to make sure that Rachel's killer or killers were put safely behind bars. How could I let down Ray and Wanda? How could I let down my family? And it'd be the biggest humiliation of all to give those who'd conspired against me the perfect opportunity to gloat at my untimely demise. No, I'd have to fight my way back, inch by inch, and I couldn't do that if I was six feet under. But how? I'd nobody to turn to for inspiration or words of wisdom. And then suddenly, from nowhere, images of my Dad flooded my mind and I heard his gentle voice calling,

'Son, I've watched you fall apart for far too long. You have the answer. You know what to do. Look at what you've achieved today. I'm proud of you. But you've lost all your power. Just think about how good you'd feel if you harnessed all that negative, raging anger and fury burning inside of you and turned it into a source of self-power, a power that would give you the strength to fight back and regain your lost confidence. It will be your only chance of finding your way back'.

I'd no idea where those words came from. Maybe I'd subconsciously arranged them to make it sound like it was my Dad, because I'd have given anything for him to have been here with me now, even for a moment. They made a great deal of sense as I thought about just how negative I'd become. There was indeed a raging anger inside of me that had brought me to my knees, but I'd allowed it to, nobody else. I'd given it permission to take away the joy of living, to fear that something bad was going to happen, to shatter my confidence and much more. Maybe tonight had to happen for me to realise that I'd always known the answer to finding my way back, turning my negativity into a source of positive energy. I felt like a modern day Scrouge in a way. I tried to picture a visit from the future if I continued to do nothing and I didn't like what I saw, a bleak landscape of bitterness and depression. I thought about what the alternative might look like and I knew what I had to do: leave the past behind and start again. Within a heartbeat, I began to feel better. I knew that it wasn't going to be easy but nothing could stop me from me from choosing to be positive again, and I was pretty sure that the rest would follow, at least I hoped it would and that it wasn't too late. I wondered why my Dad had appeared offering a way back for his son. I'd no idea. Perhaps it was some kind of reward for trying to be a good person. Maybe life gave you a break now and again, just because that's the way life is. Whatever the reason, I felt like a different person already as I got back into the warmth of my car.

I sat for a while trying to compose myself but the tears came anyway. I was physically and mentally exhausted. Thankfully, my mobile came to life with its 'Positively Fourth Street' ringtone. It was Shaun. He'd just finished interviewing Little and sounded absolutely shattered. It was just what I needed, to hear the sound of a friendly voice.

"No comment from Little, boss. Fuller talked though and didn't want a solicitor. Denies everything and called Little a 'fucking murdering bastard'. Sounds unlikely that he knew nothing but I believe him. Just a feeling that's all. Before we start interviewing again tomorrow, DCI Redmore's arranged for the three officers who found Rachel to be at the briefing at eight. You're going to want to hear what PC Dennison has to say. He's done a brilliant job recording everything in his notebook and we made sure that Little signed it on video. Oh, before you go boss, Little's brief, Harding, is already complaining about a lack of disclosure. Says that's why he's advising Little to go no comment."

Driving home, it took me a while to regain my composure, but it didn't take me long to realise the significance of Little going no comment. The saying, 'If it seems too good to be true, it probably is', came to mind. We'd found poor Rachel and the probable crime scene, together with her killer, who'd already freely admitted his guilt. A conviction would be expected given those circumstances, but I'd enough experience to know that there was much that could go wrong. It was one thing to go to trial with little or no evidence and gain a conviction against all the odds, but this was at the other end of the spectrum. I'd some serious thinking to do before tomorrow because I knew that I couldn't afford to assume anything. Would Little's confession to PC Dennison be held inadmissible? Would he go down the diminished responsibility route? Would he use the I can't remember what happened routine? Would he blame Fuller?

With Harding already complaining about lack of disclosure, the first person I'd call tomorrow would be DCI Gary Shaw. He was a national expert in investigative interviewing and he'd kindly helped me before on other cases. He was very likeable with a thick Geordie accent. It was the kind of accent that you could listen to for hours, and he'd a certain charm that was both disarming and effective. Defence solicitors would start out all prickly and unhelpful but before long they'd succumb to Gary's way of thinking. If there were any challenges to Little's interviews, then I couldn't think of anyone else I'd rather see in the witness box than Gary. The jury would love him. I just hoped that he'd be available.

PART 2

IF IT SEEMS TOO GOOD TO BE TRUE, IT PROBABLY IS

TWELVE

'I must be evil. A normal person wouldn't do that'

At last, we'd solved the mystery of Rachel's disappearance, and the crushing weight of expectation had already lifted from my shoulders. Accordingly, the drive into work was very different to all the previous days of the investigation. Selfishly, I wallowed in the realisation that because of the action I'd taken, there'd been an outcome, a conclusion and hopefully some kind of closure for Rachel's family. Although my police career wouldn't now be defined by a failure to find Rachel's body, the renewed spring in my step was short lived because I knew that this was just the beginning: we still had to gain a conviction at Crown Court. Whilst I could do my best to try and second-guess Little's defence, the problem was that there were so many variables that I couldn't control. He'd the upper hand because whilst we were duty bound to disclose all the evidence against him, we'd have to wait for his defence statement. And then there'd be the trial - the judge, jury, prosecuting and defence barristers, and witnesses - would all play their part in deciding the outcome. I just had to figure out how best to influence that outcome.

Maly, Trev and Alan were waiting for me in my office that

unexpectedly felt welcoming and familiar. I didn't talk about the post-mortem and they didn't ask. We just sat for a while enjoying a few moments of peace before the madness of the day began.

"You look different somehow. You've got a smile on your face for a change," said Maly sarcastically.

"On my way into work, I just thought what a bloody fine day it is. We should all go out for a drink sometime."

They looked at each other as if they didn't know what to say, but I was determined to show everybody that I had a new-found optimism for the future, and I couldn't think of a better place to begin than with my close colleagues. I could tell that it seemed to be working. Alan said more than usual, and Trev came out with a couple of one-liners that made us all laugh. Perhaps positivity is infectious, I thought, as I picked up the phone to call Gary Shaw. It was good to hear his unmistakable Geordie lilt once again.

"Been busy I see. Is there any way I can help?"

I told him about Little's solicitor and the issue with disclosure.

"Aye well that won't be a problem. Him an me'll get along just fine once we've had a bit of a natter."

I knew exactly what that meant. I'd seen him in action before and he was bloody brilliant at treating the process of interviewing suspects as a kind of art form. And that included bringing solicitors onside to such an extent that they'd view Gary as a friend rather than foe. It was agreed that he'd come to help DS Weir and DS Austin with interviewing Little and Fuller.

"I'll be there later on today. I'm not far away as luck

would have it. Maybe we can have a pint or two or three."

I walked confidently into the briefing room that was full to bursting. There were officers from pretty much every part of the force involved with the search for Rachel, including underwater search, forensics, intelligence, dogs, horses and, of course, my own investigation team. I knew that I'd remember this day for a long time to come, not only because we'd achieved what we'd set out to achieve, but because for the first time in years I felt calm and self-assured. I knew that even my fiercest critics would have to acknowledge that we'd two in custody for murder, however begrudgingly. That's the way the police culture worked - 'he might be an arrogant twat but fair play to him, made a bold decision and it paid off. Still think he's a twat though'. I'd no doubt that would be the collective sentiment across the force over yesterday's events.

What happened next took me by surprise. The three officers who found Rachel, all stood up together to acknowledge my entrance. It wasn't something that happened often, unless it was the Chief Constable. I'd witnessed it in other forces like West Yorkshire though, where there seemed to be more respect for rank. It was an awkward moment because they expected everyone else to do the same. But, nevertheless, they continued to stand until I'd taken my seat as the rest looked on, slightly embarrassed. I decided to let the officers give their account of what happened when they knocked on Little's door, before talking about the post-mortem. I couldn't wait.

There was silence in the room. PC Dennison volunteered to tell the story. Young, dark-haired and definitely nervous, he cleared his throat before recalling in some detail what happened when they arrived at 19 Nashcourt.

"Little opened the door. White, about five foot nine tall, chubby, early to mid-twenties, with very dark short hair. He'd quite a stubbly face with a goatee beard and moustache. Seemed friendly in a matter of fact kind of way. Didn't seem nervous at all and he happily let us into his flat and consented to our request to the search. There was a second male, Marc Fuller, who was younger, maybe late teens early twenties. Slimmer, local accent, same height, fluffy moustache."

PC Dennison's description of what he saw as they searched each room was impressive. He was spot on as he recalled the squalor and the smell, and then he paused for a moment before continuing. He took a sip of water as if he was trying to compose himself before launching into how they eventually managed to open the outside store cupboard door. I'd have done the same thing, given what he was about to say.

"Little got some keys, a few silver ones on a ring and was trying them in the lock of the door. I was standing next to him looking and thinking he's turning the key the wrong way. He said the keys wouldn't work. Little disappeared and produced some more keys and asked Fuller if they were his. Little managed to turn one of the keys but didn't open the door. Little squeezed past us and went back into the flat."

I asked the officer if he needed a break because I knew what was coming next, but he said, respectfully, that he was OK and would rather continue.

"PC Hague had to use some force to get the door open. I was stood next to him, and I could see piles of rubbish piled high to the top of the cupboard as the door opened. It was only maybe three foot by three foot. I didn't think a six-foot-tall person would be in there."

The young officer was struggling, having to relive that moment again, a moment that he'd probably never be able to forget or erase from his memory.

"Fuller was still hanging around the hallway area and said, 'I bet it stinks in there'. PC Hague indicated to me to 'sniff up'. I sniffed up, and although I haven't had much experience in dealing with dead bodies, I've smelt dead bodies before through visits to the mortuary and recognised the smell. It was like rotting vegetables. But I didn't expect to find a body in there. PC Hague took out bin bags and rolls of carpet and I helped him. And then we both stopped at the same time. We looked at each other and I said, 'Christ, it looks like a leg'. The skin had a wax like look with discoloured blotches like bruises. I thought it was a female leg as it wasn't hairy and it was quite delicate. The body was covered in an old curtain and sheet. It was crammed into the bottom of the cupboard. I didn't want to look anymore and neither did PC Hague. Didn't want to damage anything forensically. I didn't want it to get too gory."

PC Hague and DC Key sat listening, nodding every so often in agreement. DC Key looked absolutely shattered. He'd been the one to call me with the heartbreaking news, sobbing as he'd uttered the words that would change many people's lives forever. I'm not sure whether they'd any idea what they'd achieved. What might have happened if they'd not bothered to look inside the cupboard? Would Little have simply left poor Rachel to rot there indefinitely? Would she have remained undiscovered? Would Little have moved on never to be found again? But none of that mattered now because of the diligence of these three officers. They'd be always associated with finding Rachel, and I realised that despite the torrential rain, despite being told to 'fuck off' by an elderly lady who thought that I was a 'grey-haired twat', luck had been on my side. Somehow, three dedicated and humble officers had arrived at 19 Nashcourt determined to do a first-class search. And they did. PC Dennison continued.

"PC Hague, me and Fuller, went back into the flat and entered the lounge where Little was still with DC Key. My head was racing and I thought 'Oh Christ'. Little was on the sofa with DC Key. I spoke to them both. 'Based on what we've found out there, in the cupboard, I'm arresting you both on suspicion of murder'. Almost immediately, Fuller began rocking in his chair, like an astonished response, like he was taken aback by what I'd just said. PC Hague and me handcuffed them both. Little didn't resist but Fuller was anxious, not flailing but shuffling on his seat. Fuller said something like, 'murder, what you on about murder for'? Fuller looked over to Little and said, 'do you know something about this'? Little was looking down with his hands in his lap and said, 'yes'. Then he looked up at me and said, 'he's nothing to do with this'."

Alan asked the obvious question.

"PC Dennison, based on what you saw, do you think that Fuller had anything to do with this?"

"Sir, I've never been in this position before so it's hard to tell but Fuller was astonished when he'd realised what was going on. Can't think of a better word than astonished. We've talked it over since and we all think he's either a brilliant actor or he really didn't know there was a body in Little's cupboard. As we were waiting for transport, I just made small talk with Little. I don't know why but I didn't know what else to do. He talked about how he loved his grandma and that she'd be mortified when she found out. Fuller kept shaking his head saying, 'how can you talk to him after what he's done, fucking evil bastard. We've known each other since we were kids and I can't believe he's been letting me come to his flat as a friend with that in the cupboard'. Seemed really angry at Little. Seemed genuine to me."

Was it possible that Fuller knew nothing? If he was involved or knew something, why didn't he just stay away from Little's flat? Now that Little had a solicitor, would he blame Fuller? But Little had already confessed to PC Dennison. We were all about to find out what he told the officer.

"When I was alone with Little, he began to talk. He knew we were from the Rachel Moran incident. 'It's her', he said. He was clearly upset. And then he opened up. 'I need to get it off my chest. I've wanted to tell someone or someone find out for so long'. I could see sadness in his face, he wasn't crying, didn't give me eye contact and kept his face angled down. 'I can't be normal, I must be evil, a normal person wouldn't do that'. I tried to tell him that it wasn't the time to talk but he seemed to want to talk. 'The night she went missing, she was on the street and she was walking past'. I took the 'she' to mean Rachel Moran. 'She called over to me. She jogged to catch up with me as I was walking along. She told me she'd been at her Mum's, she wanted to walk with me and felt safer walking with me. I asked her to go back to my flat for a drink. She agreed. We'd been talking but we ended up arguing. During the argument I hit her across the face. She got upset because her boyfriend used to hit her. She went in the kitchen and as I walked up behind her, she swung round and slashed me on the arm with a knife'. Little indicated a mark on his left or right arm but I didn't see any mark. 'I lost it, picked up a knife and stabbed her'. He didn't say where he got the knife from, where he stabbed her or how many times. I didn't want to prompt him to tell me stuff. He'd already told me what I wanted to know."

That saying 'If it seems too good to be true, it probably is', kept coming back to me, like it was a warning to be careful. On the plus side, Little had inferred that it was Rachel in the cupboard and that he'd stabbed her. At the time he told PC Dennison, nobody knew that she'd been stabbed. That would be crucial evidence. And so, would the fact that the young officer's account of what happened was agreed by Little as a true and accurate record of what he'd said to the officer in his flat, all captured on video in the charge room. For someone so young in service, PC Dennison had dealt with a very unique set of circumstances with calm authority and intelligence. The notes he'd made of Little's confession were the best I could've hoped for. I gave a very brief summary of the results of the post-mortem, and I asked everyone not to talk to the press about Rachel's cause of death, not under any circumstances. Although Little had already admitted to stabbing Rachel, there was always the possibility that he'd told someone else what he'd done.

After the briefing, I bought the three officers a coffee in the canteen. People nodded in our direction as they recognised their colleagues who'd be forever known as the ones who found Rachel. They looked embarrassed and uncomfortable as they realised what was happening.

"You'd better get used to it. All the attention I mean. And rightly so, you all deserve it. I wanted to thank you all personally for what you did yesterday. You should be very proud of yourselves."

I could see that PC Dennison was more at ease than either DC Key or PC Hague. PC Hague was the quiet one with a very obvious respect for rank. But I sensed that it was more than that, it was a respect for everyone around him. I'd seen it before but not often. It was genuine humility that shone through in his every move, everything he said, every look he gave. PC Dennison wanted to acknowledge what the others had done, maybe because he'd received all the attention, given that he was the one who'd arrested Little and Fuller.

"Sir, it was PC Hague who insisted on searching the cupboard and taking all the rubbish out. We spent ages at every house we searched 'cos Rob wanted to do a thorough job. I don't think he's even told his wife that he was the one who found Rachel. I learned a lot from Rob yesterday."

PC Hague thought for a moment and all he said was,

"I was just doing my job."

And just as I was about to leave, I heard the unmistakable sound of DCI Gary Shaw's voice. It was good to see him and he seemed pleased to be here as he chatted to the three officers. In an instant, he managed to do what I could never do in a lifetime - put people at ease as if he'd known them forever. It was a gift, a gift that I didn't possess.

We made our way across town to Queens Gardens Police

Station. Shaun and Keith were busy preparing to interview Little again. They'd already had a confrontational meeting with Harding over disclosure and it was becoming a distraction they could do without. Time to introduce Gary to Little's solicitor. I led Harding into the interview room.

"Mr Harding this conversation is being video recorded. Is that OK?"

He nodded and shifted nervously in his seat as if he'd no idea what was coming.

"I understand from my detectives that you're not happy with the amount of disclosure you've been given so far. Is that correct?"

"Most definitely. That is why I've advised Mr Little to make no comment."

"I'm sorry to hear that. Accordingly, I've managed to obtain the services of one of the country's leading experts in investigative interviewing. This is DCI Gary Shaw from the National Crime Faculty and he'll be dealing with disclosure from now on. I wouldn't want you to think that I'm not taking your complaint seriously. Should there be any issues over the interview process, then the DCI will be the one to give evidence at the trial."

Mr Harding looked uncomfortable. I'm not sure that he realised what was happening.

"Now then Mr Harding, I'm Gary and I just thought it'd be canny for us to have a natter. We all want the same thing, for Mr Little to be treated fairly and properly and to be given every opportunity to tell the truth. Right?"

"Yes, yes of course. My point entirely but how can he when I've had virtually no disclosure of the police case against my client?"

"Aye, well the police case against Mr Little amounts to the events that occurred yesterday and if I'm not mistaken, he made certain admissions to PC Dennison. Now then Henry, it is Henry isn't it? You don't mind if I call you Henry, do you?"

"Please do."

"Well Henry, the way I see it's this, Mr Little will be asked questions, perfectly reasonable questions covering everything from his childhood to the officers discovering a body in Mr Little's utility cupboard. He'll no doubt be given Special Warnings about the presence of the body in his flat. Now then Henry, I'm just trying to help you here because judges tend to take a dim view of solicitors who wrongly advise their clients to say nothing. Can you see me point?"

Harding was way out of his comfort zone, and I almost felt sorry for him because I'd a fair idea what was coming next. Gary would no doubt be quoting the judge in the case against Imran and Hussain back in 1997, who stated that: 'There is no requirement for the police to present a prima facie case before questioning the accused or to give the defence solicitor a full briefing before questioning the suspect'. Gary often talked about this case in the past and used it as part of his presentation on interviewing suspects that he gave up and down the country. I decided to leave them to talk. Little would be given reasonable written disclosure prior to each interview that would also be recorded on video. I had to show that everything we did would be capable of withstanding the most rigorous test of integrity.

Shaun and Keith were busy preparing to interview Little again. Knee deep in paper, poring over statement after statement, I knew that Shaun would leave nothing to chance. He'd know every statement backwards and every detail of the investigation from the minute Rachel disappeared. It was a gamble putting Keith with Shaun, but he'd done a good job so far and he deserved a chance. Gary joined us with a smile on his face.

"He's a canny lad that one, got on just fine. Still won't change his advice to Little though. Still going to make no comment. Couldn't seem to get his head around the fact that the police case against Little IS the discovery of the body and his admissions."

"So why are you smiling?" I asked.

"Well, I'm a canny lad too. Knowing that he's not going to change his mind is worth its weight in gold. Gives us the opportunity to ask him questions about what his likely defence is going to be. There's a clue in the caution 'but it may harm your defence if you do not mention something which you later rely on in court'."

Gary was right of course. We had to explore every possible defence Little might rely on to save his own skin. Although the custody clock was ticking, we spent some time brainstorming what we'd do in Little's position. To be an effective police officer you definitely had to think like a criminal. Now was the time to put that theory to the test. Failing to answer any questions gave Little time to formulate his defence statement that we'd probably not see for months. Maybe it was Harding's idea; after all, Little was within his rights to say nothing. We just had to hope that it'd be held against him when it came to trial. What would we do in Little's position? And then the penny dropped. Shaun was the first to put into words what we were all thinking.

"He's going to blame Fuller. That's what I'd do. If he gets away with it, he might get a short sentence for assisting an offender but he won't get life. He's got nothing to lose as far as I can see."

But if he was going to blame Fuller, they'd have to somehow explain the reason why Little had been so desperate to take responsibility for killing Rachel when he was arrested. We all agreed that Fuller's movements would be crucial during the early hours of New Year's Day. He'd need a cast iron alibi.

Little's medical history showed that he'd suffered from depression in the past. We knew he was seen by his social worker, Rose Lister on 16 January, and complained of being depressed over Christmas having 'lost touch with reality' for a few days. Accordingly, I decided to use Rose Lister as an appropriate adult to sit in on the interviews. It would help to protect us from being accused of failing to consider that Little may well be classed as 'vulnerable', given his state of mind.

Maly was at Priory Road Police Station with detectives, Follan and Spaven, who were interviewing Fuller. Unlike Little, he was talking openly and freely about where he'd been on New Year's Eve and the early hours of New Year's Day. According to Fuller, he had a few drinks with a couple of friends, John Blampey and Sarah Edwards, who live on Allerford Drive. He left just before midnight and walked to his home on Greenwich Avenue. It took him about twenty-five minutes. When he arrived, his sister, Kersty, was already there. He stayed in his room all night and didn't go anywhere near 19 Nashcourt. His mother, Janet Devine, would be able to support his story. If Fuller was telling the truth, then the only person who knew what'd happened was Little.

We outlined the most likely sequence of events based on what we knew so far. The CCTV footage discovered by DC Bailey showed two figures that we believed to be Rachel followed closely by Little. Rachel was heading home along Hall Road to Saxcourt but then she took a short cut across a poorly lit, almost pitch-dark, grassed area. With no street lighting, the only light would be from the windows of nearby flats. That would give Little the perfect opportunity to abduct Rachel and drag her the short distance to Nashcourt, her screams, if heard, mistaken for New Year celebrations. And, as I looked at the video screen at the powerfully built Little talking to Harding in the next room, Rachel wouldn't have stood a chance. The mud on her legs was consistent with being dragged across the grass, and the bruising on her knees and shins, with struggling to break free as Little forced her up the concrete stairs to his flat. Once inside the tiny hallway, Little probably stabbed her repeatedly from behind. If Little was driven by lust then he violated her as she lay face down, dying or dead. Whilst Professor Milroy was of the opinion that Rachel hadn't been sexually assaulted, I wasn't convinced. If Little had unprotected sex with her either before or after death, then we'd find the evidence and he'd surely know we'd find the evidence. But that would be weeks away. Maybe that was another reason for Little's silence so far: he'd be waiting for the results of the DNA tests before committing to his defence statement.

Why had the attack been so vicious and frenzied? Maybe he tried to approach her with an invitation to go back to his flat, an invitation that Rachel rejected, getting home to her kittens was the only thing that mattered to her. Maybe it was the rejection. We all agreed that our version of what happened was much closer to the truth than the one given by Little to PC Dennison. He was right when he told the officer that 'I must be evil or something', and that 'I just lost it and got real mad. I grabbed a knife and stabbed her'. The rest of what he'd said though, was carefully worded to make it look like Rachel went willingly to his flat, that she was the aggressor and cut him with a knife on his arm. And yet a medical examination showed no signs of a healed wound. That was an unconvincing lie.

Gary and me watched the video screen as Shaun and Keith took their seats opposite Little and his solicitor, with Rose Lister sat to one side. Little looked full of confidence as he was told that the interview was being remotely monitored by senior officers. He stared up towards the camera. It was the first time I'd seen him since he was led handcuffed out of his flat by PC Dennsion. The pressure was on Shaun as the lead interviewer, but I'd complete faith in his ability to strike the right balance between fairness, and a ruthless determination to seek out the truth. If Little thought that he was in for an easy ride given his comfort blanket of never ending 'no comment' replies, then he was very much mistaken. I knew that yesterday Shaun had concentrated on Little's background, his state of mind, his depression and anti-depressant medication, his family and the events leading

193

up to the discovery of Rachel's body. Little must be thinking that today would be much the same.

Shaun had other ideas. Without warning, he placed an A4 size photograph on the table. It was Rachel's body, showing the numerous stab wounds to her naked back and neck. Visibly shaken, close to tears, Little wretched as if he was going to be sick. Shaun didn't say a word. It was a tactic of his to leave an awkward silence, and it was awkward, as Little bowed his head down so that his chin was almost touching the table. Eventually, Shaun broke the silence.

"Michael, I want you to look again at the photograph of Rachel. Did you do this to her? Did you inflict all of these injuries?"

Little lifted his head slightly. It was the right question to ask because if he was going to blame Fuller, then this would be the perfect opportunity for him to do so. Just for a moment, I thought that he was going to start talking. He whispered in Harding's ear and looked again at the photograph. But then came 'no comment' that was spoken in barely a whisper.

"Did Marc Fuller play any part in the murder of Rachel Moran. If he did now's the time to tell us Michael."

The question clearly surprised Little. Shaun skillfully gave the impression that we thought that Fuller was involved. But would he take the bait? Would he take the opportunity to give us a preview of what his defence statement was likely to be? There was whispering between Harding and Little.

"He's a clever lad that Shaun. It's a simple question but I'll be surprised if either Little or Harding understand the significance of what Shaun's asking."

Gary was spot on. If Little did blame Fuller at the trial, then he would have to come up with a reasonable explanation for not answering Shaun's question. There was a good deal of hesitation before Little answered with 'no comment'.

"Michael, can you please show us your arms and show us where Rachel cut you as you claimed to PC Dennison."

Little's arms were already exposed.

"There's no marks on your arms Michael. You've been medically examined and there are no scars. No scars, because I believe that you're lying. Rachel didn't cut you, did she?"

"No comment."

Shaun produced a photograph of Rachel's body crammed into the tiny utility cupboard and placed it on the table without saying a word. Harding looked and then looked way. It was a photograph that should never have needed to be taken. What Little had done to Rachel couldn't be undone. He'd taken her young life, but to discard her still warm body as if it was just a piece of rubbish was an act of pure evil. And if I were ever asked for a definition of evil, then I'd simply produce that photograph. There'd be no need for any words.

"I want you to look at the photograph. Did you alone put Rachel's body in the cupboard? Did Marc Fuller help you in anyway?"

"No comment."

Little must have realised by now that Shaun would be doing the same thing with every question. Harding understood what was happening and requested a break so that he could speak to Gary. Little was taken back to his cell.

"Now then Henry, what can I do for you?"

Harding was in a prickly mood, clearly under pressure. I formed the opinion that he hadn't represented many clients accused of murder before.

"What's Fuller saying? Does he have an alibi? You can't expect Mr Little to answer any questions about Marc Fuller without proper and full disclosure."

"Aye, well the case I was telling you about before made it real clear. All Michael has to do is tell the truth. Why does he need to know what Marc Fuller's saying? Does he want to know so that he can lie to the detectives about what happened? I'm sorry Henry but you've been given written disclosure about what the detectives will be asking Michael. You won't be getting anything more I'm afraid."

There was no doubt that Harding was in awe of Gary and had been from the moment that they'd met. Gary had a kind of hypnotic effect on most people and Harding was no different. I was pretty sure that should Gary ever fancy a change of career, he'd make a bloody brilliant used car salesman.

Shaun resumed the interview with more photographs: Rachel's black jacket and dress, Rachel's passport and personal belongings found in the drain, and Rachel's chest showing her delicate skin, pierced by Little's knife stabbing into her back with brutal force. The detectives didn't ask any questions, they just explained the content of each photograph and maintained the long silences so enjoyed by Shaun. The problem was, that whilst Shaun had been doing most of the talking and doing his best not to be emotional or confrontational, Keith had other ideas. Without warning, he moved closer to Little so that their faces were only a few inches apart, and the following is a fair summary of what he said,

"You stabbed Rachel so that you could have sex with her. You had sex with her after she was dead or lay dying in a pool of blood. You're nothing but a bully who can't handle rejection because Rachel did reject you didn't she. It was an evil thing to do. You said it yourself, you must be evil. Did you have sex with Rachel?"

Keith spat out his words with venom and contempt in complete contrast to Shaun's measured and precise delivery, and if his intention was to elicit a reaction from Little, then he succeeded. For the first time, Little lost his composure as beads of sweat ran down his massive forehead. Keith had obviously struck a nerve. The atmosphere was claustrophobic and tense.

"I'll ask you again, did you rape Rachel or have sex with her after you'd killed her? I believe they call it necrophilia."

Little looked like he was about to have a heart attack as he tried to quell his natural urge to respond. If he did violate Rachel, then he'd surely be reliving what he'd done over and over again in his mind, and I wondered just what he'd have said if he'd not been advised to say no comment by his brief. To the independent observer, it would probably seem as though it was the good cop bad cop routine, but it wasn't. Keith had every right to challenge Little over motive, and whilst there was no doubt that his questioning was robust, it fell far short of being oppressive.

"I'll take your silence to mean that you don't want to make any comment."

Harding looked behind him towards the social worker as if he was looking for guidance on how to safeguard the best interests of his rattled client. He requested a break and I didn't blame him. Shaun brought the interview to a close and it was the right thing to do. Little needed time to regain his composure, and Shaun wouldn't want his interviews to be perceived as oppressive in any way.

The canteen at Queens Gardens Police Station hadn't changed much over the years and neither had the staff, they'd just grown older. But they were always friendly and ready to acknowledge my rise through the ranks from humble beginnings. They'd no hidden agendas, they'd no egos to speak of and I felt comfortable chatting to them. As we sat down for a coffee, Keith looked nervous.

"Sorry if I went in a bit too strong towards the end. But he's a bully and I can't stand bullies."

Keith had no need to say sorry. Little was a bully and his bullying behaviour had led to the most tragic consequences imaginable. It was simply human nature to want to redress the balance somehow, to make him feel pressured and uncomfortable.

Looking back to when I was a uniformed constable working in the city centre, I came across my fair share of bullies and I hated them with a vengeance. On one occasion, it was a late Saturday night in the bus station and it was full of drunken idiots, both men and women, screaming, shouting, fighting, throwing up, and urinating. It happened with alarming regularity every weekend and most weeknights for that matter. Gradually, over time, I'd grown tired of this behaviour and whereas some of my colleagues turned a blind eye for a quiet life, I did the exact opposite. A crowd had gathered and I expected to encounter a fight of some kind. But it wasn't a fight, it was a load of muscle-bound youths taking the piss out of a poor handicapped kid. They had him by the throat and he was sobbing. I shouted for them to stop. 'Fuck off black bastard. Fucking wooden top', came the reply.

They all ran off laughing and bare-chested, showing off their impressive muscles. I made it look like I'd given up the chase to arrest them and they soon settled in a group waiting for the last bus home. I walked up behind them and without warning, grabbed the ringleader by his neck so that I had him in a stranglehold. I pulled him backwards. His head hit the ground with a sickening thud, and all hell broke loose. I managed to put out a call for assistance over the radio as I struggled to keep hold of my prisoner. Thankfully, a police dog man, who happened to be passing, came to my rescue. The mere sight of his snarling beast of an Alsatian was enough to make his mates run for their lives. Back at the police station, with only the walls of his cell for company, the bully quickly turned into a quivering wreck as his bravado melted into tears. He subsequently received a huge fine for his cowardly and brutish behaviour.

For the rest of the day, Little stuck to his no comment strategy as Shaun painstakingly explored every possible defence that Little might later rely on in court. Gary couldn't think of anything that they'd missed and neither could I. But there was a growing feeling that Little's only way out would be to blame Fuller.

I met up with Maly back in my office. It was getting late

and we were both knackered. We'd a decision to make. Whilst there wouldn't be a problem persuading the CPS over charging Little with Rachel's murder, what to do with Fuller was the question.

"I think he should be bailed for the time being. I've watched and listened to what he's had to say all day and I honestly don't think he'd anything to do with Rachel's murder. I don't think he knew she was in the cupboard. I honestly don't. I know it sounds far-fetched. Just think about it. Little's confession, his comment that Fuller knew nothing about it, Fuller's look of astonishment following discovery of Rachel in the cupboard, his utter disgust towards Little, not to mention his pretty watertight alibi."

Maly smiled and began to laugh.

"It's been a long day and I'm sorry for laughing but I've got this image in my mind of Fuller giving evidence. He swears more than anyone I've ever met. Seriously, I don't know how he manages to include the words 'fucking, bastard, cunt, twat, arsehole', in just about every sentence. Almost like an art form. Not sure what the judge and jury'll make of him. That's if we'll be able to get him to court."

We both ended up laughing. Police officers could always be relied upon to find humour in the most tragic of circumstances. It didn't mean that we were insensitive or that we didn't care, on the contrary, it was just a way of coping with all bad stuff that's all. It was a welcome moment of relief from the strain of the day. I trusted Maly's judgement but I knew that in the end, it was my decision. There was only so much second-guessing we could do. We had to go with evidence and the evidence so far pointed to Little being solely responsible for killing Rachel. Bailing Fuller would give us time to investigate his movements over the New Year period and beyond. I couldn't rule out Little's defence team from raising the possibility that she'd died later, despite Professor Milroy's opinion that Rachel had died in the early hours of New Year's Day - it wasn't an exact science by any means. Maybe that was why they were so keen to discover what Fuller had been saying. And so, we called it a day, decision made. If nothing changed tomorrow, Fuller would be bailed and I'd contact the CPS over charging Little. There was a change of leadership at the Hull branch of the CPS. Bob Marshall had moved on to be replaced by Linda Sweeting. The mere fact that Linda Sweeting was a female was enough to put my senses on high alert.

I pulled out of the station car park to head home, and my mind inevitably turned to how Wanda and Ray were coping. A parents' ultimate fear had been realised for them, and I wondered whether they'd any idea of what was still to come. If I could, I'd move heaven and earth to be able to save them from being at the mercy of the criminal justice system. There was still a bloody great mountain to climb, there was still a very long way to go before Little would be stood in the dock to answer for what he did to Rachel. The scale of the challenge that lay ahead made me feel weary and exhausted. I remembered one of the inspirational quotes I was so fond of. 'We must meet the challenge rather than wish it were not before us'. Although the words made a great deal of sense, maybe I'd just met too many challenges along the way. I was pretty sure that I wouldn't be alone in thinking this way.

Little was formally charged with Rachel Moran's murder

at 1934hrs, the next day in the custody suite of Queens Gardens Police Station. Flanked by Shaun and Keith, Little stood handcuffed and showed not a flicker of emotion as the custody sergeant read out the charge and asked him if he understood what was happening. Little didn't say a word. The custody sergeant pressed him again but Little refused to acknowledge what was being said to him. No response, nothing. As he was led back to his cell, I thought about the countless times I'd brought prisoners here as a constable, hoping that the custody sergeant would be in a good mood and wouldn't give me a hard time.

The world outside may well have changed over the years but not inside police cells. You still had to press a buzzer to be allowed in and if you were lucky, there wouldn't be a queue of prisoners waiting to be processed. Once inside, you had to satisfy the custody sergeant that the arrest was lawful and then came the search of your prisoner, that was the part I'd always hated. Needles, razor blades, knives. You never knew what they were carrying. Thankfully, I was never given the opportunity to be a custody sergeant. The job offered little or no reward, stuck inside without daylight with only prisoners for company, and the fear of losing one of them through suicide, career over.

This fear wasn't lost on my old colleagues on D relief, who were always on the lookout for the chance to have a laugh at someone else's expense. To be fair, on one occasion, I was part of the plan to set up Sergeant Barker, a bright individual blessed with an annoying habit of using long words that nobody could understand. But he didn't seem to care that my colleagues regularly and openly took the piss out of him, particularly my old mentor Alfie Banks. There'd been a number of near misses at the time, including one prisoner who'd hidden a small penknife up his arse and used it to slash his wrists, narrowly avoiding death. Sergeant Barker was on duty at the time and nearly had a heart attack. As a consequence, he became paranoid over the safety of prisoners. Perfect circumstances for us to make it look like there really had been a suicide. So as not to miss his reaction, some of us made an excuse to be in the custody area when PC Clarke came running from the cells in a blind panic screaming,

"Sarge, come quick. He's dead. Looks like he's slashed his wrists. Fucking blood everywhere."

We all followed the poor sergeant as he bolted out of the charge room at lightning speed repeating,

"Oh no, you've got to be fucking kidding me, why me for fuck's sake."

It was the only time that I ever heard him swear. He burst into the cell to be confronted with what looked like a body underneath a blanket, with a realistic looking fake arm outstretched resting in a pool of fake blood. His instinct was to preserve the scene and he didn't look closely enough to realise that he was being set up. It took the duty DI's sarcastic comments upon his inspection of the 'scene' for the embarrassing truth to sink in. Some said that the hapless sergeant was never the same again and I'd have to agree. We'd underestimated the impact it'd have on him but at that time, nobody cared, anyone was fair game.

I recognised the feeling. It was a kind of emptiness as the adrenalin that had kept me going over the past month began to subside. It happened at the conclusion of every murder case. The charging of a suspect was always symbolic because it signaled the beginning of an entirely separate phase in the investigation. The team of individuals that came together and worked tirelessly to find Rachel, would soon no longer exist. Sure, I'd keep a few, including Alan, Shaun, Keith and Trev to prepare for the trial, but the rest would return to their day jobs.

Gary declined my invitation to celebrate the charging of Little with the rest of the team because he had to move on to his next case. As I watched him drive off through the worsening blizzard of snow that had replaced the torrential rain of a few days earlier, I wished that things were different. If I could, I'd hand pick a team of detectives to work with until my retirement. Gary would definitely be one of them.

I took a deep breath as I entered the Fair Maid pub on the outskirts of the city. I'd normally avoid social gatherings, but this was one of those occasions when it would be wrong of me not to buy everyone a drink for their outstanding contributions. And, in any case, this would be the perfect opportunity to show everyone that I had a softer side to my steely character, I thought. Most of the team were already there, apart from Shaun and Keith, who were busy putting the finishing touches to the prosecution file in readiness for Little's appearance at court in the morning. I felt surprisingly relaxed and I was soon lost in conversation with Maly, Alan and Trev. They'd no idea how grateful I was to them for just being there every day. I came to the inquiry desperately looking for comfort and they'd unwittingly created a sanctuary for me, a place where I could hide from the world.

I wanted to tell them that they'd helped me to heal and how I was looking forward to a brighter future, but I didn't, and neither did I tell them that they were extraordinary human beings.

I made the effort to speak to as many of the team as I could but my thoughts were elsewhere. I couldn't stop thinking about Wanda and Ray. Ray's instinct would be to want to tear Little limb from limb, and if Rachel had been my daughter, I'd want to do the same thing. How would they cope with knowing that a complete stranger had murdered their daughter? From the extensive enquiries that'd already been made, there appeared to be no connection between Little and Rachel. They'd never met, no phone contact, no friends in common, nothing. And then there was Rachel's boyfriend Mark. I knew that we'd given him a hard time and that we needed to provide him with some support, now that we knew that he was innocent. He was going to need it. Despite what we all thought, he'd lost the love of his life and now was the time for us to see things from his perspective. I'd no idea how long it would be before the trial. It would be months away and those months would pass slowly for all those who were grieving for the loss of Rachel.

I'd already put a call into the FLO coordinator and asked for Sergeant Kay Durrant to replace Sergeant Wood and PC Holding. They'd done a first-class job but they were due back at Division. The months leading up to the trial and beyond would be a nightmare for Ray and Wanda in particular, and they deserved to have someone blessed with extraordinary gifts to be there for them. To hug them when they needed a hug, to brighten their days with a smile, to answer the million questions they'd have about the investigation, to hold their hands during the trial and much, much more. I couldn't think of anyone else I'd trust with such a demanding task. If I'd been in their position, I'd have wanted Kay to be the FLO. Just as I was about to leave, she walked in and came straight over to me. It was really good to see her. She reminded me of Bernie Orr - loyal, professional and a bloody great old school detective. The only difference was that she smiled a lot more than Bernie.

Kay took me to one side and told me how pleased she was to be working with me again. She asked me if I was OK and how I was coping. I knew exactly what she meant. We'd had long conversations before about the impact of the discipline investigation. It was an unexpected display of human kindness. I knew that I'd rest easy now knowing that Wanda and Ray would have Kay and her big heart to lean on, during the dark days that were still to come.

Even though the snowstorm was getting worse, I decided to head back to my office. I don't know why because there wasn't much more that I could do tonight and I was bloody exhausted. The familiar sight of the media circus had vanished from the station carpark as if they were never there, the tracks of their vehicles hidden by a perfect blanket of freshly fallen snow. Now that Little had been charged, they wouldn't be back until the trial.

Shaun and Keith were in my office still working away on the summary of evidence. Shaun was a perfectionist and I knew that he wouldn't put his name to something that didn't meet his high standards, no matter how late the hour. As humble as ever, he asked me to read it to see if I thought that it was OK. 'Murder – Contrary to Common Law. The Facts of this case are as follows'. His words would be spoken by a CPS lawyer at Magistrates' Court in the morning and would form the basis for the request for Little to be held in prison on remand. Shaun had done a brilliant job in presenting the evidence to date against Little that, on the surface, appeared to be overwhelming - 'I'm so glad you found her. I've wanted to tell someone for ages. It's such a weight off my chest. I saw all the police stuff on the news and just hoped they came here. I've not told anyone else. Nobody knows. I feel like I've been able to smell her body right from the start even before she started decomposing. I grabbed a knife and just stabbed her'.

I stayed for a while after Shaun and Keith had left. I looked outside. My car was already buried by the snowstorm and I wondered whether I'd make it home tonight. I couldn't remember the last time it snowed so heavily for so long. I thought about the madness of the last few days. Finding Rachel on the first day of the search. My Dad appearing from nowhere at the very moment when I'd needed him most as if he was watching over me. The inevitability of Little's no comment interviews that signaled his intention to plead his innocence at court. And, finally, the eventual understanding that I'd a pretty good idea of how to fight my way back to the person I used to be.

All the stuff on the walls, scribbled in black, was still there staring back at me: Alan's plan to search Orchard Park Estate; the list of possible suspects and scenarios; my own kick-up-the-arse words about raising the bar for Rachel; Chuck Burton's 'trust your judgement and instinct'; and Rick

Lyon's 'last throw of the dice'. I somehow felt a kind of warmth towards my tiny, sparsely furnished office, if that were possible. It sounded a daft thing to say but it had, I think, something to do with it being the place where I'd experienced every possible emotion over the past month. Whatever the reason, it felt familiar, and familiarity was a blessing to be thankful for.

THIRTEEN

'It's hard to hold a candle in the cold November rain'

The day of Rachel's funeral arrived, Friday 28 February, at St. Vincent's Roman Catholic Church, on Queens Road in Hull. It was my son, Sam's, 15th birthday. I gave him the biggest hug that I could before I left. It was something that I did much more often now. At first, my boys wondered why but they soon grew used to my regular outward displays of affection.

The journey into Hull gave me time to reflect on much that had happened since Little was remanded into custody on Friday, 1 February. My sense that I would lose control over the outcome of the case had been justified. The change of leadership at the CPS from Bob Marshall's friendly and cooperative style, to Linda Sweeting's more guarded and distant approach, proved to be the case. An early meeting with her to discuss the investigation and request that Francis Bernard be appointed as the prosecuting barrister, didn't go well. I wanted Mr Bernard because I'd worked with him several times in the past. He was eloquent, likeable, intelligent, and I couldn't think of anyone better to take on Little and secure justice for Rachel. When she refused to even consider him, I'd lost my temper for the first time in ages. It was unprofessional behaviour on my part, but the question I'd asked was a perfectly reasonable one. Why shouldn't we have a say in the choice of prosecuting barrister? I half-expected a complaint from her about my conduct but it never came. When I tried to see things from her perspective, whilst I still couldn't understand why she was so unwilling to listen, maybe it was because they only ever read about a case. How could she hope to even begin to understand the depth of horror that lay within Shaun's carefully chosen words? It was the question that I knew would drive me mad with exasperation, because I could do nothing about the system of which the CPS was an integral part. All I was trying to do was fight for Rachel because she could no longer speak for herself.

I'd insisted on keeping Shaun, Trev and a few HOLMES staff until the trial. We were still waiting for the phone call from the forensic scientist, Dr. Warner. There were so many questions still unanswered: was it Rachel's blood on the stairwell; did the fingerprints in blood inside the hallway belong to Little; was there a DNA profile of Little's semen on the swabs taken by Professor Milroy; and was there Rachel's blood on any of the knives found in the kitchen? If Little's motive had been lust, then he'd know that we'd discover the truth and wait until the forensic tests were completed, before revealing his defence statement.

I stood outside St. Vincent's with Shaun, Alan and Kay. We decided to wait until everyone else had gone in because there were hundreds of people wanting to pay their respects. I recognised Father White at the entrance to the Church. I saw Sergeant Wood and PC Holding walk in together with a few other officers who'd worked on the investigation. There was a force policy that actively discouraged the attendance of police officers at the funerals of victims, but I told all of the team to attend if they wanted to anyway. What possible harm could it do? Wasn't it the right thing to do for God's sake? I didn't agree with it because it made no sense, it was just another organisational rule that lacked compassion, and one that lacked any kind of understanding of the unique bond between a victim's family and investigator.

We managed to get a seat inside at the back of the Church. The sound of a song I'd heard before filled the air. I couldn't remember the band's name, but Shaun told me it was 'November Rain' by Guns 'n' Roses. Apparently, Mark had chosen it because Rachel loved their music. I caught some of the words that did nothing to lessen the feeling of sorrow that you could almost touch. 'Nothing lasts forever and we both know hearts can change, and it's hard to hold a candle in the cold November rain'. I wondered if the lyrics had a special meaning for her in relation to Mark. Maybe it was their song, the one they most often listened to together.

Rachel's coffin moved slowly towards the front of the Church followed by her family, Wanda and Ray, Kerry her eldest sister, John her only brother, and Vanda debilitated by diabetes. Rachel was to be buried because she'd a lifelong fear of fire. As the coffin finally came to rest, Father White spoke first.

"I bumped into Rachel in a shop on Newland Avenue just before Christmas. She greeted me with friendship and warmth. She'd grown into an elegant young woman, but I'll always remember her as a pretty, shy girl of immense beauty who brought so much joy to her parents."

He paused for a while as if he wanted us all to form a mental picture of his brief encounter with an innocent young woman who should have had a lifetime ahead of her. It wasn't difficult. He went on to pay tribute to Rachel's family.

"On a personal note, I want to salute Rachel's family. I have never been involved in anything like this before. Like all of you, I have read about and observed at a distance many horrific, family sorrows. But this was different. I was involved at very close quarters. I have watched a family torn apart by real family disaster, unimaginable family pain. But I have watched that same family rise from the ashes of desolation with courage and bravery and unbelievable resignation."

Father White's gentle Irish lilt had us all spellbound. It was the kind of voice that you could listen to forever and never tire of hearing. It was measured, and he left just enough space between his words so that they had maximum impact. The hymns gave everyone time to think about what he'd said. I couldn't sing along though because I didn't know any of them: 'Go Silent Friend', 'The Lord of Sea and Sky', 'The Day Thou Gavest, Lord, is Ended'.

Vanda moved slowly, unsteadily to the lectern. She paused for a moment, and I was hoping that she'd be strong enough to say what she wanted to say. Her voice quivered.

"I want to…I want to…. tell you all about my little sister. She's gone forever and won't be coming back. All I have left are the memories. Rachel had a passion for many things. She'd really get into something before moving on to the next thing. We shared a love of rock music and I'd describe her as a true 'rock chick' but there were some fads I was unable to share. She got into WWF wrestling at one stage. She had all the videos and magazines and would sit and watch it for hours. She once went down to London on her own to watch it. She was mad about Oasis for a while and had a Liam Gallagher key ring for ages. Recently she was mad about Al Pacino films and she made Mark buy her the Godfather trilogy. She was quite fickle in a way but that was just Rachel. She was also very funny. That is how I will always remember her. Laughing. She was like a shining star in our lives and she just made us all feel better for being in her presence. The light has gone forever. Now there is only darkness."

You could hear a pin drop as Vanda stopped to take a sip of water. She'd already shown immense courage in talking about Rachel without breaking down, and it was courageous, because there were no words to properly capture the sense of loss inside the Church. I could feel my pulse quickening and although I was determined to hold back the tears, they came anyway. And just as I thought that Vanda had finished, she did something that I wasn't expecting her to do.

"The last thing that I want to do...... if I can...... is read a poem by Henry Scott Holland."

I wondered whether she'd be able to cope with reading something that obviously meant a great deal to her. I didn't know the poem, but from the moment that Vanda gently recited the opening lines, I formed the impression that maybe Vanda had chosen it because it was what Rachel would want to say to her family if she were here now.

"Death is nothing at all. I have only slipped away into the next room. Whatever we were to each other, that we still are."

I struggled to remember every word that she said because it was heartbreaking, I wasn't ready for a poem that suggested that we'd nothing to fear from death.

"Wear no forced air of solemnity or sorrow. Laugh as we always laughed at the little jokes we enjoyed together. Let my name be ever the household word that it always was. Let it be spoken without effect, without a trace of a shadow on it. There is unbroken continuity. Why should I be out of mind because I am out of sight? I am waiting for you, somewhere very near, just around the corner. All is well."

I looked around me and there wasn't a dry eye to be seen. Vanda's chronically ill body had somehow managed to deliver the most poignant and moving eulogy imaginable. I wasn't sure that I understood the opening words 'Death is nothing at all', or the last ones 'All is well', either. Knowing that death is the one thing that we all have in common and coping with the reality of death, seemed to me to be two entirely different things as I watched Wanda and Ray walk, trembling with grief, behind Rachel's coffin as it left the Church.

FOURTEEN

'I felt like I'd just opened a door
that led to a further dimension
of despair and desolation'

Towards the end of March, the call that I'd been waiting for finally came from Dr. Warner. Semen from the high vaginal swabs taken by Professor Milroy, proved beyond doubt that Little had penetrated Rachel, either before or after death. All that I could think about was the devastating impact the news would have on Ray and Wanda. How would I tell them? When would I tell them? Where would I tell them? I knew that there'd be an expectation for me to arrest Little and charge him with rape. That would be easy, given the circumstances, but my first instinct was to simply question him about the presence of his semen inside Rachel. Not charging Little with rape would leave the door open for the prosecution to infer that intercourse took place after death. That's what I believed, because there was no evidence to show that Rachel was alive at the time, although I was pretty sure that Little's defence statement would be based around how she'd consented to sex. I wrote down the decision in my policy book, and when I read it back, it seemed to be a perfectly reasonable one to make. I just had to tell Wanda and Ray.

I called them at home and Wanda answered. When I

asked if they'd be able to come to my office, I could tell that she'd guessed I'd something I needed to say face to face, but she didn't ask why. I'd grown used to Wanda's calm approach to the darkness that she'd had to deal with since we first met. There were no outbursts, no demands, no criticism of the investigation, just a flawless display of humility and understanding. Wanda agreed to come in right away with Vanda and not Ray. Maybe she recognised the significance of my call - she wouldn't want Ray to be there if it was bad news of some kind.

Vanda had asked whether Rachel had been violated sexually, just after her body was found, and I'd told the family that we simply didn't know. I'd tried to be positive, given that Rachel was found fully clothed and that Professor Milroy didn't think that she had been. I was now about to deliver another hammer blow to the already broken family.

I stared at them both from across my desk. Wanda looked so tired, and I could see that Vanda, debilitated by her diabetes, was struggling to get comfortable. Despite the pain, her blue eyes still shone as brightly as ever. It was one of those moments when random thoughts flashed before me. How I wished that I was a kid again playing football all day long during the summer holidays, going for a pint with my Dad on a Friday night, or doing my paper round before school whilst eating a quarter of midget gems. All I was trying to do was provide some comfort for me when I should be thinking about Wanda and Vanda. I just didn't want to give them the bad news. They knew something was wrong, because I always tried to be professional and calm whenever I met them. Now, I was behaving differently, nervously, and

I just hoped that my composure would hold when they knew what Little had done.

"I'm afraid there's no easy way to say this and so I'm just going to say it."

I realised that the same words had been spoken before by one of the FLOs, Sergeant Wood, when we'd found Rachel's body. It was too late to take my words back now.

"We've had the forensic results back and there's no doubt that Little had sexual intercourse with Rachel either before or after her death. I am very, very sorry."

I felt like I'd just opened a door that led to a further dimension of despair and desolation for the family. Imagining Little stabbing a defenceless Rachel over and over again, would haunt their every waking moment and now, so would the thought of her being violated sexually, probably after death. All Wanda asked was how did I think that Little would react when questioned. I told her that we weren't expecting him to make any comment. The last thing she said was,

"Thank you for telling me."

Vanda's eyes moistened and then the tears came. Uncontrollable grief. Her mother gave her a warm embrace, and I wished more than anything that I could take away their pain. I left them alone for a while in my office, to give them some privacy. I didn't know what else to do. After they'd gone, there was just me, alone again with only my thoughts for company. Today had been a bad day, a dark day, and I'd a feeling that there were many more to come. Now that the forensic results were known, the next phase would begin. It wouldn't be long before we'd receive Little's defence statement that would be riddled with lies in an effort to save himself.

The phone rang later that afternoon. It was Ray Moran. He ranted and raged at me for what seemed like forever demanding that I charge Little with rape. All I did was listen; there was no point in trying to explain to him that I was looking beyond today to the trial. I couldn't bring myself to offer necrophilia as an explanation to Ray for not wanting to charge rape, even though I'd raised my belief with Wanda and Vanda that Rachel was dead when intercourse took place. Maybe he thought that we'd considered the possibility that Rachel consented to sex. I didn't for a moment think that Rachel went willingly with the foul smelling, ugly and overweight Little, and nobody else did either. He slammed the phone down on me and I didn't blame him for one second. There was so much pain in his voice, it felt like a bolt of lightning down the telephone line.

I was wondering whether the day could get any worse when one of the incident room staff knocked on my door and handed me a message. 'Can you please call Maggie Bloom. It's a personal matter. It's urgent'. Maggie Bloom, the champion of the grievance procedure, wanted me to call her. My heart literally stopped beating, I began to sweat, my stomach churned. What could she want with me? Why was it so urgent? In an instant, I'd convinced myself that it must be another grievance from some politically correct nutcase I'd offended and I began to panic. The level of adrenalin in my veins was at an all-time high, even for me, and then my fear turned into anger at how the organisation had reduced me to a quivering wreck at the mere thought of returning her call. I knew that I wouldn't have the will to withstand another nasty discipline investigation and resignation from the force would be my only course of action.

I picked up the phone in a rage and then I put it down. I was doing it again, feeding the anger inside of me. Stop fearing the worst, I told myself. Calm down. Be positive.

"Kwee, Paul. Thank you for calling me back."

Maggie had this annoying habit of using 'Kwee' as a form of greeting, whether in person or on the telephone. I'd no idea what it meant and so I looked it up once. I wasn't surprised to learn that it's used when someone doesn't know what else to say and it can mean anything. I often wondered why she couldn't have simply used 'hello' like the rest of us.

"Maggie, nice to speak to you again, how can I help you? You said it was a personal matter."

"Kwee, Paul, it's a personal matter for you. I was wondering whether you would give a talk at the Gender Agenda conference in a couple of weeks about your grievance. We wanted to get a senior officer's perspective and you're the only one who's had a grievance against them. We've also got a young female who's willing to tell her story about being bullied."

Although my heart was beating fast and I felt sick inside, I kept my composure.

"I'd be glad to help but can I think about it for a couple of days. I'll get back to you if that's OK."

I didn't know much about the 'Gender Agenda' movement in the force, but I knew that it'd been established to champion the rights of the so-called minority groups within the organisation, of which there were many.

I was literally exhausted. The call from Ray had taken its toll and so had the one from Maggie. The questions came quickly. Should I give the talk? Would it make any difference? Would it help me to tell my story? It was the last one that made some kind of sense and I formed a mental picture in mind of being able to say what I wanted to say. This would be my chance to stand up for myself, to regain some of my lost pride.

FIFTEEN

'Everybody has experienced the defeat of their own lives'

I rose early on the day of the Gender Agenda conference. It was late April, my favourite time of year when the spring flowers always filled me with the promise of better times to come. I sat at the kitchen table and pored over the notes I'd made of the speech I was about to give in just a few hours. They ran to over fifty pages. When I'd started, I couldn't stop. My wife came downstairs to wish me luck and asked me if I was sure that I still wanted to go through with it. I knew that her life had been blown apart as I'd sunk into depression following the grievance, and she was worried and anxious that today would send me back to the bad old days. I gave her a reassuring hug before I left.

The venue was some conference centre in Hull, away from police premises of any kind. I wasn't sure who'd be there. I wasn't sure how many would be there. I wasn't sure what would happen when it was my turn to address the audience. Would I be able to speak at all or would I freeze, stricken with fear? I looked down at something I'd written on my hand, 'Don't lose your power'. It was a reminder not to give my power away as if I'd done something wrong. It was a reminder to be proud of myself.

I arrived early as I always did for everything. I sat and

watched the car park fill with people from all corners of the force. The Chief arrived with his fellow chief officers, apart from my previous boss, ACC Bland, who was responsible for mishandling the grievance in the first place. Maggie parked her bright orange car next to the Chief's long black BMW. There was definitely going to be more people there than I'd hoped for. The realisation that my grievance had resulted from a speech that I gave, hit me hard and here I was again, about to give another speech. Should I be politically correct or should I say what I really think? Did it really matter if I offended anyone? My career was pretty much over anyway.

Maggie opened the conference with 'Kwee everyone'. A young female constable spoke before me about how she'd been bullied by her supervisor. It sounded authentic. She too had changed, and went on to describe how every part of her life had been profoundly affected by the struggle to make herself heard and be treated fairly. It felt as though that I was being set up in a way, because there was a danger that I'd be perceived as the archetypal bully that she referred to in her story. I'd a feeling that the audience wouldn't be at all sympathetic to what I had to say.

With a deep breath and a quick glance at the words written on my hand, I took the stage. My mouth was dry and I feared that I wouldn't be able to speak. Panic set in. I looked at the words again, 'Don't lose your power', but I could already feel it slipping away as the Chief, sat at the front only a few yards away, was no doubt wondering whether I was ever going to begin. But with nothing to lose and a burning desire to, at long last, be able to tell my story to an audience that had no option but to listen, I clenched my fists, stood tall and lifted my head high. I didn't bother with the notes I'd made because I knew that I wouldn't need them - I could recall every detail of the nightmare that began the moment I was first told about the grievance. She introduced me with,

"Kwee, everyone and now we have Detective Superintendent Paul Davison who's kindly agreed to tell us all about his experience."

She made it sound like it'd been a walk in the park. Memories of those dark, desperate days, weeks and months, came flooding back with a vengeance. I wasn't sure that this was doing me any good, but I had to make my appearance count for something. Maybe I could at least make chief officers think about the amount of psychological damage that has been, and is being, caused to honest, hardworking individuals by their grievance policy. But I also wanted my story to be, in the end, an uplifting one about how I'd overcome the emotional trauma I'd suffered. And so, I paused for a moment and decided to change what I'd intended to say. I didn't want the speech to be an outpouring of bitterness on my part. I was bigger than that. I wanted the audience to give me credit for maintaining my dignity as they listened to my account of what happened.

"Good morning. Before I tell you what happened to me from my perspective, I want you to look at the person sat next to you. Maybe you know them, maybe you don't. It doesn't really matter. What matters is that you will have formed an opinion about them, based on perception, in about five seconds flat. And, in my experience, that first impression will almost certainly be wrong and will, more than likely, be a negative one. Why do we do it? Wouldn't it be better to see the person behind the uniform as a human being in need of kindness, compassion, and understanding? But there's no place in the police culture for such emotional intelligence, no place for individuals who are different, and I'm not just talking about minority groups either. I'm different, and I'll be the first to admit that I'm not everybody's cup of tea. I've been called many things. Arrogant, aloof, thinks he's God's gift and much worse. The truth is, I'm plagued with debilitating shyness and I have been all my life. The arrogance and aloofness are my ways of dealing with the shyness, and the great irony in my story is that if I've a fear of anything, it's public speaking. Why am I telling you this? Because two female sergeants submitted a grievance against me following a speech I gave to an audience of Neighbourhood Watch Coordinators. The basis of their grievance was that I'd publicly humiliated them both during the speech and that my reason for doing so was because they were female. Their clear intention was to proceed to an Industrial Tribunal."

I paused for a sip of water. I felt in control and more importantly, I was keeping my power.

"So, why did I agree to speak today? Well, for one thing, I've never been able to tell my story. Nobody ever asked me what I actually said on the evening in question. And for another, in talking about my experience, maybe chief officers who are present today, might gain a better understanding of what it's like to be the subject of their grievance policy. A policy that was probably formulated with the best of intentions to allow individuals to be heard but in reality, has fallen into disrepute. There are frivolous and silly grievances flying about the force every day. I was told that a grievance couldn't lead to discipline but mine did. It led to the DCC from Nottinghamshire Police being called into investigate my alleged conduct. And, even though I was never served with a Regulation 15 notice, I was removed from my job. Following a lengthy inquiry, he concluded that I'd done nothing wrong and questioned why he'd been called in to conduct the investigation in the first place. I could go into elaborate detail about exactly what happened, but I doubt that you will be interested in me trying to persuade you of my innocence and nor should you be. If I were sat listening, I'd be more interested in whether the grievance policy is a legitimate way of settling fairly minor differences within a modern organisation. It's important because, in my view, a grievance culture has gripped the force and far too much time is being spent in attempting to resolve them."

I stopped again to collect my thoughts and to look at my audience. They didn't look at all comfortable at my very direct approach because by now I'd moved up a gear, and I was talking without a trace of apprehension or fear. It was if I could see for miles, and I knew exactly what I wanted to say and how to say it.

"Maggie has asked me to give you an example of how the emotional trauma I suffered affected me. During the course of the investigation that continued for many months, I probably suffered a nervous breakdown of some kind. Unable to sleep, going from place to place not being able to remember the journeys. I could go on. I felt humiliated. I felt as though all the hard work that I'd done over the years counted for nothing. Wherever I went, I was the Superintendent that didn't like or respect females. One Saturday morning, I took my eldest boy, Sam, who was twelve at the time, to play football at the local football ground. I also took my youngest, Cal, who was five. At the end of the game I drove home. My wife asked where Cal was and, to my horror, I realised that I'd forgotten him. Needless to say, I drove back at about a hundred miles an hour and fortunately, he was still there on his own wondering why I'd left him. When I got home, I crumpled in a big heap on the floor and sobbed for what seemed like forever."

I paused for a moment as I remembered like it was yesterday, seeing my little boy on his own sat on a bench swinging his legs. He ran towards me, jumped up and hugged me as if he was never going to let go and with tears streaming down his face, he cried, 'Why did you leave me, Daddy'.

"You're probably wondering how a grievance could lead to me forgetting my precious and innocent little boy. What if he'd vanished, taken by some nutcase? Or tried to make his own way home and got hit by a car? Whilst a broken arm can be easily fixed and be stronger than before the break, a broken mind is a different thing entirely. It's not the outcome of any investigation that causes the damage, it's the corrosive impact of the investigation itself that wreaks havoc with every aspect of an individual's life."

I wanted to say much more because I believed from the beginning that I was being bullied by the might of the organisation, but the word 'bullied' would infer that I saw myself as a victim and I didn't. Finally, after much soul searching, I'd come to the conclusion that none of this had been personal. In many ways, it was a perfect storm as Maly had pointed out. A grievance culture fuelled by political correctness, an individual in a position of power who needed to be cut down to size, and a force that didn't know how to resolve the matter. I knew that I wasn't alone. There were many other similar examples of poor Superintendents across the country being investigated for minor issues. I smiled to myself thinking about when I'd joined the force, I don't think that any of my colleagues would have known what the word grievance meant. I'd been on my feet for more than thirty minutes and there was more to come.

"Looking back, yes, this really did happen. Could the matter have been resolved the day after the meeting? Of course, it could. It would've been a simple task to ask a few people who were present what I'd said. The great irony is that I made no reference to either sergeant in my speech. Why would I? It was very much about how to deliver locally-based policing more effectively to communities across the Division. I've still no idea what their motive was for bringing the grievance in the first place. But I was told that the grievance procedure wasn't about blame, it was a means of being able to raise legitimate concerns over how people are being treated. There are many questions that I don't have the answer to. For my part, was I in any way to blame for what happened? Probably, because I'd unwittingly built up a reputation for being arrogant, ruthless, unwilling to listen and too clever by half. I was unaware of the impact that I had on people. The coaching that I subsequently received taught me to see things from the perspective of those who worked under me and, yes, I could see why I may have been perceived as an intimidating boss who demanded too much."

I wanted to tell the audience of all the positive things I'd done, though. How I'd moved heaven and earth to facilitate the transport of a young Sudanese Muslim, who was stabbed to death by an Iraqi male in Hull, back to his native country so that the body could be washed and buried within seven days. His family were poor and so I'd made sure that the force met the costs. His mother wrote a heart-warming letter of thanks to me because without my help, her son would have been buried in Hull, a place where he'd no family or ties, a place thousands of miles from home. There were of course many other similar examples that I could have given. The overwhelming human instinct to seek revenge for being wronged had had no outlet and neither had my overwhelming desire to plead my innocence. Nobody would listen to my side of the story, and so I'd contacted respected figures in the community who'd listened to my speeches in the past. I duly received many glowing letters of support complimenting my positive approach to local policing. But they were of no use because I wasn't allowed to submit them in my defence, despite them being a source of evidence to show that I gave speeches that were inspirational and that I'd never criticised any individuals publicly, male or female.

"And that takes me back to where I started, the capacity for us all to misunderstand others. So what lessons can be learned from my experience? There must be a fair and balanced response to any accusations brought against an individual. 'What would an ordinary reasonable member of the public think', is a test that should be applied. What would they make of my story? Would they shake their heads in disbelief, or would they applaud the force for setting in motion a chain of events that took months to determine that I'd done nothing wrong? Regardless of their motive for the grievance, I wouldn't imagine that the two sergeants found any joy in the process, apart from receiving a sum of money from the force in settlement for the distress they'd apparently suffered. When the force turned against me, it was the loneliest and most desolate feeling that I've ever experienced in my life. But my story has a happy ending because when I finally realised that I'd allowed the whole experience to take my power away, I decided to harness the rage that I felt inside and turn into a source of positive energy. Before I came here today, I wrote on my hand 'Don't lose your power', and I don't believe that I have. I'm actually OK now. My life as a SIO has helped and so has my family."

I deliberately stopped and took a sip of water. I felt more alive than ever. I'd finally been able to tell my story and, in the end, that's all I'd ever wanted. But above all else, I was proud of myself for staying true to the way I'd been raised by my parents. I believe that my Dad would have been proud of my conduct and I hoped that my boys, in time, would be too. I then focused my gaze on the Chief.

"Lastly, and this comment is aimed directly at the Chief, should I be faced with a decision whether to watch one of my boys play football or attend one of your meetings, then I think you'll know what my decision will be. Thank you for listening."

It was over. I walked proudly from the stage to a surprisingly generous applause given the circumstances. I sat down next to Chief Superintendent Dalton. All he said was,

"That was fucking fantastic. Well done."

I left shortly afterwards as if I was done with the police service for good. I wished that it could have been for good. I wouldn't have looked back, not for a moment. On my way home, the question that I kept asking myself though was, had the experience of bearing my soul provided closure for me? Leonard Cohen was right when he said, 'Everybody has experienced the defeat of their own lives, nobody has a life that worked out the way they wanted it to'. But I could never have imagined in my wildest dreams when I began my career back in 1982, that mine would have turned out this way. If I found some comfort in Cohen's perspective on life, then Dylan helped me believe that, in the end, all that mattered was the truth: 'The dirt of gossip blows into my face, and the dust of rumours covers me, but if the arrow is straight and the point is slick, it can pierce through dust no matter how thick. So, I'll make my stand and remain as I am, and bid farewell and not give a damn'. I thought about how the grievance had covered me in a bloody thick blanket of humiliation. But then Dylan offered hope: the arrow of truth would be able to slice through that blanket, no matter how thick. God bless Dylan.

Over the next couple of days, I received many calls about my talk at the conference. They were all positive. Apparently, my reputation had been considerably enhanced because I'd been so refreshingly honest. It was welcome feedback, but it couldn't change the fact that I hadn't fought the organisation for unnecessarily humiliating me. I'd allowed the experience to fracture my relationship with family and friends. I lost my passion for life, for the job that I used to love and for the innocence of a brand-new day. But my Dad had come to the rescue as I'd stood beneath the bridge in the depths of despair and that was something I'd never forget.

SIXTEEN

'Finally, it was here, what we'd all been waiting for'

A few weeks later, on 5 June, a fax arrived on my desk from the CPS. I glanced at the words, 'Regina v Michael Little – Defence Statement'. Finally, it was here, what we'd all been waiting for. I called a meeting with Maly, Shaun, Keith and Trev. I read out the statement in full to a nervous and expectant audience.

"The nature of the Defendant's defence is as follows: the defendant did not murder Rachel Moran."

Before I'd finished reading the last words, there was a collective 'you must be fucking joking' from everyone in the room, although it was no more than we'd expected.

"In the early hours of January 1 2003, the defendant met Rachel Moran when both of them were walking along Hall Road in Hull. The defendant had a few minutes before seen Rachel Moran in the company of another female but otherwise he has no recollection of having previously seen her. Rachel Moran voluntarily accompanied the defendant to his flat namely 19 Nashcourt on the Orchard Park Estate in Hull. At the flat the defendant and Rachel Moran had consensual sex."

Little had waited for the results of the DNA tests that

232

proved beyond doubt that his semen had been found inside poor Rachel. Rachel couldn't speak for herself now but if she were watching, I was pretty sure that she'd be screaming something like, 'no, no, no, I'd have never have had sex with that foul-smelling loathsome individual, not in a million years. Please don't let people think that I'd have betrayed my love for Mark'. At that moment, I was more relieved than ever that I was a police officer in the business of putting people like Little behind bars, instead of being a solicitor having to take instructions from the dregs of society. I continued.

"After they had consensual sex together there was an argument between the defendant and Rachel Moran. Then Rachel Moran taunted the defendant with his inability to maintain an erection. The defendant struck Rachel Moran a single blow across the face with his left hand. He told her to leave the flat. Rachel Moran continued to taunt the defendant and then struck him a single blow with a knife cutting his left forearm. After Rachel Moran had struck him with the knife, the defendant picked up another knife and stabbed her once in the left side of the back just below the level of the breast. Rachel Moran fell to the floor of the hall with the knife still in her back. The defendant struck just one blow and that blow did not kill Rachel Moran. Whilst she was lying on the floor Rachel Moran asked for help and the defendant prepared to leave the flat in order to obtain assistance."

The next part of the statement contained what we believed Little was going to do in an attempt to save his own skin. Blame Fuller.

"At this point, Marc Fuller came to the defendant's flat.

His arrival was unexpected. Rachel Moran was still alive and was lying on the floor in the hallway of the flat. The defendant admitted Marc Fuller into the flat. Marc Fuller saw Rachel Moran on the floor and said, 'He would sort everything out', or words to that effect. The defendant interpreted those words as meaning that Marc Fuller would summon assistance for Rachel Moran."

I stopped for a while because there was more. I looked up to stunned silence. Not one word remotely resembled his confession to PC Dennison. Before I carried on, I knew what was coming next and so did Maly,

"Let me guess, Marc Fuller suddenly and for no reason stabs Rachel to death. This should be good."

"When the defendant was in the living room of the flat, Marc Fuller attacked Rachel Moran whilst she was lying on the floor in the hallway of the flat. Using a knife Marc Fuller stabbed Rachel Moran, a number of times. The defendant did not know or foresee that Marc Fuller intended to carry out this attack. The defendant did not ask Marc Fuller to attack Rachel Moran. He did not in any way assist Marc Fuller to carry out this attack or otherwise participate in it. Rachel Moran died as a result of the stab wounds inflicted on her by Marc Fuller. Subsequently the defendant and Marc Fuller placed the body of Rachel Moran in the bath. Later and acting together, the defendant and Marc Fuller concealed Rachel Moran's body in the store cupboard outside the flat where the police subsequently discovered it. The defendant stabbed Rachel Moran once. The single blow did not kill her. Rachel Moran was killed by Marc Fuller who stabbed her with a knife inflicting a number of wounds upon her as a result of which Rachel Moran died. The defendant was not a participant in the assault. The defendant did not kill Rachel Moran and is not guilty of murder."

We all tried to digest Little's defence but it wasn't in a calm measured way, it was more of the same outpouring of frustration at the unfairness of the justice system. He was allowed to say nothing in interview, he was allowed to wait for full disclosure of the prosecution evidence before making his defence statement, and he was allowed to blame an innocent human being, whose only mistakes were to befriend Little in the first place and be in the wrong place at the wrong time.

My immediate thoughts turned to Wanda and Ray. Little's lies would be another body blow, but at least we knew what to concentrate our efforts on now - Marc Fuller's movements in the early hours of New Year's Day. We already knew that he'd an alibi provided by members of his family, who'd given statements to support his claim that he was at home.

I read out Linda Sweeting's comments about Little's defence statement.

"There is nothing in the statement that causes me great concern. In order to persuade a jury that this is what happened, they will have to be sure that Marc Fuller went to bed then got up again and went out in the middle of the night without anyone in the house hearing him, returning before anyone awoke, again without disturbing anyone, then continued to behave entirely normally throughout January."

On paper, her words made sense but we all knew what a top flight defence barrister would be capable of: they could convince you that black was white, they could cast doubt were there was certainty, they could pretty much twist anything to their advantage. They did it for a living and so they ought to be bloody well good at it. And then there was Marc Fuller and how he'd come across in the witness box. Having watched a video of his interviews, Maly was right, the words 'fucking', 'bastard', 'twat', 'cunt', counted for about eighty percent of what he said and I tried to imagine him giving evidence at court. I'd a feeling that there was much in Little's statement to cause concern. Could Fuller have left the house without it being noticed? How would he have travelled to Little's flat? On the pushbike discovered in the bathroom? By taxi? On foot? They were all questions that'd have to be investigated over and over again. How would Fuller's family stand up to a ruthless grilling in the box? The questions came and we realised that, although his defence statement was a load of rubbish, it'd be taken seriously by a jury. That was their job. They'd have no idea before the trial about the case and they'd be presented with a set of circumstances: two males are found in a flat with a dead body in the outside store cupboard. Would they believe Little's confession to PC Dennison, when his defence in court was going to be about as far removed from what he'd said to the young officer as you could imagine?

Little's defence team had made a glaring error though, by failing to account for his convincing admission of guilt at the time of his arrest. 'I need to get it off my chest. I've wanted to tell someone or someone find out for so long. I must be evil, a normal person wouldn't do that. I lost it, picked up a knife and stabbed her'. Why hadn't they made any comment as to why he'd admitted responsibility if it wasn't true? It was either incompetence on their part, or maybe it was deliberate so that they could argue diminished responsibility, insanity or depression for taking the blame on behalf of his friend Fuller. I was pretty sure that there'd be another defence statement and that we'd have to wait until the trial to receive it. Little was going to fight every inch of the way for his freedom.

The last thing I read out to my deflated audience was 'Date of trial 13 October 2003 – Hull Crown Court'. The trial was going ahead earlier than I anticipated and it was going to be in Hull, which was not what I'd expected. In a case like this that had already received a huge amount of media coverage locally, I'd have put money on the most likely venue to be Sheffield. Maly stayed behind after the meeting and we both had to accept that the outcome of the case was by no means a foregone conclusion. I still didn't know who was going to be Queens Council for the prosecution, and neither did we know who was going to defend Little. More than ever, I wished that I'd been able to choose the barrister to prosecute Little. I imagined a scenario where there were a number of likely candidates before me, like in an interview, and I asked them just one question, 'Why do you want this case'? I'd be able to tell in about five seconds whether any of them really wanted justice for Rachel, or whether this was just another case to them. I imagined Rachel helping me to choose, urging me to go with someone blessed with humility, a quiet way about them and a kind face. All I could do is hope that the one chosen by Linda Sweeting fell into that category. In such formal and intimidating surroundings, the jury would form an impression of the prosecution case by the opening address from Queens Council, who'd be stood before them, resplendent in wig and gown.

SEVENTEEN

'Tasmanian devils by any chance?

The next few months leading up to the to trial were defined by an escalation in serious and violent crime in Hull, that seemed to be never ending. A gang of white racist males, who called themselves 'Hull Cruz', terrorised the city, usually during the hours of darkness. Their M.O. was to drive around in high-powered cars looking for suitable ethnic minority targets to intimidate. Their preferred choice was usually Iraqi males, although they weren't particularly bothered, anyone who wasn't white was seen as fair game. The problem was that the police response was to chase the gang around the city, which is exactly what the they wanted. The end result was usually the same - no arrests and some frustrated traffic cops.

On one occasion, the gang deliberately drove into two innocent Iraqi male asylum seekers. They were tossed in the air like rag dolls. The gang got out their cars and beat them with baseball bats, laughing as their latest victims lay on the ground pleading for help. Miraculously, one escaped with bruising but his friend sustained serious fractures to both legs. Back at Division on LPTs, Shaun came to see me in utter desperation.

"Boss, can you have a look at this. It's been crimed as just another assault. I've got no staff to help me investigate. It's just me. Bloody ridiculous. The Sirrs brothers are taking the piss."

The Sirrs brothers were the gang leaders and they'd been getting away with it for far too long. It was yet another example of how LPTs weren't working; serious crimes were being pretty much ignored. I made the decision to class the assault as attempted murder, and I formed a small team of dedicated detectives, led by Shaun, to investigate the gang. Before long, most of the gang members were in custody charged with a range of offences from disqualified driving to attempted murder. Their ultimate downfall was to order the intimidation of witnesses to the attack and other similar assaults, by firebombing their homes. They used their girlfriends to make the arrangements during visits whilst they were on remand, but what they didn't realise was that we'd installed covert listening devices and heard every word that was said. Shaun did a brilliant job and was able to charge very serious crimes: witness intimidation, arson with intent to endanger life and so on. They'd been caught by good old-fashioned detective work, and there was little doubt in my mind that they'd be subsequently found guilty and handed substantial prison sentences.

Not long before the trial, I received a call from Trev at home. There'd been another brutal murder of a young female that had occurred in Highcourt flats on the Orchard Park Estate, not far from Saxcourt where Rachel had lived. The weapon used to inflict over sixty wounds was probably a carving knife of some kind. Trev didn't know any more, apart from that the occupier of the flat was Tony Campbell, who'd vanished. My thoughts quickly turned to the similarities with Rachel's murder. Did we have a copycat killer on the loose or was it just pure coincidence? Pinging his mobile phone showed that he'd gone to Grimsby and seemed to be heading up to Scotland, where his parents lived.

"I knew what you'd say, boss. Get yourself to Scotland. Bag already packed and I've handpicked a few trusted detectives to go with me."

The victim was Tina Wright, a 21-year-old local girl. The familiar face of Tony Dickinson met me at the front door to her flat.

"I hope you're ready for this. It's probably one of the most vicious attacks I've ever seen. Whoever killed her tried to clean up the blood but they must've given up. Come and see for yourself."

Tony wasn't kidding. Her body was mutilated beyond recognition, and it lay in a gigantic pool of blood that almost covered the filthy floor.

"She must've been alive for most of the time due to the amount of blood, her heart would've still been beating."

If I was ever in danger of assuming that I'd seen everything, I was very much mistaken. The Tasmanian Devil was everywhere. Pictures on the walls, a Tas duvet, an infant sized Tas toy dressed in Tas baby clothes, a Tas carpet and literally hundreds of Tas toys of every conceivable description. And there were hundreds of fluffy spiders too arranged neatly on shelves, in cabinets, on the mantelpiece, in the kitchen.

Later that day, Trev called to say that they'd arrived in Scotland but had no idea where Campbell was. He'd not made contact with his parents. The only other possibility was a pub in Falkirk called the Goose where, according to the local police, he'd assaulted someone years ago. With nothing to lose, Trev went to the pub and just as they entered the bar, they caught sight of a bewildered looking Campbell, an eighteen stone heavily tattooed skinhead, who was just about to take a sip from a freshly pulled pint. After Trev had introduced himself, Campbell paid the detectives an unexpected compliment.

"Fair play to you coppers. I've only just got here myself. Can I finish me pint?"

Trev called to say that they were on their way back with Campbell.

"You'll never guess what he's got tattooed all over his body."

"Tasmanian devils by any chance?"

"How did you know that?"

"Oh, just a guess my friend, just a guess."

In interview, he admitted killing Tina Wright but claimed it was self-defence. According to Campbell, Tina came willingly to his flat for sex, but when he was unable to maintain an erection, she'd taunted him and said that she was going home. But before leaving, she went to the toilet and came back with a fluffy spider. When she told Campbell that she wanted to keep it, he went berserk at the thought of losing one of his precious toys and they argued. It was an argument that led to Tina's death at the tender age of 21, the same age as Rachel. He used a knife from a block of knives just as Little did. He claimed that Tina Wright picked up the knife first to attack him, just as Little accused Rachel of doing when he was arrested. I wondered whether the jury would see through his lies when he eventually appeared at court. I was trying to imagine how the jury would come to terms with how a young life could be lost over a fluffy bloody spider, but that trial would be after Little's. Campbell and Little had no previous convictions to speak of and yet they'd both committed the ultimate crime. After Campbell was charged, Trev and I tried to make sense of why Little and Campbell had acted without mercy and been so brutal towards defenceless young females, but we didn't have any answers. The only conclusion we came to was that the world is full of bloody nutcases.

PART 3

THE CRIMINAL

JUSTICE SYSTEM

ON TRIAL

EIGHTEEN

'There was something about him that was deeply unsettling'

Tuesday, 14 October 2003, arrived like any other day. The trial should have started yesterday but when it came to Crown Court, things rarely happened when they were supposed to. I didn't sleep much as I'd lain awake contemplating what was about to happen. I'd no control over the outcome of the trial now. All that could've been done to properly investigate Rachel's murder had been done. It would now be down to Godfrey Morton QC, who'd be prosecuting the case, and although he came highly recommended by Linda Sweeting, my first impression was that he was no Francis Bernard. Maybe I'd not wanted to be impressed with him simply because I didn't know him and that he wasn't my choice. I just hoped that he'd prove me wrong. The first question I'd asked myself when I'd met him for the first time was, did he have the 'likeability factor'? I wasn't sure. He was shorter than I'd expected with sharp features and fair hair. His handshake was reassuringly firm, though, and there was a calming presence about him that would find favour with the jury. Had he a firm grasp of the case? Absolutely. And the more I'd pressed him on certain aspects of the investigation, the more he'd responded with a style that was methodical and logical, without a hint of theatrics. Maybe it wasn't my place to give him the third degree and Shaun, who'd accompanied me to the meeting, tried to nudge me accordingly. But I had to for Rachel's sake, for Wanda and Ray, for the investigation team, and for my own peace of mind. I'd convinced myself that it would make a difference to the outcome, but it was too late for that now. We'd all have to put our faith in Mr Morton.

The journey into Hull was a lonely one. I'd rather have been doing anything other than walking up the steps to the front doors of the Crown Court, situated at the corner of Lowgate. Lowgate was the gateway into the old part of the city with its narrow-cobbled streets that led to the River Humber. I must have walked them countless times as a young constable. The area used to be my foot beat, and I liked nothing better than spending time alone wandering along the riverbank. It made me feel closer to my Dad, who'd spent most of his adult life at sea.

The sense of anticipation was overwhelming because selfishly, I wasn't sure what'd happen to me and my career should Little be found not guilty. But as I approached the imposing building set back beyond its wide-open courtyard that was pretty much filled with reporters, this was not the time to show anything other than absolute and unshakeable confidence. And so, with a hefty dose of aloof arrogance, I walked up the steps and into a different world.

I saw Rachel's family stood together in the foyer. I went over and introduced myself to Kerry, their eldest daughter, who I'd not met before and who'd travelled up from

Southampton. I could hear myself saying all the right things - 'don't worry, we've got a really strong case, we've left nothing to chance' - but in reality, I'd no idea just what the next couple of weeks would bring. I wasn't sure that Ray was listening as he paced up and down. I knew from Kay that Ray hadn't coped well with the long wait for the trial to begin and I could see that he was in pain, the pain of living each second as if it were a lifetime. Wanda was her usual self, but the months of turmoil had taken their toll. It was as if she no longer had the strength to smile, laugh or cry. Before I left to take my place in court, Ray asked me what I thought about Little's defence in blaming Fuller. I told him not to worry. I didn't have the heart to tell him that there'd almost certainly be another twist, given that Little had changed his barrister.

It was time for the trial to begin. I sat next to Kay. My view was unrestricted with the witness box only a few feet away. The judge would be to my left but in an elevated position, prosecuting and defence barristers to my right, and Little would be sat behind a glass partition, again to my right. The press gallery was bursting with a collective sense of anticipation. This was their time. It was what they'd been waiting for since Rachel's disappearance. I recognised many of the faces. I'd come to know them by their first names as they'd always wanted more from me, more than I was willing to give during the past nine months.

Mr Morton swept into the room with a purposeful stride looking taller than I remembered in his wig and gown. I was hoping for a reassuring glance of some kind but he just looked away, no doubt deep in thought about his opening speech. And then it was the turn of Little's barrister to make his grand entrance. Mr Ahmed QC, who was a good deal smaller than Mr Morton, marched in with a swagger flanked by numerous aides. It was as if he was trying to send a message that his gang was bigger and more streetwise than ours. He didn't acknowledge Mr Morton but he looked straight towards me as if he knew who I was, and stared for what seemed like forever. There was something about him that was deeply unsettling as if his presence radiated a wave of electricity that sent a shiver down my spine. I formed the impression that he couldn't care less about what people thought of him - he wasn't here to win friends or play by the rules - he was here to fight. In all my time as a SIO, I couldn't remember feeling like this, I couldn't remember ever coming across an individual like Mr Ahmed and he'd not even uttered a word. All I could say was,

"Fuck it Kay, I've got a bad feeling about this."

Little took his place in the dock dressed smartly in dark trousers, a white shirt that was too small for him, and a black tie. He looked straight ahead avoiding eye contact with anyone in the courtroom. It was the right thing to do, because I'm not sure what Ray's reaction would be if their eyes met. Everyone stood as the court usher uttered the words,

"The court will rise."

The imposing figure of Lord Justice Hooper, dressed in bright red robes and a bushy white collar, acknowledged Mr Morton and Mr Ahmed from his elevated position. I'd done some research on him and he was about as eminent as they come, having presided over some of the biggest trials in English legal history. That had to be a good sign, I told myself. Members of the jury - six men and six women - were sworn in. They'd have absolutely no idea what the trial would be about until Mr Morton's opening address. Lord Justice Hooper delivered an unusually strong warning to the jury,

"I must say first of all that, although you may discuss this case among yourselves as the case progresses, what you cannot and must not do is discuss the case with anyone else. It is a case which may attract considerable publicity. You must not visit any of the locations mentioned in the trial. You must not go on the Internet to look up this case. You must try the case on, and only on, the evidence you will hear in court."

Mr Morton stood ready to begin. Mr Ahmed looked bored and uninterested. Little sat motionless, staring straight ahead behind the glass screen. He'd gained a considerable amount of weight since the last time I saw him, back in January, being interviewed by Shaun. It made him look more powerful if anything but at the same time more unappealing, if that were possible. Members of the jury glanced nervously between Little and Mr Morton. The press fixed their gaze on Little. Members of Rachel's family, who were not giving evidence, craned their necks to get a sight of the chubby defendant. Ray looked ready to explode.

"Members of the jury, I am Mr Morton representing the Crown. It is my job to present the case for the prosecution. My learned colleague, Mr Ahmed, is here to represent the defendant Michael Little. What you are about to hear comes with a warning because, in many ways, I am sorry that you will have to learn of how an innocent young woman, Rachel Moran, lost her life in the early hours of New Year's Day this year. It will, I am sure, have a profound effect on you as caring human beings for a very long time to come because the manner in which she was murdered by the defendant, Michael Little, was brutal, savage and without mercy. You will hear evidence from the pathologist in graphic detail of the number of stab wounds inflicted upon Rachel Moran, more than twenty, all from behind. You will hear evidence of the severe force used to cause the fatal injuries. You will hear evidence from the forensic scientist that Michael Little had intercourse with Rachel Moran. We will never know whether that was before or after death."

I looked across at Ray and I felt so very sorry for him. No parent should ever have to listen to how their precious child was helplessly mutilated and violated. He stood up to leave, unsteady on his feet and shaking. Kay went after him.

"You will hear evidence of how the police discovered Rachel Moran's body stuffed in a small utility cupboard on the landing of Michael Little's address, 19 Nashcourt, on the Orchard Park Estate in Hull. You will hear from the police officers who found Rachel at the bottom of the cupboard, wrapped in a blanket and curtain. You will hear how they removed household rubbish that was dumped on top of her decaying body. And you will hear evidence of Michael Little's confession to PC Dennison."

Mr Morton had been right to deliver his warning because, as he repeated the words 'You will hear....', I knew that the jury would be entering a dark and unforgiving world that'd be about a million miles away from anything they'd ever experienced before. I wished he'd done more than issue a warning though, because they needed to know that after the conclusion of the trial, they might never be the same again. They'd have to look at photographs of Rachel's body in a fetal position at the bottom of a filthy cupboard that could well have been her grave. That sight alone would be enough. I knew that the moment I'd opened the cupboard door and touched her delicate skin would be one that I'd never forget. How would they be able to go back to their everyday lives and put the experience behind them? It was a question that I didn't know the answer to, but as I looked at the jury with their eyes fixed on Mr Morton, I felt sorry for them. If I was anything to go by it wasn't the brighter side of life that left a lasting impression, it was the opposite.

"So, who was Rachel Moran...I am sorry to have to use her name in the past tense... and how did she have the misfortune to have crossed the path of the defendant? She was the youngest child of Wanda and Ray Moran. Mr and Mrs Moran have three other children, Kerry, Vanda and John and the family home is 56 Hall Road in Hull. Rachel lived with her longtime boyfriend Mark Shepherd at 22 Saxcourt on the Orchard Park Estate. There is only a mile or so between the two homes. I will, if I may, use some of Wanda Moran's words to describe what Rachel was like. 'Beautiful is how I'd describe Rachel. She has this innocence in a kind of child-like way because she always sees the good in everyone. As older parents, did we spoil her, maybe, but it was hard not to, she made us all feel better for just being in her company'."

I recognised the words; they were taken from her video statement. Mr Morton paused for what seemed like forever. If he intended to move everyone in the courtroom, then I was pretty sure that he'd succeeded. But something he said got me thinking again about how Little had managed to lure Rachel into his flat, 'She always sees the good in everyone'. Could this endearing quality have contributed in some way? Maybe Little managed to catch up with Rachel, told her how lonely he was being on his own at such a time of celebration, and perhaps she took pity on him for a moment. That's all he'd have needed to pounce on a vulnerable pretty girl who clearly had other things on her mind. Others would have told him to 'fuck off', but that wasn't Rachel and, in any case, she wouldn't have been able to scream with his hand over her mouth. But this was speculation on my part because we'd no evidence. All I knew was that Rachel wouldn't have gone willingly.

"Members of the jury, at about one forty-five on the morning of New Year's Day, Wanda Moran was stood outside of 56 Hall Road, pleading with Rachel not to walk back home to feed her two kittens. It was bitterly cold and Rachel was only wearing a thin dress and black leather jacket. Mark Shepherd, Rachel's boyfriend and the person with whom she lived, was supposed to have stayed in to look after them but he had decided to go to a party at an address on Bransholme in Hull, a few miles away. Rachel was angry with Mark for not staying in and she was determined to walk back alone, despite her mother's pleas not to do so. And then something happened. A cruel twist of fate. To call it a coincidence would be to grossly underestimate the significance of what I'm about to say. It is the Crown's contention that as Wanda pleaded with Rachel not to walk home alone, the defendant walked past and overheard their conversation. Wanda, who will give evidence later, will tell you that she thought about asking the 'young man' to walk with Rachel for safety, but the defendant had already gone on his way. You will hear evidence that just after two o'clock, the defendant was caught on CCTV at Jacksons Supermarket further along Hall Road, followed closely by Rachel. There are reliable witnesses who positively identify the defendant. There is no doubt that it was the defendant. You will be shown the footage. You will also be shown CCTV footage that is of a poor quality but nevertheless shows what the Crown believe to be Rachel, followed moments later by the defendant. At this point, Rachel was only a few hundred yards from home. You see, at Jacksons Supermarket the defendant is ahead of Rachel and a short time later, Rachel is ahead of the defendant. It is the Crown's contention that the defendant somehow managed to lay in wait for Rachel so that she was in front of him. We will never know what happened next, but again it is the Crown's belief that Michael Little forced Rachel against her will into his flat. Once inside, he murdered her by stabbing her repeatedly with a knife using severe force. Why did he did do this? What possible motive could he have had? Well, we will never know because Little refused to answer questions put to him by the police. But you will hear evidence from the Forensic Scientist that the defendant's semen was discovered inside Rachel. At some point, Mr Little had unprotected sexual intercourse with Rachel and we will never know whether he committed the act against her will when she was still alive, or whether he did so after she lay dead on the floor. Members of the jury, you may, with respect, draw your own conclusion as to why the police took the decision not to charge the defendant with rape."

Mr Morton paused for what seemed like forever, and I believe it was designed to allow the jury time to form a mental picture of the horror inflicted upon Rachel as she fought for her life.

"Members of the jury, I invite you all to ask yourselves what you think the defendant should have done at this point. Did he call the police? No, he did not. He thought only of himself. He wrapped her body in an old blanket and one of the curtains from his bedroom, and then he cold-bloodedly and without remorse, forced her body into the tiny cupboard and left her there to rot whilst he simply carried on with his life. Wanda Moran will tell you later about how she rang her daughter's home telephone over and over again with no answer, and then did the same thing with her mobile phone with same result. And this is, you may think, an important point because it suggests that Rachel did not reach her home, and it is the Crown's position that Rachel could not have answered her mobile phone because she was either dead or lay dying."

I had to hand it to him he was doing a first-class job. He wasn't anything like Francis Bernard, but his delivery was measured and precise and easy to understand. There was nothing to dislike about him and I was beginning to have confidence in him. But would he be a match for Mr Ahmed, who I'd yet to see in action?

"And now I must come to the substance of this trial. The police discovered Rachel's body in the store cupboard belonging to Michael Little's flat following a search of a number of dwellings on the 28th of January. The defendant

254

immediately, and without being questioned by the police, admitted responsibility for stabbing Rachel. 'I can't be normal. I must be evil. A normal person wouldn't do that. I just lost it, I picked up a knife and stabbed her', is what he said to PC Dennison. Marc Fuller, a friend of the defendant, was also present in the flat but he had nothing to do with Rachel's murder, he was there only by coincidence. He was at home with his family when the defendant acted alone in taking Rachel's life. Did the defendant accept responsibility when interviewed by the police? No, he did not. He made no comment. And has he done the right thing by pleading guilty in order to lessen the distress to Rachel's family? No, he has not. In an effort to save his own skin he is now attempting to place the blame onto Marc Fuller. He is now saying that his friend was responsible. But his friend could not have been responsible because he was simply not there. You will hear from Mr Ahmed in due course and he will try to convince you of Michael Little's innocence by blaming Marc Fuller. Members of the jury, I will not pretend that you have an easy task ahead of you because you do not. It will be challenging and it will demand a great deal from each and every one of you. It takes courage to sit on a jury. How many of us want to decide the fate of another person's life or freedom? How many of us want to hold that kind of power? All that is required of you over the coming days is that you consider the evidence. But I believe in trial by jury and, if I may, I would like to quote Lord Denning, who said, 'Trial by jury has been the bulwark of our liberties too long for us to seek to alter it. Whenever a man is on trial for serious crime or when in a civil case a man's honour or integrity is at stake then trial by jury has no equal'."

I was definitely warming towards Mr Morton. From his measured and dispassionate delivery, it was already clear that there'd be no place for speculation, only what he could prove beyond reasonable doubt. Maybe that was why he hadn't raised the issue of Little's motive for attacking Rachel with such ferocity.

Yes, of course I had my own view. We were all convinced that he'd wanted sexual intercourse with Rachel. Although there was no connection between Rachel and Little, maybe he'd watched her walk past his flat from his bedroom window and became obsessed with fantasies about what he'd do to Rachel if he ever had the chance. After Little's arrest, I did some research on so-called lust murders,

'It is not enough for these types of killers just to kill; they have a compulsive need to act out their fantasies with their victims and their victim's bodies......such fantasies can include necrophilia'.

Had necrophilia been Little's motive? The typical profile of such an offender certainly fitted Michael Little perfectly, and it also fitted what he did to Rachel,

'The disorganised offender is usually below average intelligence. He is generally a loner type, who usually is not married, lives alone in close proximity to the crime scene. He experiences difficulty in negotiating interpersonal relationships and is described as socially inadequate. He acts impulsively under stress and will usually select a victim from his own geographic area. He is described as sexually incompetent without meaningful relationships. He uses a blitz style of attack, which catches the victim off guard. This

256

spontaneous action in which the offender suddenly 'acts out' his fantasy does not allow for a conscious plan or even thought of being detected. This is why the crime scene will be disorganised. The disorganised offender usually depersonalises his victim by overkill type of wounds to parts of the body that contain a strong sexual significance to him, including the neck'.

Little used a 'blitz' style of attack to cause 'overkill' type of wounds to her neck, and I was convinced that Little had sexual intercourse with Rachel after she was dead. If the jury wondered why Mr Morton had warned them that this case would have a profound effect upon them then, judging by their glum faces, it was beginning to sink in. I wouldn't have blamed them for wanting to be anywhere but sat in this courtroom.

Mr Ahmed didn't waste any time in jumping to his feet. It was as if he didn't want to give the jury time to digest Mr Morton's carefully chosen words that had the ring of truth running through them from beginning to end. If ever there was a case that cried out for a guilty plea, this was it. But Mr Ahmed had other ideas. His first line of attack though, to ask for more time to prepare Little's defence, was dismissed by Lord Justice Hooper.

"Mr Ahmed, I have carefully considered your request for the trial to be adjourned. I understand that the defendant has, for some reason, seen fit to dispense with the services of his previous defence team. That is, of course, his right. But it should not follow, and I will not allow it to follow, that there is a presumption that the trial should be adjourned to facilitate the instruction of a new team. My ruling is therefore that the trial will proceed. Please be ready with your opening speech at, shall we say, two o'clock."

Over lunch, I took a walk down Lowgate and headed towards the River Humber. The wind strengthened and began to bite as I got closer to the water. The area wasn't as familiar as it'd once been as a young constable, when I'd felt comfortable amongst the weather-beaten shabbiness of the forgotten buildings. The café that I used to take refuge in from the rain was still there, but I almost didn't recognise it now that it was called 'Café Gelato'. They must have knocked the old one down and started again. The view from the pier hadn't changed though, apart from the massive new structure called The Deep built at Sammy's Point, where the River Hull merged with the Humber estuary. It'd opened last year and it was a brave attempt to put the city on the map for being one of the UK's biggest and best aquariums.

My thoughts, inevitably, turned to the trial. This should've been a straight forward guilty plea, but I'd a strong sense that this was going to be a dog fight to the bitter end. There was already a degree of nervous tension in the courtroom that I'd never experienced before, and we'd yet to hear from Mr Ahmed. I wondered whether I'd agree with Lord Denning's view that 'trial by jury has no equal', when the jury eventually reached their verdict.

At two o'clock precisely, Mr Ahmed was up on his feet prowling around with his aides. It was obvious that he couldn't wait to begin his opening speech. Would he be presenting a different defence? I didn't have long to wait for the answer.

"Members of the jury, there are two victims in this case.

Rachel Moran and the defendant Michael Little. Michael Little because he sits here before you unjustly charged with the murder of Rachel Moran. He is not guilty. His so-called friend, Marc Fuller, committed the murder by stabbing her to death. There were two people inside 19 Nashcourt when the police discovered the body of Rachel Moran. The prosecution has made much of the defendant's alleged confession. Yes, he did say that he had stabbed her. The prosecution wants you to believe that that must mean that he is guilty. It does not. The defendant only admitted responsibility because he feared for his life and that of his family. Why? Because Marc Fuller threatened to kill Michael Little and do harm to his family if the defendant did not immediately confess to the police that he murdered Rachel Moran and acted alone."

And there it was, finally, as I'd expected Mr Ahmed had spotted the weakness in the previous defence statement: how to explain Little's confession to PC Dennison. If Mr Ahmed could then cast doubt on Marc Fuller's alibi, then the outcome of the trial would no longer be a foregone conclusion as I'd hoped for on the day we found Rachel's mutilated body. It was, to be fair, the only way that they could even try to attack Little's honest admission of guilt at the scene, and I was annoyed at myself for not realising this at the time we'd interviewed Little. The judge could then have alerted the jury to the fact that Little had 'failed to mention something that he later relied on in court'. This was a shining example of everything that was wrong with the criminal justice system. It was like playing a game of poker were the prosecution must show their hand at all times, whilst the defence are allowed to keep their cards close to their chest before laying them on the table as Mr Ahmed was doing so skillfully. We'd had to disclose the CCTV evidence and the fact that Little had sexual intercourse with Rachel, but the rules of the game allowed Little time, not only to formulate his defence, but to change it during the trial with no advance warning. Surely the jury would take this into consideration, I told myself, but would they?

Mr Ahmed continued with his flamboyant delivery that was in complete contrast to the measured and precise style of Mr Morton. He talked as if it was just a matter of time before his defendant would be found not guilty. I was sure that he looked across at me and winked through his steel-rimmed glasses.

"The prosecution has made much of the CCTV evidence, but I submit that it wasn't Michael Little on the footage at Jacksons Supermarket. The defendant was at a party in another part of the city and did not leave until around four in the morning. Marc Fuller had his own key to 19 Nashcourt. Marc Fuller met Rachel Moran on Hall Road in order to sell her some cannabis. It was a pre-arranged meeting. He then persuaded her to go back to the defendant's flat for a drink. When Michael Little returned home he found them both sat in his living room talking and drinking. The defendant had never seen Rachel Moran before. Mr Little then went into his bedroom and Rachel Moran followed him and began to kiss him. They had consensual sexual intercourse. Marc Fuller felt betrayed by his friend and they argued. In the hallway, Marc Fuller lost control and stabbed Rachel Moran repeatedly as he held her face down on the floor. Marc Fuller told the defendant to clear out the store cupboard to hide Rachel Moran's body and they placed her in there together. Ever since, the defendant has lived in fear of what Marc Fuller would do to him and his family. That is why he was so willing to take responsibility for killing Rachel Moran when the police came. The prosecution will rely on Marc Fuller's apparent surprise at the discovery of her body in the cupboard. But do not be persuaded by this argument because Marc Fuller had a month in which to perfect this reaction. And it must have been very plausible because the police were taken in by this performance and released him from custody. Even when the prosecution learned that the defendant's position was that Marc Fuller was responsible, did the police look into this further? No, is the answer."

I hardly dared to look across at Ray to see his reaction. The inference that Rachel had been a user of cannabis, and the allegation that she willingly had sex with a complete stranger, must be torture for a father to hear. The problem for Mr Ahmed though was that we'd had months to carefully examine every aspect of Rachel's past and there was nothing to suggest that she'd ever used cannabis, or any other drug for that matter. We'd also had months to test Marc Fuller's alibi and it was absolutely watertight. The defence hadn't once suggested that Rachel died at any other time than the early hours of New Year's Day. Marc Fuller was at home according to his mother, Janet Devine, his mother's boyfriend, Jesus Inglesias Mandrinan and his sister, Kersty. They were all seen on a number of occasions and they were of good character. I knew what was coming next.

"The prosecution will rely upon Marc Fuller's alleged alibi

to show that he could not have murdered Rachel Moran because he was not there. How do they know this? Well, they will try to convince you, members of the jury, that Marc Fuller was at home in Greenwich Avenue. They will produce a number of witnesses. His mother, her boyfriend, and his sister, who will say that he was at home. But they all have an interest in protecting Marc Fuller, particularly his mother, Janet Devine, because there can surely be no stronger bond in life than that between mother and son. They will lie to you in an effort to protect Marc Fuller. The prosecution do not have any other independent witnesses who can corroborate Mr Fuller's alibi. Indeed, there is CCTV footage showing Marc Fuller on Hall Road as he waited for Rachel Moran. Members of the jury, I will not pretend that this trial will not be challenging, daunting even, but all that I am asking of you is please listen to the evidence and after hearing all the evidence, make up your mind whether the prosecution have made you sure beyond reasonable doubt that the defendant murdered Rachel Moran. I am confident that you will reach an entirely different conclusion, which is that Marc Fuller should be on trial today and not the defendant."

Finally, Mr Ahmed had laid his cards on the table. It was going to be a simple strategy: to attack Marc Fuller's alibi by attacking his family in the witness box. And I knew that because the jury would be hearing this for the first time, in fairness to the task they were asked to perform, they were duty bound to examine the evidence presented to them by both sides. It was one of those sharp intake of breath moments as a shiver ran down my spine. The outcome of the trial would have nothing to do with what the evidence looked like on paper, it would depend upon Mr Ahmed's ability to discredit and cast doubt on the truth spoken by ordinary human beings, who'd be no match for the experienced and battle-hardened barrister. Mr Ahmed continued for what seemed like forever saying how he was going to show that Rachel's relationship with Mark was in trouble and that she was open to 'offers' when she had sex with Little.

In the end, I left with Kay before he'd finished. I'd had enough for one day. It was getting late and there'd be no time to call Wanda, the first prosecution witness. We went for a drink in the pub directly across the road from the court, The Three John Scotts. Sitting by the window, I could see the court building emptying. Rachel's family trudged slowly arm in arm as if they'd no idea where they were going.

I recognised other people from another case I had running at the same time. It was again a female victim but from a completely different world. She was a sixty-two-year-old prostitute called Carol Ives, who was brutally assaulted and left for dead in a rubbish skip. When she was found, her body temperature was barely high enough to keep her alive, and her face was beaten so badly that it'd left her permanently disfigured. It was a miracle that she'd survived. I wasn't hopeful of a conviction for attempted murder though. We'd charged a local fireman, but the evidence was mostly circumstantial, apart from a spec of blood on one of his shoes that bore a mixed DNA profile. It was by no means conclusive evidence but, surprisingly, the CPS agreed that it was a case that should be put before a jury.

Kay was good company and I told her that I felt safe around her and that I wished that all female officers could be like her. We both tried to put a positive spin on the day's proceedings, but in the end, we accepted that the we just had to hold our nerve and hope that because every aspect of the investigation had been conducted to such a high standard, then the jury would be somehow guided to reach the right verdict.

"Do you believe in what I've just said or do you think it's a load of rubbish?"

"Well, I kind of know what you mean that somehow things will work out because good must always win over evil, otherwise we're all fucked."

"Couldn't have put it better myself. I just hope you're right. Not guilty would be catastrophic, unthinkable, wrong and yet entirely fucking possible if today's anything to go by. Ahmed's going to fight to the bitter end."

Kay didn't disagree with me. We just ordered another drink to take the edge off the day.

NINETEEN

'As he uttered the denial, tears rolled down his face'

The second day of the trial began with Wanda giving evidence. Mr Morton treated her with the respect that she deserved as she spoke quietly, with a great deal of dignity, about what Rachel was like as a child and young woman. He probed her sensitively about what happened on New Year's Eve, how she'd pleaded with Rachel not to walk home alone and how she'd continued to call her until nearly four in the morning.

"I must apologise for what I must do next. I am going to show you the clothing that Rachel was wearing that night and I would like you, if you will, to say whether you agree that the items are indeed the one and the same. Is that alright?"

A glass case was brought in that wasn't visible to the public gallery where Ray was sitting. The dress Rachel was wearing and her new jacket were inside. Fortunately, the claret-coloured dress didn't show the heavy bloodstaining, but the jacket made Wanda put her head in her hands as if she couldn't bear to look. It was covered with white paper arrows. They'd been placed there by the forensic scientist to show the location and angle of entry of each and every one of the numerous cuts made by the knife as it'd pierced through the jacket and into Rachel's body. Wanda confirmed that those were the clothes Rachel was wearing the last time she saw her daughter alive. Mr Morton asked Wanda to confirm that the female figure captured by the CCTV footage at Jacksons was Rachel. As the screen flickered into action, there was an eerie silence in the court as the burly figure of Little came into view at 1.59am, followed at 2.01am by Rachel. It was the first time that Wanda had seen the footage, and her reaction was distressing to witness because there was no outward show of emotion to help her cope with what she was seeing. I knew that it was all inside because she'd felt so guilty for so long letting Rachel go, and now she was seeing Rachel walking as if she were still here. With barely a whisper, she said,

"Yes, that is my precious daughter Rachel."

"Mrs Moran, I would now ask that you help members of the jury to understand what state of mind Rachel was in before she left you intending to walk home to look after her kittens."

"She was angry, angrier, than I'd ever seen her before. She loved her kittens and she'd had a blazing row with Mark, her boyfriend, for not staying in as agreed. You see they didn't have much money and so her Dad gave her a ten-pound note to buy a drink. She went to the National Pub with her brother, John. Mark was going to stay in to save money. I told her to call me when she reached home. She said she would but she never called. I thought she'd forgotten because she was in a bad mood. But that was not like Rachel. If she reached home safely, she would have called me. Definitely. If she decided to go and see Mark, then she would have called me to put my mind at rest. I called and called until I went to bed around four. I didn't want to go to bed because I sensed that something was wrong."

It was the last question asked by Mr Morton and I understood why he'd done it. He'd painted a picture of an angry Rachel determined to get home despite the cold to care for her kittens. I just hoped the jury understood: going for a drink with Little willingly would be the last thing that she'd have done even if she was attracted to the defendant, which was about as likely as Little pleading guilty in the next minute and apologising to everyone for wasting their time.

Mr Ahmed remained seated. There would be no cross-examination. His plan of attack was going to be to undermine Rachel's relationship with Mark, leaving the door open for the jury to entertain the notion that she was the kind of person that might well have had sex with Little willingly. He wouldn't need Wanda for that with Rachel's brother, John, up next followed by her boyfriend, Mark.

John struck a formidable figure in the witness box. Six feet, five inches tall, well-built with an upright stance, he was at the other end of the spectrum to the diminutive, round-shouldered Mr Ahmed. His evidence to Mr Morton's questioning was delivered in a clear and articulate voice. It was to the effect that he went to the National Pub with Rachel around 7.30pm and they stayed until 12.15am. During that time Rachel drank no more than three pints of lager and described her as merry but not drunk. They called in to toast the New Year with some friends on Fairfax Avenue, before returning home to 56 Hall Road at about 1.10am. He went to bed but then became aware of Rachel arguing on the telephone with Mark. Rachel asked him to talk to Mark but he didn't want to get involved.

I wasn't sure how forceful Mr Ahmed would be with John because you couldn't fail to be impressed by his understated, confident performance so far. He was clearly used to speaking in public and it looked like he'd given evidence many times before.

"Were Rachel and Mark happy? Did they have a strong relationship? Why did they not go out together on New Year's Eve to celebrate together?"

"Which question do you want me to answer first, Mr Ahmed?"

It was a good response from John, one that Mr Ahmed didn't expect.

"Mr Moran, I will ask the questions, not you. Let me put it another way, describe for me if you will, Rachel and Mark's relationship."

"I would describe it as a stable one with a history of them breaking up only for them to make up the next day."

"Was Rachel a sociable person?"

"Yes, she was, although she could be shy around people she didn't know."

"Tell me if you will, was Rachel open to offers from other men?"

Before Mr Ahmed had finished the sentence, I could see John seething with rage at the question that was posed in an attempt to ruffle John's composure and again, raise the idea in the juror's minds of an unfaithful Rachel.

"Mr Moran, I'm still waiting for an answer."

"No, absolutely not."

He thought for a moment before adding.

268

"You can press me all you like but I will not be swayed. Rachel would not have been open to offers as you put it. Not under any circumstances."

Undeterred, Mr Ahmed continued with this line of questioning but John held up remarkably well. He didn't give an inch as he fought to defend his little sister's reputation. I expected Lord Justice Hooper to step in and direct Mr Ahmed to move on but he didn't. The wily barrister was testing the waters with the learned judge to see what he could get away with. He'd obviously used this tactic time and again, and if the prosecution witnesses that were to follow, particularly Marc Fuller and his family, were hoping for an easy time in the witness box then I'd a feeling that they were in for a nasty surprise. Eventually, John was free to go and he couldn't hide his disgust as he shot Mr Ahmed a glance that was full of hatred and I didn't blame him for one second. I'd have done the same. John left the courtroom with his head held high.

Mark Shepherd was up next, and I wondered how the shy and reserved young man would be able to hold his nerve in open court. It would be the most daunting thing that he'd ever faced in his young life. Would the jury understand? Would they judge his inability to express his emotions as not caring about Rachel as I'd done? Dressed smartly in a black suit and blue shirt, he took his place in the witness box. He looked up for a moment at the packed courtroom. It must have been overwhelming and the last thing he'd ever expected to happen when he'd fallen for Rachel over three years ago. It was hard to watch as Mark struggled to read the oath.

"Sorry, I'm… too nervous."

The usher read it out slowly and deliberately for him to repeat after her. It was an act of kindness that didn't seem to belong in the courtroom. Mr Morton led him through a number of questions designed to settle Mark's nerves before moving on to New Year's Eve. They were framed in such a way that Mark only needed to give one or two-word answers, which was just as well because talking wasn't one of Mark's strengths.

"Some might think it odd that you chose not to spend New Year's Eve as a couple and therefore were not as close as you have already described in your statement to the police. Would that be fair comment to make?"

"No."

"Can you tell the court why?"

"Rachel wanted me to stay in to look after our kittens, Speedy Tomato and Batman."

"So, you are telling the court that it was because of the need to care for the kittens that Rachel insisted that you stay at home. Was she so fond of her kittens?"

"She treated them like babies. She didn't like leaving them overnight. If she ever did, she'd leave the light and tele on for them."

"Can you tell the court why you did not do what you had both agreed and went out to a party on Bransholme?"

"Just did, don't know why."

"And how angry was Rachel when she spoke to you on the telephone after she realised that you had gone out leaving the kittens alone?"

"Mad, really mad. She'd have wanted to feed them. She'd

270

have wanted to make sure they was OK. Couldn't hear her proper though. The noise from the party was too loud."

"The defence have already introduced the possibility that Rachel might have been open to 'offers' from other males, as my learned colleague has already stated. What have you to say about that?"

"No, definitely not."

The words were spoken more clearly than at any time during the questioning. It was the last thing he would have wanted to hear, but I understood why Mr Morton had raised the issue first: it was a way of warning Mark what to expect from Mr Ahmed.

"And how determined would Rachel have been to return home?"

"Very. Nothing would've stopped her. She'd have walked home no matter what."

Mr Ahmed couldn't wait to get stuck into the young man who'd be no match for the condescending barrister.

"Your relationship with Miss Moran was on the rocks was it not, Mr Shepherd?"

"No."

"It was because she did not invite you to go out with her."

"Didn't have no money to go out."

"You slagged her off on the telephone when you argued. Is that right?"

"No."

"Your girlfriend could not be trusted could she because you were not getting along."

Mark was becoming increasingly agitated at the inference that Rachel couldn't be trusted to remain faithful to him. I knew what was coming next.

"Is it therefore not possible that Miss Moran could have had consensual sex with someone else?"

Mr Ahmed had gone too far. Mr Morton leapt to his feet to object, stating clearly that there was not a shred of evidence from Rachel's past to show that she was anything but faithful and true to Mark during their time together. Lord Justice Hooper, however, allowed the question to stand and directed Mark to answer.

"No."

As he uttered the denial, tears rolled down his face. Mark's ordeal was over and he walked out of the courtroom, sobbing uncontrollably. It was another one of those moments when I was glad that I was a police officer and not a barrister defending the Little's of this world. Mr Ahmed had taken advantage of a shy and reserved vulnerable young man, and maybe the rules of the game allowed him to do so, but that still didn't make it right. I wouldn't want to change places with Mr Ahmed, not for anything.

The last witness before lunch was Nathan Tempest, a close friend of Little's. His evidence would be crucial for a number of reasons: he was with Little on New Year's Eve and told us that the defendant was 'agitated' and in 'a mood' mainly because a girl they met preferred Tempest; he used to live with Little at 19 Nashcourt but moved out because he couldn't put up with the squalor; and he was adamant that it was Little walking in front of Rachel on the CCTV footage at Jacksons. But how would he withstand the pressure from Mr Ahmed? After all, it was one thing to provide a statement to the police but quite another to give evidence at Crown Court.

Dark, neatly trimmed hair, fresh-faced and dressed in a purple shirt and brightly coloured tie, he didn't look anything like what you'd expect a close friend of the defendants to look like. His testimony was given at break-neck speed. Mr Morton had to ask him to pause several times so that the jury could follow what he was saying. Whereas John and Mark stood completely still in the witness box, Nathan Tempest rocked backwards and forwards on the balls of his feet when considering what to say, and then he swung his shoulders from side to side when answering. I wasn't sure whether it was due to nerves or whether he was enjoying the occasion.

Eventually though, Tempest gave a valuable insight into Little's inadequacy in forming relationships with women.

"He was always keen to find a girlfriend for the evening but I never saw him succeed. He was no good at chatting up women and he didn't handle rejection well. He'd often sit down in a dejected state or simply slope off."

Tempest offered his view that the two females Little claimed to have been his former girlfriends, were pure fantasy.

"He told me that one was a schitzo who'd pulled a knife on him and cut him with it, he then accidentally cut her taking the knife off her. But I never saw her, nobody did."

Would the jury recognise the similarities between that story and the one Little gave to PC Dennison?

"Mike bragged about another girl, a six-foot blonde supermodel who all the other lads used to fancy whenever they went out together. But nobody ever saw her."

The description fitted Rachel and there was every likelihood that Little had seen Rachel walking past his bedroom window and fantasised about being her boyfriend. Tempest's 'fantasy' theory was supported by the fact that we hadn't been able to trace or identify any previous partner for Little. I just hoped that the jury would understand the significance of the words 'didn't handle rejection well', because I believed that Rachel's fate was sealed the moment she'd rejected Little.

Mr Morton saved the most important questions until last.

"Mr Tempest, how would you describe the defendant's mood on New Year's Eve?"

"He seemed OK until we got chatting to some girls. Mike fancied one of them but she made it clear she wasn't interested."

"What was his reaction to being rejected?"

"Not good. Mike mouthed stuff so she could hear like 'fucking slag'. He got real agitated like he always does when he gets a knock back. Then he left without saying anything."

"Are you able to tell the court how much alcohol the defendant had consumed by this point?"

"Not sure. Two maybe three pints. But he wasn't drunk."

"So, would it be reasonable to say that when the defendant left, he was in a bad mood because he had received a 'knock back' from the young lady in the pub."

"Yes."

Mr Ahmed responded by ripping into Tempest. I felt sorry for him, because I didn't suppose for one minute that he knew what he'd be letting himself in for all those months ago when he'd willingly given us his evidence. It was ruthless.

"Mr Tempest, what you have told the court is a pack of lies from beginning to end. The defendant was in a good mood. After all, it was New Year's Eve. You say his flat was filthy. How so? Young men living on their own in my experience do not spend all their time cleaning. Do you? And then we come to the CCTV footage. How do you know for certain that it was Michael Little? The quality is poor. Could be anyone. Why don't you start telling the truth?"

Mr Ahmed had done it again. He'd delivered a mini speech laden with different questions for the benefit of the jury. But he'd added a considerable amount of venom to his voice that wasn't present with the other witnesses. His questioning was oppressive, but the beleaguered young man stood his ground as Mr Ahmed relentlessly pursued Tempest's reasons for identifying Little on the CCTV footage. There was a moment of light relief though when, after Tempest described Little's clothing on New Year's Eve,

"His baby blue long sleeved shirt, black trousers and black shoes."

Mr Ahmed posed the question,

"How can you tell it was the blue shirt he was wearing from the footage?"

"I can't."

Mr Ahmed sensed a small victory but it was short lived because without a hint of irony, Tempest fired back with,

"The footage is in black and white."

Tempest remained steadfast and wouldn't be swayed by the increasingly animated Mr Ahmed. He was adamant that it was Little on the footage by his clothing, the way he walked with a slight limp giving him a rolling gait, by his build, and just because he was his friend who he spent a lot of time with. But at least Tempest had kept his composure during the bitter and unnerving browbeating in the witness box. How would Marc Fuller react under similar circumstances, I wondered, as we all headed out for lunch.

Despite our best efforts Marc Fuller was reluctant to give evidence, and there was the very real possibility that the judge would have to order his arrest as a hostile witness in order to bring him to court. I bought a copy of the Hull Daily Mail and sat alone in the pub opposite the court. There was an artist's impression of Little that almost filled the front page with the words 'I can't be normal, I must be evil. A normal person wouldn't do that', in big bold letters running down the side. The story of the opening day of the trial ran to some full five pages. It was something I hadn't seen before, such a significant amount of space given to a local trial. Everyone read the HDM. Everyone would be talking about it. The coverage by its investigative reporter, Rick Lyon, was elaborate, accurate and comprehensive. How would the jury be able to avoid being told about what was in the newspapers or listening to the radio or watching TV? I recalled the warning from Lord Justice Hooper about not trawling the Internet - he should've included the need to avoid the Hull Daily Mail as well.

Towards the end of the afternoon, Mr Morton produced a number of prosecution witnesses to show that after leaving the Goodfellowship Pub on Cottingham Road, Little went to a party at 11 Exchange Street, off Beverley Road. They described him and what he was wearing in exactly the same way that Tempest had done. Little was, apparently, quiet and subdued whilst there and left alone sometime after midnight but no later than 1am. Little had told Tempest on 4 January, however, that he'd left the party at Exchange Street shortly after 4am. Although Mr Ahmed tried his best, the jury must have been in no doubt about Little's clothing and the approximate time he left the party to head home. Other witnesses were called to identify Little on the CCTV footage at Jacksons.

The last witness was DC Bailey, the unassuming detective who'd spent day after day sifting through countless hours of CCTV footage collected from all over the city. His evidence put everything into perspective for the jury. They were given maps highlighting the location of Exchange Street showing that the most likely route Little would've taken on foot to go home, would be up Beverley Road, along Cottingham Road and then Hall Road, passing number fifty-six. As DC Bailey talked, Rachel's family must have been in agony wondering what they'd done to deserve the coming together of Little and their daughter, at the precise moment when Wanda had pleaded with her not to go. DC Bailey told the jury how long it'd taken him to walk from Exchange Street to fifty-six Hall Road, and from there to Jacksons. The timings all fitted.

The footage of Rachel almost within touching distance of arriving home to her kittens and safety, came next. This would be the first time that any of the family had seen the last moments of Rachel's short life. The court fell silent as DC Bailey explained to the jury and Lord Justice Hooper, who had to leave his chair to obtain a closer view, what he was sure they were looking at: Rachel followed seconds later by Little. It was heartbreaking to watch because Wanda and Ray must have wished for the power to stop the video, as if it were real life, and prevent the need for the chilling evidence from the pathologist, Professor Milroy, that would be heard tomorrow. I was proud of the way DC Bailey defended his position. He'd remained calm during Mr Ahmed's expected and persistent challenges over the officer's unshakeable belief that the male captured on CCTV at Jacksons and later near to Rachel's home, was Michael Little.

On balance, despite Lord Justice Hooper's tolerance of Mr Ahmed's conduct towards witnesses, the second day had been a pretty good one for the prosecution. My thoughts though were with John and Mark in particular; they had every right to be angry and frustrated at the suggestion that Rachel was open to 'offers'. On the journey home, I wondered whether they would find any comfort tonight in having given their evidence. Probably not, because they'd be overwhelmed with the desire to restore Rachel's reputation that had been so cruelly called into question by Mr Ahmed. And if I could play them both Dylan's 'One Too Many Mornings', there'd be no need to explain why because the words 'it's a restless hungry feeling that don't mean no one no good', would speak for themselves. His use of 'restless' captured perfectly how I imagined they'd be feeling: the complete absence of peace. I understood a long time ago that suffering of any kind inevitably leads to a state of perpetual restlessness. There would be no peace for Rachel's family, no peace for Mark. It would be human nature for them to live each day hoping for peace to come but it wouldn't. Whatever the verdict in the trial, it couldn't bring Rachel back.

TWENTY

'I will sit through it all, as it's the very least I can do for her'

I wasn't looking forward to the third day of the trial. The three officers who'd found Rachel would be on first followed by the pathologist, Professor Milroy, and finally, the forensic scientist, Dr. Warner. It would most certainly be the worst day for Rachel's family, and Kay had already tried to persuade them not to be in court for the pathologist's evidence in particular. They knew that she died from multiple stab wounds, but that's all they knew. The precise details of Little's frenzied attack would be unbearable for them to hear.

I arrived early to have a coffee with Carol, who was due to give evidence at her trial in court 2. I hardly recognised her as she approached me in the foyer. The last time I saw her was after she was released from hospital, her face unrecognisable, distorted by deep lacerations as a result of the brutal attack. I'd called in to see her at home, and even though I could see that she was in pain, she was already back on the game as a male client knocked on her front door. He was a good deal younger than her, and the only person embarrassed out of the three of us was me as I'd said goodbye and wished her

279

well. With a cheeky grin on her face, she'd closed the door with, 'a girl has to make a living'.

I could see that she'd made an astonishing recovery. She told me that business was as brisk as ever but that she only worked from the comfort of her home these days. Real life never ceased to amaze and surprise me, I thought, as she left with a 'thank you' for what had been done to get this far. Maybe she was referring to the fact that we'd managed to charge the fireman with a very similar attack on another female, who was attempting to call the police as he assaulted his brother in broad daylight. He was already on remand in prison for that offence but, of course, the jury wouldn't be allowed to know this before the trial. Whatever the reason for her gratitude, I was proud of the investigation and the risks we'd taken to bring him to justice. Whether he was convicted though would be an entirely different matter. Talking to her had made me feel better. She might well be an aging prostitute, she may well not be educated, and she may well not have had a privileged childhood, but there was something about her that I found refreshing. No hidden agendas and no political correctness to worry about.

PC Hague struck a humble and respectful figure in the witness box, and that was exactly the kind of person I'd judged him to be when I'd met the three officers following the discovery of Rachel's body. I remembered PC Dennison doing most of the talking whilst PC Hague sat quietly listening. I could tell then that he'd no ego to speak of just like many other officers I'd come across on the investigation - the underwater search team immediately came to mind. The arrival of PC Hague at Little's door was a stroke of luck, because there would have been no way that he'd have failed to search the store cupboard thoroughly as others might have done. For a long time after the discovery of her body I'd suffered nightmares imagining officers turning up at 19 Nashcourt and failing to open the cupboard, or failing to take out all the rubbish that was piled on top of her.

Ready and waiting to hear, for the first time, from the officer who found Rachel, I looked across to see her family sat together, hand squeezing hand, for comfort. Although they knew that Rachel was found in a cupboard, PC Hague was about to describe in some detail his reaction to the smell of 'rotting vegetables' as he opened the door. How he 'reeled backwards' when he 'reached out and touched what he thought was a plastic dummy and realised it was soft human skin'. And his 'disbelief at how a body could be crammed into a three-foot by three-foot space in a fetal position'.

Mr Morton paused for a while before moving on to the differing reactions to the discovery from Little and Fuller. Maybe he did it so that the jury would have time to think about the unspeakable cruelty of leaving a body to rot in a cupboard indefinitely, as if it was just a piece of rubbish. Or maybe he wanted to emphasise the most crucial part of PC Hague's evidence: the complete contrast between Little's almost immediate admission of guilt, to Fuller's look of astonishment and then his disgust at what Little had done. PC Hague told the court that Fuller looked genuinely shocked when he realised that a body had been found in the cupboard, he wanted to leave and called Little 'an evil bastard'. Mr Morton asked him to recall what was said between Little and Fuller,

"Fuller said 'do you know something about this' and Little replied 'yes'. Little looked at Fuller and said 'he's nothing to do with this'."

Mr Ahmed, as expected, tried to suggest that the officer had got it wrong and that Little had in fact said 'you knew something about this didn't you'? But PC Hague wouldn't be swayed despite Mr Ahmed's many attempts to try and get the officer to change his mind. Mr Ahmed was wasting his time though, because the more he repeated the same line of questioning, the more composed and steadfast the officer became. It was amusing, in a way, to watch the contrast between the calm, unassuming, down to earth policeman, and the hard-nosed barrister struggling to impress the jury with his animated performance. If I were a member of the jury, I'd believe every word that PC Hague said. As he left the witness box and walked past me, I was reminded that the force was blessed with many officers in the same mould as PC Hague.

PC Dennison was just as fresh faced as I'd remembered him to be. His evidence would be crucial because it mattered how the young officer, despite still being in his probation at the time, had dealt with Little's confession - the jury had to believe that at least some of what Little said to the officer was true. And it mattered that PC Dennison was the one who'd arrested Little and Fuller and remained inside the flat with the two suspects - he was therefore qualified to offer his opinion on their differing and contrasting behaviours when Rachel was found.

Mr Morton set the scene by asking the officer to read from his ONB the notes he'd made of Little's confession.

Notes that Little had read and signed as a true and accurate record of what he'd said, all captured on video. I was acutely aware that this would be the first time that Rachel's family would learn of the precise details of Little's confession to PC Dennison. But they would have to listen knowing that he'd subsequently given two other versions of what happened in an attempt to save his own skin. The inference in all three though, was to paint Rachel as a female who would willingly have gone to his flat for a drink, either with Little in his first two accounts, or Marc Fuller, in his latest. Only Wanda, Ray and Mark would know just how unlikely and out of character that would have been for Rachel. If the jury believed that, then they'd have to come to the conclusion that Rachel had been forced against her will into 19 Nashcourt.

"Thank you for reading from your notebook officer. Can you tell the court when you were able to record what Mr Little said to you after being cautioned several times?"

"Immediately after I booked him in at Queens Gardens Police Station."

"Did Mr Little make any mention of consensual sexual intercourse with Miss Moran?"

"No."

"Did he undergo a medical examination whilst in custody? And if he did, were there any signs of a wound on his left arm inflicted by Miss Moran as alleged by Mr Little."

"Yes, he was and no, there were no wounds."

"Is it fair to say that you did not ask him any questions because he was under caution?"

"Yes. My instinct was to try to get him not to talk. I told him that but he just kept on talking as if he really did want to get it off his chest. Just to tell someone."

"Now I would just like your opinion. When you witnessed the reaction of Mr Fuller, did you believe him to be putting some elaborate act or did he seem genuinely surprised?"

"It seemed to be real. It was just the way he hung around the cupboard before we opened it and the light-hearted way he said, 'I bet it stinks in there'. The way he became instantly agitated rocking backwards and forwards and the hatred towards Michael Little."

"What do you mean by hatred?"

"Well, he called Little 'an evil murdering bastard', and pleaded to be taken out of the same room that we were sat in together."

"Did you believe his initial comments when he said, 'I must be evil. I just grabbed a knife and stabbed her'?"

"Yes, I did. He seemed relieved to have told someone."

PC Dennison possessed a gentle way about him that made you want to believe every word that he said, and I wondered whether Mr Ahmed would challenge his integrity over the contents of the officer's notebook.

"Officer, surely it is possible that you misheard the defendant. Could he not have said, 'you knew something about this didn't you'? as opposed to, 'he'd nothing to do with this'."

"No. It was Marc Fuller who looked at Little and said 'did you know about this'? Little replied, 'yes' before telling me that Fuller had nothing to do with it. I haven't got this wrong."

"Did the defendant look in anyway frightened of Marc Fuller, was there tension between the two of any kind?"

It was obvious that PC Dennison had no idea what Mr Ahmed was referring to: the officer wouldn't know about Little's latest change of direction in blaming threats from Fuller as the reason for his admission of guilt. He hadn't been allowed in court before giving evidence, and it would have been against everything that the officer stood for, for him to proactively read a newspaper, listen to the news, or ask somebody about what had been said in court. Eventually, with a puzzled look on his face, PC Dennison gave his answer.

"Yes, there was tension. When Fuller realised a body had been found in the cupboard, his mood changed towards Little. He was definitely angry with Little and said something about them being friends and how could his friend let him keep coming to his flat with 'that thing' in the cupboard. I wouldn't say he was frightened of Fuller. Why would he be frightened of Fuller? There were three police officers there and they were both handcuffed."

It was an honest response in the circumstances and not one that helped Mr Ahmed's mood. I looked at the jury, and if I wasn't mistaken, there was a half-smile on the faces of a few its members. Mr Ahmed, realising that he would be wasting his time to continue, sat down with a dismissive,

"No further questions."

PC Dennison, with still less than three years' service, had just given evidence as one of the primary witnesses in a murder trial, and he'd been calm and professional despite the growing intensity of Mr Ahmed's adversarial style of questioning. He could never have imagined this scenario, not in a million years, and if the coming together of Rachel and

Little by pure chance was a tragedy, then the arrival of PC Dennison and his two trusted colleagues at 19 Nashcourt, had been a stroke of luck for the investigation. DC Key wasn't called as a witness and so it was time to break for lunch.

In the court foyer, I caught a glimpse of Carol, who must have just finished giving her evidence. I called over to her because she seemed to be alone with no one to support her. She pretended not to hear me and almost ran out of the court building in an effort to get away. I soon discovered why, she was trying to hide the tears that were streaming down her face. I persuaded her to come for a drink in what was fast becoming my favourite pub, just a short walk across the road. Sat in my usual seat by the window, she covered her face with both hands,

"Never fucking again, never fucking again."

She'd been ripped to pieces by the defence barrister, and she told me that he'd made her feel much worse than any punter had ever done. The giving of evidence had clearly brought back vivid memories of the moment she'd asked for payment from her attacker, and the savage assault that followed. It was the first time I'd seen her cry and the tears kept on coming as a few of the lunchtime drinkers looked on wondering whether I was the cause of her distress.

I thought about Natalie Clubb, Rachel and the many other cases I'd dealt with and they all had one thing in common: they'd all been unable to protect themselves from the evil perpetrated by others. And all we had to fight back with was a criminal justice system that treated the innocent with contempt and without mercy. I didn't have the heart to tell her that everything would be OK because I knew that it wouldn't be. The damage had already been done. A brutal battering for just doing her job, followed by humiliation in the witness box. I said goodbye to her knowing that our paths would never cross again. Although it wasn't much, I'd provided a shoulder to cry on at one of the lowest times of her life, I thought, as I left the sanctuary of the pub for the stiffness and formality of the court.

Before the afternoon session began with Professor Milroy's evidence, I spoke to Wanda and warned her about what to expect. She had a fair idea but told me that she'd a 'burning need' to learn as much as possible about how her daughter died. Thankfully, she told me that Ray had decided against hearing the pathologist's evidence. The last thing she said was,

"I will sit through it all as it's the very least I can do for her."

Professor Milroy struck a commanding figure in the witness box. Still brimming with confidence, his clear and articulate delivery suited the occasion as he described what he saw when he'd opened the door to the store cupboard at 19 Nashcourt, and his thought process about how best to remove Rachel's body in order to preserve any evidence. I was impressed. Before moving on to the post-mortem, he asked the jury to refer to some three-dimensional body images that showed the position and number of stab wounds inflicted on Rachel. They were much better than a two-dimensional outline diagram of a body normally used in trials, and were the next best thing to photographs. The jury's first thought must have been that they were looking at a dressmaker's mannequin, but their facial expressions changed as they realised that the numbered red marks indicated stab wounds: 1 to 17 on her head and neck, 18 to 26 on her back and 27 on her chest.

"The cause of death was due to multiple stab wounds to the neck and chest. In broad terms, these stab wounds are present on the back. Some of them have penetrated into the chest cavity, the ribs, the lungs, heart and other organs of the chest. The result of these stab wounds is they have actually damaged the lungs and the aorta, the largest blood vessel in the body, which runs from the heart down the body, supplying all the major organs. This causes blood loss both internally and externally."

Mr Morton asked the question that I liked to think was for the benefit of Rachel's family. How quickly would Rachel have died?

"As the person loses this blood, they will go into medical shock. There will be a collapse of their blood circulation and they will lose consciousness and die soon after."

I hoped that to hear the words, 'lose consciousness and die soon after', would be of some comfort to Rachel's family. But as I looked towards the public gallery, I wasn't surprised to see some of them leave the courtroom, only Wanda remained. They must have guessed what the next question would be.

"Can you please tell the court, in your opinion, how severe was the attack?"

"The wounds were made by a knife with a long blade, measuring between seven and twelve inches, with a three-inch-wide blade at its widest. That's sort of a large carving knife. It would appear to have a single sharp edge because a number of wounds have a sharp edge and a blunt edge."

Professor Milroy paused for a moment and looked up towards Wanda as if to say, 'I'm sorry but I must answer the question'.

"Severe force was used in the case of four wounds to the back, when the blade penetrated to the front of Miss Moran's body. One of the blows cut through a rib. Track marks made by the knife entering Miss Moran's body varied in direction. These wounds are running in multiple directions, going upwards and forwards through the chest. They show signs that Miss Moran put up a struggle. But the pattern of the sixteen wounds to her head and neck indicate the body was motionless at the time."

Wanda had both hands covering her face. Kay was sat next to her with her arm around her shoulders. Finally, Wanda had heard in graphic detail the brutal nature of Rachel's suffering that Professor Milroy timed around the early hours of New Year's Day, about the time that she went missing. He concluded his evidence by stating that only a small amount of alcohol was found in Rachel's urine, and there was no evidence of illegal drug misuse of any kind. I hoped that Wanda would find some comfort in knowing everything. At least she now knew that Rachel was dead when the wounds to her head and neck were inflicted, and so did the jury. The moment Professor Milroy had delivered this news at the post-mortem back in January, I knew that his words would leave an everlasting impression, a mental image of the frenzied attack on a lifeless Rachel. It was an image that never left me, and I wondered whether it ever would.

And if the effect on me was profound, I couldn't think of the words to describe what Wanda must be experiencing.

Little kept his head bowed during the Professor's evidence. Mr Ahmed remained seated. No cross-examination. It meant that he wasn't going to challenge the likely time of death. He was going to have to rely on casting doubt on Marc Fuller's alibi if he was to convince the jury that the defendant was telling the truth. If Professor Milroy's evidence was difficult for Rachel's family to contemplate, then Dr. Warner's would be just as heartbreaking.

"I can say for certain that Michael Little had unprotected sexual intercourse with Miss Moran. It could have taken place shortly before Miss Moran was stabbed to death or it could have happened sometime after. I cannot be sure."

With those words, I felt that my decision not to charge Little with rape had been the right one. The only thing that was beyond doubt was the presence of Little's semen inside poor Rachel. The jury would have to decide whether it was as a result of consensual sex, rape or necrophilia. In response to Dr. Warner being shown a knife from Little's kitchen measuring thirteen inches long with a nine-inch blade, she said that its dimensions were consistent with the multiple stab wounds inflicted upon Rachel.

"No blood was found on the knife but I can't exclude the possibility the knife was blood stained and subsequently cleaned."

Perhaps the most distressing part of her evidence was when she talked about Rachel's jacket and dress displayed in a glass cabinet, clearly visible to the jury but not to open court.

"There were thirty-four stab cuts to the back of the jacket. They were associated with saturated bloodstaining. As a result, the jacket was virtually rigid with dried blood. If the material was crumpled then a single stabbing action could look like two cuts or more. The plum dress Miss Moran was wearing was also heavily bloodstained. It wasn't cut because it had a low back."

"Do you have an opinion on as to why the straps on Miss Moran's dress were not severed? It may assist you to look at the image showing stab wounds 17 to 22 on the left side of Miss Moran's back and 23 to 26 on the right side. If you were to superimpose the likely position of the straps onto the image then would not the knife have cut the straps?"

It was a good question, and all we could think of was that the straps simply fell from her shoulders and onto her upper arms during Rachel's struggle to break free. Dr. Warner came to pretty much the same conclusion but qualified her answer with, 'I can't say for certain'. The jury would be left in no doubt that Rachel was fully clothed when she was stabbed repeatedly from behind. And there was no doubt in my mind that Little's motive had been lust and that the frenzied nature of the attack was part of the overkill associated with a 'lust murderer'. Dr. Warner continued with her view on where she thought Rachel had been killed.

"It was most likely in the hallway. The nature and distribution of blood in the hallway and bathroom indicate that attempts were made to clean up a large volume of blood, which was shed predominantly, if not solely, in the hallway. If some kind of detergent was used it would have been possible to completely wash it all away. However, there was a trace of blood on a wall in the hallway that belonged to Miss Moran."

Unfortunately, the fingerprint in blood on the door jamb was inconclusive, and the blood distribution up the stairwell was from a separate unrelated incident. Dr. Warner was as impressive as ever. Her opinion that Rachel was killed in the hallway supported the prosecution case that Little murdered her whilst she was fully clothed seconds after he'd forced her into his flat. Again, Mr Ahmed remained seated. He couldn't argue with the presence of Little's semen inside Rachel, or her blood on the wall. And he couldn't argue with her conclusion that Rachel was killed in the hallway, because that was part of Little's defence.

Shaun Weir was the last witness of the day. Tall and immaculately dressed, he radiated a wave of confidence and professionalism that you could almost touch, without him saying a word. Mr Morton spent some time on asking the officer to summarise for the court the wide spectrum of questions that were put to Little, including the one most relevant to his latest defence: 'Did Marc Fuller play any part in the murder of Rachel Moran? If he did, now's the time to tell us Michael'. If I were sat on the jury, I'd be wondering why he'd not answered the question. It would've been the prefect opportunity to do so. In hindsight, at that stage, Little probably hadn't come up with blaming Fuller as his defence.

Before Shaun left the stand, Mr Morton asked the officer one final question,

"Did you give Mr Little a Special Warning with reference to the presence of Rachel Moran's body in the utility cupboard?"

"Yes. He made no comment."

"Can you explain to the court what a Special Warning is and why it was given?"

"Yes. Mr Little failed to give an explanation for why Miss Moran's body was in his flat. Section 36 of the Criminal justice and Public order Act, 1994 provides for such a warning to be given in these circumstances."

"And am I right in saying that it is for the court to decide whether an adverse inference should be drawn from Mr Little's lack of cooperation."

"I believe so."

Mr Ahmed fired back with a statement, rather than a question.

"My client was well within his rights to make no comment, if that was the advice of his solicitor."

I had to admit that he was right. In many ways, Special Warnings were just a repeat of the caution given by police officers to suspects upon arrest. But nevertheless, Mr Morton had quite properly highlighted Little's complete lack of cooperation for the jury to consider. Whether or not they'd hold it against him, would be an entirely different matter. It would depend on the judge's view of the significance of the defendant's no comment replies in his summing up of the evidence. We'd just have to wait to see.

I'd a feeling that Mr Ahmed would raise the issue of lack of disclosure - as Harding had done during Little's interviews - as the reason for his client's no comment replies to every question. That's exactly what he did in cross-examination, but Shaun was more than ready with a perfectly formed answer that Gary Shaw would've been proud of. I caught some of the jurors nodding as if in agreement. After all, written disclosure was given to Harding and Little prior to each interview, all captured on video. It'd all been submitted as evidence to show the thoroughness of Shaun's interviewing prowess. Maybe that was why Mr Ahmed abruptly ended his cross-examination. Shaun stepped down with his head held high. I was pretty sure that my trusted colleague had left a favourable impression on the jury.

The last act of the day was what I feared - the need for Lord Justice Hooper to treat Marc Fuller as a hostile witness for the prosecution and issue a warrant for his arrest. It was the only way we would be able to guarantee his attendance at court tomorrow.

I called in to see Mr Morton before heading home. I wanted to tell him that he was doing a first-class job and that I'd every faith in his ability to secure a conviction. But I didn't. There was still this inescapable reality that we came from very different worlds. Yes, it was true that I'd achieved much in my life given that I was brought up on a council estate in east Hull: Detective Superintendent with three degrees to my name, including a PhD. But the gulf in intellect was massive and I felt my power slipping away in his presence. Even though my confidence had grown over the past few months, I still wasn't ready to believe that it had and I understood that there was a difference. I asked him how he felt about the way the case was going. All he said was,

"Tomorrow should be an interesting day."

Mr Morton's response was measured to say the least, and I couldn't blame him because he clearly had absolutely no idea what Fuller was going to say, or how well he'd behave in the witness box. And neither did we. He'd refused to speak to any of my investigation team before the trial.

On the way home, I imagined that I was a member of the jury and I started to panic. This was only the third full day of the trial and the prosecution case would surely depend upon Fuller's performance in the box tomorrow, and the credibility of his family to provide him with a cast iron alibi. It would also depend upon Mr Ahmed's ability to challenge their evidence. The months of waiting had come to this, the months of thinking that surely Little would be found guilty, and now I wasn't so sure because, in the end, it was down to twelve members of the jury. Ordinary people leading ordinary lives. Who would they believe? It was a question that I never expected to be asking myself when we'd charged Little with Rachel's murder. But Crown Court was an unforgiving environment, only the strong survived. The battle between Mr Morton and Mr Ahmed was far from over.

TWENTY-ONE

'I wouldn't protect a murderer'

I had a feeling that Friday, 17 October, was going to be a day that I'd remember for a long time to come. I woke with a deep sense of foreboding that sent my stomach into meltdown. It was as if it was me that was on trial. The journey to court was a lonely one with only the familiar voice of negativity for company. But whereas the impact of that voice had at one time been profound, it no longer had the same effect. I'd gradually won that battle by refusing to give in and by choosing to be positive every day.

A call from Shaun though brought some good news. Marc Fuller was in custody but it was tempered by the bad news: he was aggressive, agitated and couldn't stop swearing. The scene was set. I walked into the court building with a familiar nod from security. Two of my trusted detectives were stood with Fuller. He was pacing up and down, dressed in a white baggy t-shirt, jeans and a baseball cap, spitting out words that appeared to be directed at no one in particular, 'and you can fuck off, what you looking at, silly twat'. What on earth would the jury make of him? What would Rachel's family think of him? I'd never felt so apprehensive about a witness giving evidence before and the irony was that he was supposed to be on our side. I could see Rachel's family looking on, they'd have no idea that it was Fuller.

It was time for Fuller to give his evidence. He swaggered into court with absolutely no regard for the formality of the occasion, glaring at just about everyone in the room. But he seemed to take a particular disliking to Mr Ahmed, and I was pretty sure that he muttered something to the effect of 'little fat twat', as he sauntered past the impassive barrister. Then he stopped for a moment and turned to Little and mouthed 'evil bastard'. Lord Justice Hooper must have been well aware of Fuller's conduct but chose to ignore it, at least for the time being.

Fuller stood in the box only a few feet away from me, trembling with rage, as if it were a Saturday night in the city centre of Hull, and he was ready to fight anybody, just for the sake of it. It wouldn't take much to send him over the edge, I thought, as Mr Morton braced himself before standing to address Fuller, who'd at least removed his baseball cap for the occasion. Mr Ahmed stared at Fuller, eyeing his prey looking for a weakness, and he must have been delighted with Fuller's performance so far - hostile and aggressive, with absolutely no 'likeability' factor. Mr Morton opened with a question that I hadn't expected.

"Did you murder Rachel Moran?"

It seemed to take Fuller by surprise and just about everybody else for that matter.

"I didn't kill no-one. It's that evil bastard over there who killed her not me. Fucking nothing to do with killing no-one."

It was an emotional outburst, his hands clenching the witness box rail as if he was about to leap towards Mr

Morton. If this was going to be his reaction towards the prosecuting barrister, I couldn't begin to imagine what it would be when it was Mr Ahmed's turn to cross-examine him. Lord Justice Hooper warned Fuller about his language.

"It would help us if you tried to calm down. The swearing is not helping anyone."

"I didn't come here to be accused of something I haven't done. Fucking not right. Sorry, not right."

Mr Morton did his best to guide Fuller through his movements on New Year's Eve and the early hours of New Year's Day. It took some time but he got there in the end. Fuller arrived back at his mother's home on Greenwich Avenue, just after midnight and didn't leave again until late afternoon. His mother, Janet Devine, his sister, Kersty and his mother's boyfriend, Jesus Mandrinan of Spanish origin, would be able to corroborate his story. Also, there were phone calls from his two uncles, one timed at 12.15am and the other some fifteen minutes later, both answered by Fuller before handing the phone over to his mother. Finally, Mr Morton sat down with a look of relief that his questioning of our troubled witness was over. If the jury believed Fuller and they subsequently believed his family, then there would be no way that he could have been in two places at once. But Mr Ahmed's cross-examination of Fuller was yet to come, and by now, his language had descended into expletive after expletive, despite being threatened with contempt of court by Lord Justice Hooper. Fuller replied with,

"Go on then, see if I care."

Mr Ahmed was ready to pounce. The jury looked bemused, and the question I would be asking if I were in their position would be, is this normal to allow a witness to behave in such a way in Crown Court? They must have read my mind because the foreman of the jury passed a note to the judge via the court usher. Lord Justice Hooper cleared the court and addressed the jury.

"Members of the jury. I have considered the question that you have asked in your note. The behaviour of Mr Fuller is indeed worthy of comment and you are right to ask whether or not it should be allowed in this courtroom. I am sure that both Mr Morton and Mr Ahmed would wish to call witnesses that show obedience and courteousness towards the court at all times but in reality, that is not always possible. I am prepared to allow Mr Fuller a certain degree of latitude in his choice of language only because it is likely that that is his normal way of expressing himself. In addition, and more importantly, you may think that what Mr Fuller has to say in its entirety, including his colourful choice of words, should be heard in order for the defendant to receive a fair trial. Thank you."

The jury had their answer. But it wasn't his foul language that was worrying me, it was what the jury would make of his brooding and aggressive presence in the witness box. Mr Ahmed was about to accuse Fuller of stabbing Rachel to death in an act of extreme violence, and I wondered whether an independent observer would think it likely based on his performance so far. Probably.

Mr Ahmed stood and edged forward, to get as close to Fuller as possible. His response was a sign of what was to come over the next hour or so.

"What you fucking looking at. Who the fuck are you?"

"I'm Mr Ahmed representing the defendant, Mr Little."

"How can you defend that podgy evil bastard?"

I looked at Lord Justice Hooper and with a shake of the head, he again warned Fuller about his language. Mr Ahmed had carefully laid his trap and Fuller was about to walk right into it as gasps of astonishment rang around the court. This was high drama and if it had been on the TV, nobody would believe it, not for one minute. But this was really happening and I could feel the case slipping away from me.

"Mr Fuller, what you have told the court is nothing but a pack of lies. It was you who murdered Rachel Moran in a fit of jealously because your friend Michael Little had consensual sex with her. You stabbed her repeatedly, didn't you?"

For a moment, I thought that Fuller was going to bolt from the witness box and attack Mr Ahmed. But his reaction was not what I expected, and it provided a moment of light relief amidst the ugliness of the encounter.

"The last thing I killed was a fucking wood pigeon on Sutton golf course."

I was struck by his response, it sounded raw, authentic and very real. He was either telling the truth, or he'd the imagination to pull a cracking one liner out of thin air whilst under the intense scrutiny of the court. I knew that he was being honest but would the jury? Mr Ahmed pressed on with his tactic of provoking Fuller at every opportunity and, for the most part, it worked.

"I put it to you that you were not at home, you were caught on CCTV on Hall Road about 1am. You were waiting for Miss Moran because you had arranged to deal her some cannabis. You are a dealer in cannabis are you not? I'll remind you that you are under oath to tell the truth."

"Yes, but that's got nothing to do with it. I wasn't fucking anywhere near Hall road."

Lord Justice Hooper duly warned Fuller about the potential risk of prosecution by his admission in court, but given the circumstances, I had no interest in pursuing Fuller for such a minor crime. Mr Ahmed showed the CCTV footage. It was the first time I'd seen it, and it showed a male sitting on what looked like an electricity supply box, before moving off in the opposite direction to Nashcourt.

"This is you, isn't it?"

"Not me. Looks nothing like me."

"When Miss Moran turned up you persuaded her to go to Michael Little's flat and smoke the cannabis. You let yourself in with a set of keys given to you by the defendant. Mr Little returned home unexpectedly and found you having a drink and smoking the cannabis with Miss Moran. You became violently jealous when Miss Moran followed the defendant into the bedroom. When you realised that consensual sex had taken place between them, you flew into a rage, picked up a carving knife from the kitchen and stabbed Miss Moran repeatedly in the back, neck and head. Didn't you?"

"You're lying. Get your facts right. Little twat. I was at home. Ask my Mam, ask my sister, ask my Mam's boyfriend."

"And when you had murdered Miss Moran you threatened to murder the defendant if he did not take the blame."

"How could I threaten Podgy when I wasn't even there? I

was at home how many times do I have to say. Are you fucking deaf?"

Mr Ahmed moved on to when Rachel's body was discovered, and he accused Fuller of putting on an elaborate act for the benefit of the police appearing to be shocked and surprised. Fuller started shaking as if he'd just been given a jolt of electricity. I was only a few feet away and it was very real. I felt sorry for him because I knew that he was innocent and yet here he was, a witness for the prosecution, now being accused of murder and being ripped to pieces by an unrelenting barrister.

"Look, I've never seen the lass in my life. When the coppers came, I felt like I was superglued to the floor. I couldn't believe it."

He pointed towards Little.

"All that bastard was doing was talking about his favourite video, Lord of the fucking Rings. It was unreal."

In an afterthought, Fuller began to fight back.

"Answer me this clever twat. If I was guilty like you say, why would I hang around Podgy's flat waiting for the coppers to come? We'd seen the tele that morning. That grey-haired copper was on saying how they was going to search every house on the estate. I wouldn't be that stupid. If I was guilty, I'd have been miles away."

It was a fair comment and I could see the jury scribbling away. Mr Ahmed seemed, for the first time, to be momentarily put off his stride. He'd clearly not thought about how to counter Fuller's authentic sounding plea of innocence. It was a comment that anyone could understand. Why would you wait for the knock on the door that you knew was coming and hope that Little would take the blame. It didn't make any sense.

"Mr Fuller, I will ask questions. Not you."

Mr Ahmed's comment was an acknowledgement that he'd unwittingly handed a slim lifeline to Fuller. The balance of power had moved ever so slightly.

"Let me now turn to your so-called alibi. A pack of lies from start to finish concocted with your family after you were bailed by the police."

"Foul gossip and slander that is. You're a liar, a fucking horrible little liar."

By this point, it wasn't as if Lord Justice Hooper had simply given up trying to curtail Fuller's colourful language, as far as I could see, he didn't have much choice but to give the jury every opportunity to witness all aspects of Fuller's character. They had a limited amount of time to watch Fuller fighting to protest his innocence, and it wouldn't be long before they would have to make a decision about whether Fuller was telling the truth. I realised that the judge was bending over backwards to give Little a fair trial and thereby limit the likelihood of an appeal should he be found guilty, or at least that what I told myself.

Mr Ahmed's hostility towards Fuller continued unabated, and I wondered how long it would be before Fuller decided enough was enough and storm out of the building. I wouldn't have blamed him. He cut a lonely, pathetic figure being wrongly accused, in the most intimidating of circumstances, of slaughtering a young female who he'd never set eyes on before. Being accused of something you hadn't done had to be right up there with life's worst nightmares, and I could forgive Fuller's ugliness in the box as I tried to imagine what would be running through his mind. Will Podgy be found not guilty? Will I be arrested again and charged with her murder? Why won't anybody listen to me? Why is that little fat twat being so aggressive? Finally, though, his ordeal was over and with obscene gestures to anyone who would look at him, including the jury, he was gone. There was no doubt that Mr Ahmed had gained the upper hand and he sat down with a contented grin on his face. He'd achieved what he'd no doubt set out to do: revealed to the jury, Fuller's quick and unstable temper so that they would at least consider the possibility that he was capable of stabbing Rachel and threatening Little. I knew what was coming next. If Little had any chance of being found not guilty, Mr Ahmed had to cast doubt on Fuller's alibi by discrediting his family, and Janet Devine, Fuller's mother, would be the perfect target. What mother wouldn't want to protect their son?

Lord Justice Hooper rightly adjourned for lunch. Everybody needed a break from the heightened tension that suffocated the courtroom. I didn't want to see anyone. I just wanted to escape so I headed for the nearest record store in Whitefriargate, a long-cobbled street just off Lowgate. I had it in my mind that buying a CD would make me feel better having endured the worst morning for the prosecution so far. I wondered what it would be like to work in a record store for a living. I'd be useless at selling CDs though, because I still hadn't come to terms with the demise of the LP. Maybe I could open up my own record store and start a campaign to bring back vinyl's, I thought. I still had my own turntable and numerous LPs from my younger days, and there was a warmth from their sound that couldn't be matched by CDs. Then I got lost in how I'd play really cool music, loud and hand out strong coffee for free. For a moment, I almost forgot that I had to go back and listen once again to Mr Ahmed, who I already knew would be someone that I'd never forget.

Janet Devine was the complete opposite of her son. Quietly spoken and reserved, she told Mr Morton that Marc came home just after midnight on New Year's Day. She remembered her two brothers calling shortly afterwards to wish her a happy New Year and that Marc had answered both times. She recalled Marc coming down for breakfast as she prepared a family dinner and staying in for most of the day. The jury must have wondered whether Fuller really was Janet Devine's son, and her unexpectedly respectable and dignified presence in the box, can't have been what Mr Ahmed would have wished for. He'd got some work to do if he was to undermine her story, and I wondered if he'd treat her with more respect than he'd shown to her son. It wasn't long before he reduced her to tears though, as he forced home his accusation that she was supporting her son's false alibi. And then he delivered a rambling summary of what he thought had happened. Janet Devine just sobbed as he accused her of,

"Getting together with your daughter and boyfriend to get your stories straight after your son was bailed. You then lied to the police in your first statement and when they came back you gave them more lies. Now you stand here lying to the court."

Finally, he asked a question.

"I know it is very difficult for a mother once she is faced with siding with justice or her son. Would you side with justice or your son?"

Lord Justice Hooper asked her if she needed some time to compose herself. She acknowledged his act of consideration and sipped from a glass of water before whispering her answer.

"I wouldn't protect a murderer."

It was a cleverly worded question, 'Justice or your son', as if it had to be one or the other, not both. The CCTV footage was played again, and Janet Devine told the court that she was certain that it wasn't her son sat on the electricity supply box. She must have hoped that there would be no more questions but Mr Ahmed had only just begun. He asked whether she knew for certain that her son stayed in the house after the phone calls from her two brothers, one from Scotland and the other from North Yorkshire. In fairness to Mr Ahmed, I'd have asked exactly the same question,

"Was it possible that your son could have gone out again without you knowing? Were you not in your bedroom with your boyfriend and Marc, in another?"

She of course had to accept that she couldn't be certain, neither could Fuller's sister, Kersty, or his mother's boyfriend. Mr Ahmed was equally brutal with all of Fuller's family, apart from his two uncles, whose testimony couldn't be disputed - their phone calls were logged and timed at just after midnight, with a fifteen-minute gap between them.

I left the court before the end of Jesus Mandrinan's testimony, because I'd had enough of watching perfectly decent people being destroyed for one day. Janet Devine and her daughter had already been humiliated and fled the room in floods of tears. It was late Friday afternoon, time for a rest over the weekend. I was spot on to think that today would be a day that I'd never forget. It'd been a shameful day for the criminal justice system.

Driving home, I recalled what Mr Morton quoted in his opening speech: 'Whenever a man is on trial for serious crime, then trial by jury has no equal'. That might well be true, but I was pretty sure the Janet Devine's of this world were never given a second thought. The system couldn't care less about them. Even if Little was found guilty, a verdict that was becoming increasingly unlikely after today, the damage had already been done to Fuller and his family. Would I reopen the case should Little be freed? Not in a million years.

TWENTY-TWO

'It'd been an accident. I was drunk. It was an argument that went wrong'

Monday, 20 October, was the last day of the prosecution case. In the morning, Mr Morton produced his last witness, Alan Briggs, a career criminal who was placed in a holding cell with Little following his remand into custody in January. Briggs told the court that Little spoke freely about Rachel and admitted to him that,

"It'd been an accident. I was drunk. It was an argument that went wrong."

He asked him what he'd done with her body.

"I just locked it in a cupboard."

Briggs was shocked by Little's lack of emotion,

"He just didn't seem to care."

This, according to Briggs, led to an argument between them resulting in Little head-butting him. Finally, although Briggs made his living by being dishonest, a fact that Mr Morton purposely didn't try to hide, it was evidence of Little's violent nature. Mr Ahmed accused him of lying to the police in the hope of gaining a shortened sentence. The problem was, though, that my officers had told Briggs that there would be no inducement in return for his evidence. It clearly wasn't what Mr Ahmed wanted to hear.

I knew what was coming in the afternoon. The jury had heard yesterday about the challenge to Fuller's alibi that, according to Mr Ahmed, he was caught on CCTV sat on the electricity supply box at the junction of Inglemire Lane and Hall Road. But if he had been at home on Greenwich Avenue and answered the phone calls from his uncles around 12.15 to 12.30am, would it have been physically possible for Fuller to travel either of the two most likely routes to that location by 1am?

Mr Morton wanted to answer that question and he took up most of the afternoon doing so. He produced large maps of the area, showing that the distance between Greenwich Avenue and the location of the CCTV, was nearly six miles and would take about an hour and fifty minutes to walk at a brisk pace and about thirty-five minutes on a bicycle. Accordingly, Mr Morton argued that Fuller couldn't have walked that distance but accepted that he could have travelled there on his pushbike. Mr Ahmed reminded the jury that Fuller owned a bicycle and that it'd been discovered in the bathroom in Little's flat when they were arrested. Although Mr Morton did his best that he could in the circumstances, Mr Ahmed and his team had obviously done their homework. They would have received disclosure about the timings of the phone calls answered by Fuller, and they'd know how long it'd take on a bike to reach the location of the CCTV on Hall Road.

Little's defence team had made a mistake in insisting that Fuller was the person caught on the CCTV footage. It looked nothing like him, there was no bike in sight, and they hadn't bargained for Mr Morton recalling DC Bailey to give his expert opinion on whether the clothing worn by the person on the footage, was similar to what Fuller had been wearing - an olive-green tracksuit top and blue bottoms. DC Bailey, whilst holding Fuller's top stated,

"Having viewed a considerable amount of CCTV footage, it's my belief that this top would turn out to be darker on the screen than the one shown."

In other words, although the film was in black and white, the tops didn't match. And if it was a pre-arranged drug deal, then why hadn't Fuller insisted on meeting at Saxcourt? It would have been about half-a-mile less distance for Fuller to travel in the freezing cold. It just didn't make any sense, and I hoped that the jury would come to the same conclusion.

Another day over and Little was up next. He had to give evidence, because the defence case depended upon the jury believing Little, whilst failing to accept Fuller's alibi. It sounded so simple when I thought about it, but it'd been anything but simple so far. If Little possessed an ounce of decency, he should plead guilty in the witness box tomorrow and throw himself at the mercy of the court. But he would be fighting for his life with the assistance of the very capable Mr Ahmed and, after watching Fuller's performance, he would be thinking that he'd every chance of being found not guilty. Mr Morton would have to give the performance of his life if he was to recover lost ground and discredit Little's pack of lies.

TWENTY-THREE

'Eyes blinking, mouth dry, beads of sweat rolling down his forehead'

At exactly 11am on Tuesday, 21 October, Michael Little was brought to the witness box flanked by two burly prison guards. Little made them seem small by comparison. Smartly dressed and hair combed neatly for the occasion, he stood only an arm's length away from me. The days leading up to this moment had, without doubt, been the most extraordinary ones that I'd ever witnessed in Crown Court. If it were possible to capture the unimaginable levels of adrenalin coursing through the veins of Rachel's family, and the witnesses interrogated by Mr Ahmed, then there would surely have been enough to fuel a rocket to the moon and back. But today was somehow different, more tension if that were possible, like a volcano about to explode.

This was the moment that Rachel's family had been waiting for, to see the person who stole their daughter give his evidence. I'd already warned them of what to expect. Little would be well groomed on how to play the jury and they'd have to endure the agony of listening to lie after lie. Their long wait was about to be over as Mr Ahmed cleared his throat and faced Little. I thought that I'd seen every trick in the book, but then Little made an elaborate gesture of revealing a rosary that hung around his thick neck for all to see. Mr Ahmed stood, ready to face his client, and it was obvious that his demeanour had softened. His body language suggested that there was a side to him that we'd not seen before. I knew that it was all part of the game, but would the jury be taken in by what I felt sure was about to happen? Mr Ahmed's plan would be to portray Little as a pathetic individual, a victim of society that hadn't given him a decent education, hadn't found him meaningful work, and had almost given him no option but to stay in bed all day, smoking cannabis, drinking alcohol and eating takeaway meals. And that's exactly what he did during the first hour or so of questioning.

For the most part, Little spoke quietly in a surprisingly high pitched voice that didn't seem to go with his huge frame. There were tears as he recalled the death of his stepfather seven years ago that he claimed led to his depression and the need to regularly take LSD, amphetamines and ecstasy. And two bicycle accidents that left him disabled and in need of further medication. Mr Ahmed must have been satisfied with Little's performance so far. The deliberate ploy of revealing Little's drug abuse before Mr Morton had the chance to do so was a bold move and, because Little wasn't telling lies, he looked as though he was actually telling the truth.

It was time for phase two of Mr Ahmed's plan - to question the defendant in elaborate detail over what he claims happened from leaving the party at Exchange Street to the discovery of Rachel's body. It would allow Mr Ahmed to attempt to show Little as a vulnerable young man, a victim of

Fuller's bullying, remorseful over his inability to save Rachel from the frenzied attack perpetrated by his so-called friend, and someone deserving of the court's sympathy. There would be more tears along the way in the hope that the jury would recognise the contrast between the aggressive foul-mouthed Fuller, surely capable of such violence, and the quietly spoken, rosary clad defendant. I knew that Mr Morton would be listening closely for any mistakes made by Little, and so would I.

Little argued that he left the party at Exchange Street around 4am, and therefore couldn't be the person caught on CCTV at Jacksons much earlier. That was his first error of judgement because a number of reliable witnesses had already given evidence to say that it was, without any doubt, Little on the footage. But it was when he was questioned about what happened when he arrived home to discover Fuller already inside his flat drinking with a female he'd not met before, that revealed the extent of his lies. They were subtle, and only Rachel's family and Mark, would know for definite that Little wasn't telling the truth.

"She was sipping alcopops and Marc was drinking lager."

Rachel never drank alcopops and rarely drank at all except on special occasions.

"She asked me if I'd a BMX racing game."

Rachel had no interest whatsoever in BMX racing, WWF wrestling maybe, but not BMX.

"She followed me into the bedroom and asked me if I thought she was good looking."

Rachel would never ask that question in a million years, she couldn't care less what she looked like.

"She began to kiss me and we ended up having sex."

Rachel never had unprotected sex with Mark ever since the unwanted pregnancy, so why would she with a complete stranger? It was a pity that the jury didn't have access to some kind of virtual courtroom lie detector machine for the next act of Little's performance.

"Marc came into the bedroom and went berserk. We ended up arguing in the hallway. He grabbed a knife from the kitchen and made slashing motions towards me. She came between us and pushed me away saying that she'd sort it."

Mr Ahmed paused for Little to recover his composure because he was sobbing, tears rolling down his chubby cheeks.

"Marc lunged forward and connected with her. He just lost it stabbing her in the back over and over again. She fell to the floor and he straddled her and began stabbing her head and neck."

Again, another pause.

"I watched as she kicked against the door in the hallway as she struggled for a while but then she was dead. There was nothing I could do."

I looked across to Rachel's family and they were all still there, heads bowed with hands covering their faces. How could they sit and listen?

"Marc turned on me with the knife in his hand. Blamed me for what he'd done. He said it'd been me he'd wanted to kill and not her. He said he could easily kill me too but there'd be two bodies and when the police turned up, they'd know it was me."

I couldn't believe what he'd just said. Why would Fuller

be waiting in Little's flat for the police to come?

"I was frightened for me life and so I did what he told me to do. He threw me a towel and told me to clean up the blood and clear out the store cupboard. We put her in there together. I couldn't do it on my own because my injury to my shoulder. He told me to dump some of her stuff in the drain."

The last question to Little was,

"The prosecution will no doubt make much of the fact that you changed your story three times. How do you account for that?"

"I had to take the blame when the police came. He'd a knife in his hand. He'd just stabbed her to death. I was frightened for me life and my family. He told me if I didn't take the blame, he'd kill me and harm my family."

His three-hour performance was over. Some of what Little had said was true. The frenzied attack with the knife was authentic because, apart from the fact that the knife was in the hand of Little and not Fuller, that's what happened. The defence team had prepared him well for Mr Ahmed's gentle approach, but I wondered how Little would fair at the hands of Mr Morton, the English gentleman with his impeccable manners and flawless use of vocabulary. Would he give him the third degree or would it be benign and unchallenging? I'd no idea. I managed to get hold of Mr Morton over lunch and he was reassuringly aware of Little's mistakes. Just before I left, he looked straight at me,

"You have no need to worry Detective Superintendent. I am more than ready for Mr Little."

I was deep in thought when I heard the tannoy announce

that all interested parties should go to court 2. This must be it, the verdict. Somehow, I knew it'd be not guilty and that the brave prostitute's ordeal had been for nothing. And, of course, I was right. What the jury didn't know, though, was that the fireman was on remand for the other similar assault that he'd already pleaded guilty to. As he was handed down a custodial sentence by the judge for that crime, one of the female jurors began to cry. Maybe she realised that they'd reached the wrong verdict, but based on the evidence alone, they probably had no choice but to have had reasonable doubt. I looked for Carol but she wasn't in court. Perhaps she knew what the verdict would be, or perhaps she had clients to attend to and couldn't afford to let them down. I told myself that I'd call in to see how she was doing sometime but I knew that I wouldn't.

With the afternoon session about to begin, I wondered how much more drama was to come. I couldn't remember a time when the sun refused to shine day after day for so long. I told myself that maybe it was Rachel watching from above, full of anger and pain at the lies that were being told, and that clouds had gathered over the court to protest on her behalf. And, for whatever reason, as Little took the stand once again, the heavens opened. Thunder, lightning and torrential rain, smashing down from above.

Little bowed to the judge and jury in an attempt to show some respect and humility. Mr Morton turned his head and nodded to the exhibits officer to come forward with two long carving knives protected inside cylindrical plastic containers. After Little identified one of the knives as being the one that killed Rachel, came the line of questioning that her family had been waiting for. Gone was his polite, almost gentile approach to be replaced by what I could only describe as an Exocet missile type of attack - you might see it coming but you could do nothing about it. There was a steely, unsettling menace to his voice as the questions came with military like precision, one after the other, each one chosen to strike a blow for Rachel.

"You murdered Miss Moran and you are evil. That is the truth."

"No."

"Do you agree that the person who murdered Rachel is evil?"

"Yes, but it was Marc, not me."

"But it was a wicked thing you did in concealing her body all that time."

"Yes."

"If you were innocent as you claim, why did you not call the police?"

"Because I was frightened of what Marc would do."

This was exactly where he wanted Little, the opportunity to raise with him why his defence statements had changed over time. Surely the jury would question the honesty of someone who not only changed it once, but twice.

"Mr Little, that brings me to the differing versions of your defence. Would you agree that they are very different?"

"Yes."

Mr Morton proceeded to be the master of Little, not with sledgehammer like blows favoured by Mr Ahmed, but by his keen intellect that allowed him to formulate exactly the right question at exactly the right time. It was impressive.

"You agree that you told the officers that you saw Miss Moran walking along Hall Road and jogged to catch up with her. Is that what you told them?"

"Yes."

"You agree that you told the officers that you were on your own with Miss Moran. You made no mention Mr Fuller being there?"

"Yes."

"You made no mention of having sexual intercourse with Miss Moran, did you?"

"No."

"And do you remember telling the officers that you must be evil and that Mr Fuller had nothing to do with it?"

"Yes."

"Was that the truth?"

"No."

"So, you admit lying to the police?"

"Yes."

"You have in front of you your first defence statement dated early June, submitted after forensic tests proved beyond doubt that you had sexual intercourse with Miss Moran. Is that right?"

"Yes."

"Can you please for the benefit of the court read what it says?"

Little struggled to do what Mr Morton asked claiming that he'd difficulty reading.

"Do you agree that you are again saying that you met Miss Moran on Hall Road and that she went with you to your flat for a drink?"

"Yes."

"Do you agree stating that you were alone with Miss Moran and Mr Fuller was not there?"

"Yes."

"Do you agree that you stated that suddenly Mr Fuller arrived unexpectedly after you had stabbed Miss Moran once and then he stabbed Miss Moran repeatedly?"

"Yes."

"And was that the truth?"

"No."

"So, you admit to lying yet again, this time in a formal statement to the Crown Prosecution Service?"

"Yes."

"And now you are saying that you did not meet Miss Moran at all on Hall Road and that you took a different route home. Is that correct?"

"Yes."

"And now you are telling the court that Mr Fuller murdered Miss Moran and threatened to kill you if you did not take the blame. Is that correct?"

"Yes."

"Can you tell the court at what point between your confession to PC Dennison in January and your defence statement in June, did you realise that you were no longer living in fear of Mr Fuller?"

"What do you mean?"

"You are blaming Mr Fuller in June. Do you see my point?"

It was a good question and it unsettled Little. There was an awkward silence before the judge reminded Little that he must answer the question.

"Couldn't get to me in prison. Told me family I was protecting somebody and they told me to tell the truth."

"But were you not afraid for your family? You have told the court that Mr Fuller threatened your family. Is that not right?"

"They just told me to tell the truth."

"Is your latest version the truth?"

"Yes."

"But how will members of the jury able to tell when you are lying and when you are telling the truth?"

Little didn't answer. Eyes blinking, mouth dry, beads of sweat rolling down his forehead, he looked like he was about to have a heart attack. Mr Morton waited for an answer. There was silence in the room as everyone looked at Little. Mr Morton nodded to DC Bailey to play the CCTV footage at Jacksons. It was perfectly timed.

"That is you on the footage. Do you agree?"

"No, it's not me."

Little's voice was reduced to a whisper and the judge asked him to speak up for the benefit of the jury. DC Bailey played the image of Little walking ahead of Rachel about ten times.

"Are you saying that all of the witnesses who know you and viewed the footage, and are certain beyond doubt that it is you, are mistaken or lying?"

"Yes."

DC Bailey played the footage showing Rachel ahead of Little, near to Saxcourt.

"Are you saying that is not you as well?"

"Yes."

Mr Morton paused for a sip of water. Little looked relieved, maybe hoping that his ordeal was over, but it was far from over,

"You say Miss Moran asked you if you had a BMX game. She had no interest in BMX. Tell us precisely what was said so that we may understand why Miss Moran came to ask for the game."

Mr Morton waited for an answer. Little just looked down and remained silent. The judge reminded Little that he must answer. By now sweat was pouring down his chubby face and there were damp patches under his arms.

"She just did."

"You say you had consensual unprotected sex and yet Miss Moran did not even have unprotected sex with her boyfriend. Take us through, again, as precisely as you can remember, how it happened."

"She just followed me into me bedroom and started kissing me. Then it happened."

"So, what you are telling the court is that Rachel Moran, a beautiful young woman, willingly consented to have intercourse with you, a person she had not met before. Is that really your evidence, Mr Little? Is that what you are asking the jury to believe?"

With the jury's eyes fixed upon him, Little took a sip of water. What would his answer be? Without waiting for a reply, Mr Morton held up photographs of Little's flat.

"Do you agree that your flat is filthy and disgusting?"

It was a good question and it got me thinking about my decision to keep the flat for the trial. The judge had already turned down Mr Morton's request for the jury to be given the opportunity to visit the scene. The judge's reasoning was that it would be too prejudicial to Little's defence. In reality, a decision to allow such a visit might well provide grounds for an appeal should Little be found guilty. Whilst I had to accept that the judge was being scrupulously fair to both sides, I didn't stop me from wondering what the jury would think of the inside of 19 Nashcourt.

"Do not bother to answer. The photographs are there for all to see."

Mr Morton was on top form. He was urging the jury to look at the photographs again. I just wished that there was some way of letting the jury experience the appalling stench.

"You say that Mr Fuller threatened to kill you. Did he stay for the whole month of January and threaten you every day to make sure that you did not go to the police?"

Little seemed surprised by the question. It was obvious that he'd not given much thought to what his response would be, given that the fear of Fuller was crucial to his defence.

"No."

"Then why not simply go the police and tell them everything? Fuller would have been arrested. And you and your family would be safe."

Little didn't know what to say, and Mr Morton was in no mood to help him as he left a long and awkward silence.

"You did not go to the police because you alone murdered Rachel Moran. That is what happened."

"No, Marc killed her. Not me."

It was an unconvincing reply.

"When you knew the police were coming to search for Rachel, why didn't Mr Fuller leave?"

Little's humiliation at the hands of Mr Morton finally turned to anger as he shouted,

"What you asking me for, ask him."

Mr Morton braced himself for the conclusion of his cross-examination and with a venomous delivery he spat out his contempt for Little's lies. Rachel's family must have been secretly punching the air inside as they'd just witnessed the cool annihilation of the person who they were convinced had stolen their precious Rachel.

"Elements of what you told PC Dennison are true. I believe that you did come across Miss Moran on Hall Road. I believe that you were telling the truth when you told the officer that you lost it and stabbed her. I believe that you were telling the truth when you told the officer that Mr Fuller had nothing to do with it. Everything else that you have told the court is a pack of lies. What you failed to tell the officer was that she did not come with you to your flat willingly did she? No, you somehow forced her against her will into your filthy flat because she would have nothing to do with you and because you cannot deal with rejection. You failed to mention that you murdered Miss Moran in the hallway very soon after you entered through the front door. You failed to mention that you had unprotected sexual intercourse with Miss Moran, either after she was dead or lay dying, because that was the only way that she would not have been able to resist your disgusting advances towards her. Your testimony today has been shameful. You are an evil wicked man who then stuffed Miss Moran's body in a stinking cupboard as if she was just a piece of rubbish. And you are now accusing an innocent man in an attempt to save your own skin. Mr Little, I am giving you the opportunity to come clean. Tell the truth. If you do not, then I believe that you were telling the truth when you told the officer that you are evil and that a normal person would not be capable of carrying out such a wicked and brutal crime."

Mr Morton had performed beyond my expectation. He couldn't have done anymore. Little was never going to suddenly breakdown and admit what he'd done. It might work that way on TV, but not in real life, there was too much at stake. The portrayal of Little as the innocent, rosary-wearing victim, petrified of Fuller, had worked to an extent at the hands of Mr Ahmed's gentle and sympathetic questioning. But his confidence had crumbled under the spotlight of Mr Morton's sustained and microscopic analysis of how the three very different versions of his defence, varied. I just hoped that the jury realised that the latter two versions were a blatant attempt to pervert the course of justice. The tension subsided and ebbed away like a giant balloon had just burst. Little left the stand sandwiched between his prison guards, only to be greeted by, 'You're a liar' from Kerry Moran, shouted at the top her voice. Lord Justice Hooper decided not to acknowledge her outburst. There was a feeling of anti-climax now, deflation almost, as my adrenalin levels returned to normal. I knew the feeling well, like an unwelcome old friend.

The storm was still raging as I drove home. It felt as though winter had arrived early, with the fading light and pouring rain that gave a bleakness to the vast open landscape before me. The only comfort tonight would be a glass of whisky in front of a roaring open fire in the only place that I belonged, at home with my family. But any thoughts of an evening of reflection before the closing speeches tomorrow were shattered by a phone call from Trev.

"Boss, you're not going to believe this but I was just about to leave when I got a call from James Danby. After reading Fuller's alibi in the paper, he said he had to call. Turns out that he lives next door to Fuller and says he saw Fuller leave the house just after midnight and not come back."

I turned the car round and I wondered if things could get any worse. I had a bad feeling, because even though Little hadn't done himself any favours when giving evidence, I'd no idea what the jury were thinking. Was it too close to call? Would this new evidence cast doubt over Fuller's alibi? Seeing Trev on his own in the incident room, brought back memories of when I'd gone to Courtland Road to take over the case as SIO. His 'must do' tray was still piled high.

"Boss, what do you want to do with Danby? It'll blow the whole case apart."

"We both know there's only one thing we can do. Take a statement off Danby and let Mr Morton and Lord Justice Hooper know."

Although we'd have to wait to see exactly what he had to say, Trev was right, it did have the potential to blow the case apart given that the prosecution case relied heavily on Fuller's alibi being watertight. I called out DC Bailey and DC Forbes to take a statement from Danby. They would provide corroboration for each other should Mr Ahmed question what a potentially highly significant witness had said. Every word that Danby was going to tell the officers had to be recorded as faithfully as possible. I knew that we would only get one chance to get it right.

Whilst we waited for them to return, we sat in my office and talked. I hadn't seen much of Trev during the trial, and it felt good to talk to my old friend who'd been with me every step of the way. All the inspirational stuff I'd put on the walls was still there. Trev always saw the funny side of everything and today was no different as he pondered over some of my quotes. All he did was chuckle to himself. I knew what he'd be thinking - 'what a load of bollocks'. You could take the person out of the police culture, but you couldn't take the police culture out of the person, sprang to mind.

The two detectives weren't smiling when they returned, but there was good news and bad news. The bad news was that Danby claimed to have seen Fuller leave his mother's home around forty-five minutes after midnight, on foot. He'd kept watching out of his window for about twenty minutes and Fuller didn't return during that time, although it was possible that he could have without him noticing. The good news was that they'd done some digging, and there was definitely no love lost between the two families. Danby's mother's boyfriend had called Fuller a murderer, an accusation that had reduced Fuller's mother to tears. Fuller's response was to assault the boyfriend for which he'd received a caution. Also, Danby had a colourful past with convictions for firing an air gun at a teacher and assault.

"If he's telling the truth, how's Fuller managed to get across to Hall Road and appear on the footage at one o'clock as they claim. Must've bloody flown there or he's an Olympic sprinter on the side."

Trev was right to be frustrated because we all knew that this would present a perfect opportunity for Mr Ahmed to revisit Fuller's alibi, should Lord Justice Hooper decide to reopen the case. This was a devastating blow. I hadn't seen it coming, and there was no way that we could have planned for a witness to come forward at the eleventh hour. There would be no sleep tonight, I thought.

TWENTY-FOUR

'The gasps of astonishment just kept on coming'

As Mr Morton read through Danby's statement, he made notes with a fountain pen. I hadn't expected him to use anything but a good old-fashioned ink pen that was clearly a Mont Blanc. Every barrister seemed to possess the same pen. Maybe it was something given out as some kind of acknowledgment that they'd finally made it to the top. All he said was,

"This is indeed unfortunate timing."

In his chambers, Lord Justice Hooper looked less grand without his robes, but I could still see his bright red braces beneath his suit jacket. Again, another symbol of the privileged legal profession, I thought. Following a brief discussion, I knew what was coming, the decision to produce Danby as a witness, followed by Fuller and his family. Just before I left the judge said,

"Thank you for bringing this matter to my attention. It was exactly the right thing to do in the circumstances."

I believe that his words were meant as a compliment, but all I could think of was how was I going to break the news to Wanda and Ray. Everyone seemed to sense that something was wrong as the tannoy broke the news that there'd be a delay in court one. Rachel's family had a right to know about the events of last night. They looked petrified and exhausted as I approached them huddled together in the foyer. They'd suffered so many setbacks to get to this point, in touching distance of the verdict, and now they would have to endure witnessing round two of the battle between Fuller and Mr Ahmed. They must have hoped that after Mr Morton's demolition of Little, maybe things were beginning to turn their way. But as I pulled Ray aside and explained what had happened, it was as if I'd delivered a knockout blow. He winced with pain, and to steady himself, he put his hand on my shoulder and gripped it tightly. I told him that I was sorry and tried to reassure him that we still had a strong case. But in reality, I was really worried because this was exactly what Mr Ahmed wanted, another opportunity to plant the seed of reasonable doubt in the minds of the jury.

It felt like one of those times when if somebody had said to me the words I'd heard so many times before, 'we are where we are', as a philosophical comment to explain the sudden appearance of Danby as a witness for the defence, I'd probably have given them a smack in the mouth. Why, with the unprecedented level of media coverage, had he chosen to come forward at this late stage? He had to be lying, and our only chance would be to show that he was giving evidence to get even with Fuller for assaulting his mother's boyfriend. I never underestimated a human being's instinct to seek revenge.

James Danby took the stand to a packed courtroom that had no idea what he was about to say. I'd never heard of this happening in a murder trial before, but this really was happening before my eyes, and I was convinced that the outcome of today would determine Little's fate. The tension that had subsided yesterday was back with a vengeance as Mr Ahmed stood to address the baby-faced, smartly dressed, clean-shaven, young man.

"Can you please tell the court what you saw as you looked out of your window in the early hours of New Year's Day."

There were gasps of astonishment as it began to sink in just what Danby was claiming to have seen. It was as if he'd just lobbed a hand grenade from the stand. Would it explode and blow a gigantic hole in Fuller's alibi, or would it fail to ignite the puzzled jury? Mr Ahmed did a good job in portraying the witness as a family man, who felt duty bound to come forward when he'd read the details of Fuller's alibi in the Hull Daily Mail. The completely over the top coverage of the case in the local Mail, had grown with each day of the trial and, although I was powerless to prevent it, I'd a feeling that there would be unintended consequences of some kind. And now Danby was going to give evidence having probably read details of exactly what each witness had already said courtesy of the local paper. He would more than likely have seen the staggeringly provocative front page of Saturday October 18: 'WAS THIS MAN THE KILLER?' in bold letters next to a picture of Fuller. He might as well have been sitting in court the whole time, I thought, something that would never be allowed prior to giving evidence.

But Danby's testimony seemed to differ from what he'd told DC Bailey and DC Forbes - that he'd seen Fuller leave around twelve forty-five. He was now saying, a few minutes after midnight, which of course would have given him time to travel from Greenwich Avenue to Hall Road on a bike but not on foot. Danby saw Fuller walking in the general direction of Hall Road, but accepted that Fuller could have returned to collect his bike without him noticing. Mr Ahmed had got what he wanted, an independent witness to cast doubt on Fuller's alibi. Danby looked confident as if he was enjoying the occasion. His smugness didn't last long, though, because Mr Morton was in cutting edge form.

"Mr Danby, why have you come here today? Is it because you want to exact some kind of revenge on Mr Fuller for him assaulting your mother's boyfriend?"

From Danby's look of surprise, I guessed that he didn't think we knew about the assault and the bad blood between the two families, and I don't think that Mr Ahmed did either. Gasps of astonishment again. The jury must have been wondering what the next revelation would be. He denied it and told the court that he'd called the police only after reading about Fuller's alibi. This gave Mr Morton the opportunity to dent the image, so carefully crafted by Mr Ahmed, of a stand-up, law-abiding family man, whose only reason for his appearance in court was 'to do the right thing'.

"You have a list of previous convictions. On one occasion, you assaulted a teacher before shooting him with an air rifle hitting a thirteen-year-old child at the same time. You are not all what you seem, are you Mr Danby?"

Without waiting for a reply,

"You are a liar and you are wasting the court's time. Who knows why you have left it so late to come forward? Is it because of the feud between your two families? Or is it because you do not like Mr Fuller? Do not bother to answer."

I had to hand it to Mr Ahmed, you would never say that he gave up without a fight, and he demanded that DC Bailey be recalled so that he could challenge him over the timings recorded in his statement. Mr Ahmed suggested to the officer that he'd made a mistake and it should have been eleven forty-five and not twelve forty-five, when Danby saw Fuller leave. But the one thing that I admired about the DC Bailey's of this world was their honesty and attention to detail. If Danby said twelve forty-five, then that is what he would have written down. DC Bailey would not be swayed and concluded by stating,

"I'm certain that is what he'd told us."

The end of another day of high drama or so I thought. Mr Ahmed had other ideas. As Lord Justice Hooper was about to adjourn the case until tomorrow, Friday, October 24, he asked permission to address the court. What was he up to, I wondered? Another witness maybe to support Danby's last-minute evidence?

"My Lord, based on what we have heard today from Mr Danby, it is clear to me that there must be a retrial. In the interests of justice there must be a retrial. Why should the defendant sit accused of murder when the real killer walks free? I demand, in the strongest terms, that the police reopen the case, investigate Marc Fuller more thoroughly and charge him with murder."

The gasps of astonishment just kept on coming. It was a clever ploy to use at this late stage though, because he'd spoken the words, 'retrial', 'investigate Marc Fuller' and 'charge him with the murder', and they couldn't be taken back. They were meant to leave an impression on the jury. And even though I felt sure that the judge would have none of this nonsense, I knew that he would have to go away and give Mr Ahmed's demand due consideration and produce reasons for his decision in writing.

If Danby's late appearance plunged Rachel's family into even greater depths of despair, what must they be thinking now? It was a question that I didn't know the answer to and so I took them for a coffee in the court canteen whilst we waited for the judge to return with his ruling. My instinct was to tell them not to worry but there would be no point, they were already way beyond what could be described as worry. And so, I simply explained that the judge was bending over backwards to make sure that there couldn't be any grounds for an appeal when Little is found guilty. My last comment, 'when Little is found guilty', seemed to be of some comfort to them and that's why I'd said it. I guessed from the beginning of the investigation that, as the SIO, they would look to me for reassurance that justice would be delivered for Rachel. At least that's what I'd have done.

Lord Justice Hooper swept back into court. Mr Morton gave nothing away. Mr Ahmed, on the other hand, looked hopeful. I wondered whether he really cared about any of this, or whether it was just some elaborate game of chess to him and that this was just his latest dramatic move in an early attempt to checkmate his learned opponent.

"I have considered very carefully Mr Ahmed's demand for a retrial and I must deny his request for the following reasons."

Before he could say any more, there was a deafening sigh of relief that caused the judge to pause and it wasn't just from Rachel's family either. I was so relieved that I pretty much missed the reasoning behind his decision.

On the journey home, I recalled some of what he'd said. 'This case must be decided by the jury. Should the jury find the defendant not guilty then that would be the point at which the Crown Prosecution Service must decide on the most appropriate course of action'. He'd said much more of course but it didn't matter. What mattered was that the trial was going ahead, and if I could have had a conversation with Mr Ahmed, he would have probably told me that it'd been worth a try and that there was still everything to play for as he looked forward to meeting Mr Fuller once again.

TWENTY-FIVE

'Are you going to stab me like you stabbed Rachel?'

To say that it was a nervous and anxious wait overnight for the morning to arrive, would be a bloody massive understatement. I woke early before dawn and sat with a coffee watching the sunrise. It was one of those days when a shimmering blanket of mist covered the fields that surrounded the village, and it felt like I was the only person alive. The peace and quiet gave me time to think about the progress I'd made to get back to the person I used to be. Part of my recovery plan, was to read the great authors again as I used to do during my time at University. Dostoyevsky, Hesse, Fitzgerald, Salinger and many more, had all played a part in expanding my council house-perspective mind, and I'd devoured book after book as if each day were my last. But it wasn't until recently that I'd realised why I'd taken so much pleasure from reading back then. It was something C.S. Lewis said, 'We read to know we are not alone'. Reading had been the perfect antidote to the isolation of University life, and I was hoping that retracing my earlier steps would do the same thing for me now.

If there was a prize for the most obnoxious and foul-mouthed witness ever to give evidence in Crown Court, then

Fuller would surely win it by a mile. I couldn't help thinking, though, that he'd have to go some to beat his initial performance as I watched him make his second appearance in Court 1. It felt as though the balance of power had already moved in Mr Ahmed's favour as he turned to acknowledge Fuller's entrance. With a 'fuck off you little fat twat', expletive directed aggressively towards him, and 'evil murdering bastard', spat out with a great deal of venom at Little, Fuller stood trembling and agitated in the witness box.

I told myself to be prepared for anything because I'd no idea what was going to happen. The court was, once again, packed to capacity. The press must have thought that all their birthdays had come at once, the opportunity to report on a case that beggared belief. And if I thought that the claustrophobic feeling of anticipation that had gripped the court so far had reached its pinnacle, then I was very much mistaken.

Mr Morton did his best to put Fuller at ease but it had no effect. At least Fuller knew why he was giving evidence the first time, but he clearly had no idea why he was here now.

"Why you asking me these fucking questions again? I haven't killed no-one."

The judge warned him again about his language but Fuller continued anyway. His behaviour was threatening to spiral out of control, and Mr Ahmed hadn't even begun his cross-examination. Mr Morton managed, eventually, to guide Fuller through his movements on New Year's Eve. His testimony was the same as it had been the first time.

And then it was Mr Ahmed's turn. It was clear from his animated body language and sweeping hand gestures, that this was going to be a performance that would be better suited to a play in a West End theatre.

"Not you again for fuck's sake, what do you want this time?"

The opening expletive from Fuller, was the beginning of about an hour of Mr Ahmed trying his very best to antagonise and goad an already deeply troubled Fuller. And with every question came a response that was more venomous than the last. Fuller was at boiling point when Mr Ahmed, at long last, revealed the testimony of Danby. I thought for a moment that Fuller was about to bolt out of the box and attack Mr Ahmed, who must have sensed the same thing because he shouted,

"ARE YOU GOING TO STAB ME LIKE YOU STABBED RACHEL?"

I put my head in my hands. This surely couldn't get any worse. Mr Morton leapt to his feet.

"My Lord, this is indeed outrageous. I must protest in the strongest terms at my learned colleague's behaviour towards Mr Fuller."

With Mr Morton's timely intervention, the moment had passed. Fuller's reply lightened the brooding atmosphere.

"Do you know what you are? You're a stupid little man."

For once, Mr Ahmed was lost for words, and I sensed that everyone wanted to give Fuller a round of applause. He seemed genuinely astonished to learn of Danby's evidence in much the same way as he had been, when he'd delivered the one liner I'll never forget, 'the last thing I killed was a fucking wood pigeon on Sutton Common'. There was a raw, if unattractive honesty to his answers, and I wondered if Mr

Ahmed had made a grave error of judgement in browbeating Fuller. It was human instinct to protect the vulnerable, and whatever the jury thought about Fuller, he'd showed glimpses of a frightened young man beneath his aggressive exterior. The judge thanked Fuller for his evidence, and the last thing he shouted to Little was, 'fucking murdering bastard'.

Mr Ahmed treated Fuller's mother and sister in exactly the same way that he had done the first time with exactly the same outcome, floods of tears and absolute humiliation for telling the truth. Mr Morton had the last word though, because he recalled Danby who clearly had no idea why. He seemed to be much more nervous than before, and his evidence began to crumble under Mr Morton's laser-like questioning. Although he still maintained that he'd seen Fuller leave his house a few minutes after midnight - even though he'd told DC Bailey it was twelve forty-five - his replies were unconvincing and evasive. Mr Morton had him exactly where he wanted, squirming under the intense scrutiny of Crown Court. But what would the jury make of Danby? I'd no idea.

It was late Friday afternoon and everyone looked exhausted, including the judge, who must have been more than ready for a large gin and tonic and a well-earned rest. Finally, it was over, only the closing arguments and the judge's summing up of the evidence before the verdict. It was going to be a bloody long weekend.

TWENTY-SIX

'So, who was the killer?'

Over the weekend, I continued to fulfill the promise I'd made to read again. I started with Fitzgerald's Great Gatsby. 'Heightened sensitivity to the promises of life', 'extraordinary gift for hope', 'with the sunshine and the great bursts of leaves growing on the trees, I had the familiar conviction that life was beginning over again with the summer'. Reading those words again, as I'd done so many times before, stirred in me a feeling of hope that maybe there were brighter days waiting just around the corner. But I knew that only a guilty verdict would diminish the restlessness and provide the opportunity for me to find peace. Not guilty, would haunt me forever. I'd be constantly turning over in my mind whether I'd been up to the challenge, whether I'd been good enough. I couldn't even begin to think about what a 'Not guilty' verdict would mean for Rachel's family.

The courtroom was once again ready and waiting. The final chapter in this extraordinary trial that had already witnessed the most dramatic scenes imaginable, was about to begin. The jury wouldn't be hearing from any more witnesses, thank God, only Mr Morton, followed by Mr Ahmed and, finally, Lord Justice Hooper. The game of chess was reaching its climax as we all waited for Mr Morton's closing speech. The tension was already unbearable.

"Members of the jury, the defendant Michael Little brutally murdered Rachel Moran by repeatedly stabbing her to death. It was a frenzied, vicious and cruel attack on an innocent young woman and it is the Crown's position that the defendant had sexual intercourse with Rachel as she lay dying or when she was dead. Little did it, as clear as night follows day."

He proceeded to do precisely what I expected him to do - outline why, based purely on the evidence. It was a persuasive, compelling argument because it was the truth. Mr Morton was on his feet for over an hour. There were no theatrics, no bloated performance, only a machine-gun like delivery framed in perfect crystal-clear language. He concluded this part of his summary of the evidence with,

"And so, you see, members of the jury, when you consider carefully the evidence against the defendant, it is indeed as clear as night follows day that Michael Little killed Rachel Moran and I invite you to say that he is guilty of murder."

Mr Morton paused for what seemed like forever. I felt sure that it was a tactic to give the jurors time to digest his narrative delivered with the expertise that only a barrister with his intellect could provide. And, if I was impressed by his opening, I was even more so with what was to follow. Mr Morton's contempt for Little that had manifested itself to some extent in his cross-examination of the defendant, was given free reign,

"Not content with killing Rachel, he seeks to rob her of

her reputation by saying that she followed him into the bedroom and was the instigator of a sexual act between them, an act of consensual sexual intercourse."

He went on to question what kind of a human being would wish to inflict more pain and suffering on Mark Shepherd and Rachel's family by such a despicable accusation that could only be corrected by Rachel,

"An evil man driven by lust and by the desire to save his own skin."

It was a masterstroke to point out to the jury the depths of the defendant's evil. Rachel was dead but he'd created many more victims with his lies in an effort to save himself. I wondered whether members of the jury would view the betrayal of Rachel's memory, or the blaming of Marc Fuller and the humiliation of his family, as the more damning aspect of his bid for freedom. That would only hold true, I thought, if they were convinced of his guilt. Finally, Mr Morton spent some time on the belated appearance of James Danby.

"Members of the jury, I must now turn to the testimony of Mr Danby. I do not know why he felt compelled to come forward with his less than convincing story of having seen Mr Fuller leave his home in the early hours of New Year's Day. Is he to be believed? I think not. He had every opportunity to follow progress of the case in the newspapers and would know the Crown's position in relation to the whereabouts of Mr Fuller. I believe that it was a blatant attempt on his part to mislead this court. Mr Fuller was at home when the defendant murdered Rachel Moran. Michael Little acted alone."

Mr Morton couldn't have done any more. He'd restored my faith in the criminal justice system, at least for the time being. I hadn't seen him in action before the trial, but I liked to think that he cared about the outcome as much as we did. Maybe he did, maybe he didn't, maybe he was this bloody good all the time, but I had to admit that my initial impression of him was wrong. He was every bit as good as Francis Bernard, just in a different way. The one thing that they both had in common though, was the gift to make people believe in them and that they'd always be there to fight the battle between good and evil.

I knew that the jury would be in for a rollercoaster ride as Mr Ahmed stood to his face his eager audience. Little had given him an astonishingly far-fetched defence to work with that was obviously concocted after disclosure of the prosecution case. And to be fair to Mr Ahmed, you couldn't blame him for glossing over the weight of evidence against his client, because Danby's late testimony was his only glimmer of hope if he was to cast doubt on Fuller's alibi. If the jury believed his alibi, then they would have to find Little guilty, regardless of how unpleasant Fuller had been in the witness box.

Mr Ahmed concentrated his efforts on criticising the police for failing to investigate Fuller, questioning the honesty of Fuller's mother and sister, painting Fuller to be a violent individual more than capable of murder, and suggesting that Rachel was 'open to offers'. I winced when he casually and intentionally tried to destroy Rachel's reputation again, it was a cruel thing to do in the presence of Rachel's family. Ray reacted badly and stormed out of the courtroom.

I decided to leave before Mr Ahmed had finished. Ray was in the foyer surrounded by his family, who were doing their best to restrain him from going back into court and throttling the diminutive barrister. It wouldn't have been a fair fight. Ray would've won, easily. Mr Ahmed was given a police escort out of the building for his own safety.

The end of another long day and for me, it was still too close to call. It shouldn't have been. The Hull Daily Mail hadn't helped by their latest front-page headline: 'SO WHO WAS THE KILLER?' beneath full size sketches of Fuller facing Little. They must have written it in real time from the courtroom to get the late edition printed. I bought a copy on the way home and it was the last thing I wanted to see. I knew that they were only reporting what had happened in court, but it didn't stop me from being bloody annoyed with the Mail. The day had begun brightly with Mr Morton's brilliant final speech, but the Mail had reported every last detail of Mr Ahmed's outrageous allegation about Rachel. God knows how many people would read it and believe that there was some truth in it simply because it was in print. And regardless of the verdict, I knew there would be those who would choose to think the worst of Rachel, just as there had been high-ranking police officers that questioned whether I knew where Rachel was all along and that the search had been an elaborate smoke screen. Although I was able to live with vultures in the police, Rachel's family would be deeply hurt if they thought that even one member of the public believed that Rachel had been 'open to offers'.

TWENTY-SEVEN

'This didn't look good.
Panic set in'

Lord Justice Hooper began his summing up of the evidence at ten o'clock on Tuesday, October 28. The mood in the courtroom seemed less intense in a way, maybe because everybody knew that they'd heard the last of Mr Ahmed and were looking forward to the measured and gentle eloquence of the learned judge. I knew that this part of the trial was, in many ways, the most important, because the judge would guide the jury through the evidence at some length, assisting the jurors along the way with his observations. Mr Ahmed would be listening carefully to every word spoken looking for grounds upon which to make an appeal, should the verdict be guilty. I'd been to the Court of Appeal before and it wasn't something that I wanted to go through again. The judge had to get it right, balancing the need to be fair to both sides.

"Members of the jury, if, after considering all the evidence I am about to go through at some length, you are sure the defendant is guilty, you must return the verdict of guilty. If you are not sure, your verdict must be not guilty. It is for the prosecution to prove the defendant is guilty, he does not have to prove his innocence."

For the first time, Maly, Alan, Shaun and Trev joined me in the gallery. Kay decided to sit with Wanda and Ray. The end really was in sight and they would be in need of her support. Had Mr Morton done enough to make the jury 'sure' of Little's guilt? Had the investigation been as rigorous as it could have been? I knew that this would happen though, with each point raised by the judge, questioning whether we'd covered every angle, whether we'd missed something. Glancing at my trusted colleagues settled my nerves, because they were outstanding and had been at the top of their game throughout. So, in the end, I just sat back and listened safe in the knowledge that we'd done our very best for Rachel. I looked up the definition of 'sure', once - 'completely confident that one is right'. Lord justice Hooper used that word about a thousand times over the next six hours or so. I tried to look at the evidence from the jury's perspective for anything that would make them sure of Little's guilt. Buried within his mammoth summing up, he managed to provide them with the key to the whole thing.

"The whereabouts of Mr Fuller on New Year's Eve, you may think, is an important matter. That is evidence you will take into account in deciding whether or not the prosecution have made you sure that the defendant murdered Rachel Moran."

The judge directed them with, 'that is evidence you WILL take into account'. Had Fuller and his family done enough? Would the jury believe them? Or had Danby's late testimony given them reasonable doubt? Over lunch in the court canteen, we agreed that pretty much everything else didn't really matter unless the jury didn't believe Fuller's alibi. And if they didn't, then they would be faced with a much more complex task: how to decide upon the credibility of Mr Ahmed's insistence that Fuller left his home, somehow managed to travel over five miles to meet Rachel over a drug deal, had gone to Little's flat, let himself in, sat patiently whilst Little had sex with Rachel, flown into a jealous rage, stabbed Rachel to death, and then gone home without any of his family noticing his absence. It sounded ridiculous as we discussed whether the jury would seriously consider it to be a possibility. But that was our perspective and we'd no idea what they were thinking. After all, the judge had repeated over and over again that they must be sure.

By mid-afternoon, Lord Justice Hooper asked the jury to retire to consider their verdict. Would they return with their decision before the close of play today? I'd had quick decisions before, but somehow it just didn't feel like one of those occasions. For one thing, almost immediately, they returned and asked to see the dress that Rachel had been wearing. And they wanted to watch all the relevant CCTV footage over and over again. Eventually, the judge decided to send them home for the day with a serious warning not to discuss the case with anyone.

Ten o'clock the next morning came around in a blink of an eye as if I'd sat there all night. I couldn't remember driving home, being at home or driving back to the court. It brought back memories of the dark period of the grievance when my mind had been numb and I couldn't cope with day-to-day living. It wasn't a good feeling. It was a warning sign that I was on the edge again. The level of adrenalin in my veins was at an all-time high. Surely the verdict would be this morning, I told myself. It was a cruel form of torture. Waiting and waiting. The jurors were obviously in no mood to be rushed as they asked to see Rachel's jacket again and the dress she was wearing. Lord Justice Hooper called them back towards the end of the day. They still hadn't reached a unanimous verdict and so they were sent home for the second time. This wasn't a good sign. They'd been deliberating for what seemed like forever. Panic set in. I knew that the judge would eventually accept no less than a ten to two majority, but if that couldn't be achieved, then it would be a hung jury and a retrial.

I managed to speak to Ray and Wanda in the foyer before they left. They asked what a hung jury meant. Somebody had told them that it might be a possible outcome, given the length of time the jury had been deliberating. I could tell just by looking at Ray that he wouldn't have the strength to endure another trial that would be many months away. He was broken by the loss of Rachel and there was nothing anyone could do for him. I knew that he valued honesty, and so I told him that I really wasn't sure why it was taking so long and that a hung jury couldn't be ruled out.

Another unbearable wait for the morning to come and, if it was unbearable for me, what would it be like for Rachel's family? It must have seemed as though there was some kind of conspiracy to make them suffer in ways that they could never have imagined. The months of waiting, news that Little had sex with Rachel, Little's ever changing defence statements, the betrayal of Rachel's reputation during the trial, and finally, the long wait for a verdict that might well be not the one that they so badly needed. This was serious. My colleagues agreed. We'd enough experience between us to recognise the signs, all was not well, it was taking too long.

On the drive home, I resigned myself to the very real likelihood of either a not guilty verdict or a hung jury. Needless to say, I didn't sleep. I'd lain on the settee, glass of whisky in hand, contemplating what the future would hold for me in a post 'Not Guilty' world.

TWENTY-EIGHT

'We'll shelter her with tenderness'

Ten o'clock, again, sat in exactly the same place as yesterday. There had to be a verdict today, there just had to be. The old clichés came to mind about how the tension was at 'fever pitch', 'claustrophobic', 'crushing', but there were no words to describe the gut-wrenchingly menacing feeling of foreboding that gripped my stomach. It was one thing contemplating a not guilty verdict or a hung jury, but it would be quite another to live with the consequences.

At precisely ten-fifty, the tannoy summoned all interested parties to Court 1. Could this be what we'd all been waiting for? The court fell silent as the foreman of the jury stood to address the learned judge.

"Members of the jury, have you reached a verdict upon which you are all agreed?"

"Yes."

Lord Justice Hooper told Little to stand.

"And do you find the defendant Michael Little guilty or not guilty of the murder of Rachel Moran?"

The foreman cleared his throat and paused as he looked up at the judge.

"Guilty."

The court erupted in a deafening round of applause and

cheers, but for me, the outpouring of relief quickly turned into raw emotion. I began to sob, uncontrollably, and there was nothing I could do about it other than put my hands over my face. It wasn't what I wanted to happen but I knew that I wasn't alone. As far as I could see, just about everybody else was sobbing too, including some of the jurors. Kay hugged me before leaving to find Wanda, who'd remained out of court for the verdict. I looked for Ray and he was being consoled by somebody that I didn't know. There were many ordinary members of the public, who'd been in court every day hoping for this moment.

The judge tried in vain to restore order to his courtroom. Mr Morton was on his feet ready to read Wanda's personal impact statement before sentencing. Little stared straight ahead as he had done for most of the trial - the foreman's verdict had no visible effect on him. Eventually, the judge managed to bring calm to the proceedings and invited Mr Morton to begin. I knew that Wanda wouldn't be able to speak, and I wasn't too sure about our barrister, either as he briefly and uncharacteristically, lost his composure. I didn't envy him the task he was about to perform, because it would be the first time the court would hear of the devastation caused to Rachel's family from the person who'd given birth to her, nurtured her, and watched her grow into a fine young lady.

"Through the months after Rachel went missing and then was found to have been murdered, our family has suffered in different ways. For my husband, Ray, it has destroyed him and feels that he has nothing to live for. He is broken inside and spends most of his days visiting Rachel's grave. It has become an obsession for him. He will never be the same man again. For myself, I now have a new phobia, a total fear of losing someone else close to me or them being harmed. I am a physical wreck. I do not eat or sleep properly anymore and I never will. I cannot use knives. I cannot visit places that I used to go with Rachel. I shop out of town to avoid being stopped by people asking about Rachel because it's too painful."

There was much more about the effect on John, Vanda and Kerry. The stress had caused Vanda's poor health to deteriorate. John was full of misery and rage, and his hopes for the future had been diminished by his poor attendance at work. And for Kerry, she was looking forward to spending more time with her baby sister, time that they'd never had due to the age gap; there was a crippling sense of being robbed of that opportunity.

"The rumours, assumptions and lies about my daughter, who is not here to defend herself, cause all the family distress. As a parent, I want to protect and defend my precious daughter Rachel. Life will never be the same again. We have not just lost Rachel, but lost part of each other."

Mr Morton paused again trying to compose himself. But the final part of Wanda's statement deepened the emotion in the courtroom, if that were possible.

"We'll shelter her with tenderness, we'll love her while we may, and for the happiness we have known, forever grateful stay. But should the Angels call her much sooner than we've planned, we'll brave the bitter grief that comes and try to understand."

Finally, he was able to sit down. He looked absolutely

shattered. The court fell silent as Lord Justice Hooper spoke directly to Michael Little.

"You have been found guilty by the jury of the brutal murder of 21-year old Rachel Moran. Having killed her, you then hid her body, knowing full well the additional suffering you were thereby inflicting upon her family. You have given evidence that Rachel Moran voluntarily had intercourse with you. I am quite satisfied that she did not consent and we will never know whether the act took place before or after death. You are an evil man. The sentence I pass upon you is imprisonment for life."

Everyone stood as Little was led away to face a lifetime behind prison bars. Justice was done and all that was left would be for the judge to, hopefully, commend some of my officers, particularly PCs Dennison, Hague and Key. But I was mistaken. The judge did something that I'd never come across in Crown Court before, he asked for the SIO to take the stand. Kay had returned by now and she looked at me and said,

"That's you. Go on."

It was a bloody awkward moment. I was still far too emotional to speak. With all eyes on me, I walked slowly desperately trying to compose myself but it wasn't working, if anything, it made it worse. As I stepped onto the stand, Lord Justice Hooper's demeanour changed. He was smiling as he asked how I'd arrived at the decision to search Orchard Park Estate. He considered it to be, 'an inspired decision'. It was probably the most unexpected thing that'd ever happened to me. He seemed oblivious to the fact that tears were still streaming down my face as I tried to speak. 'For fuck's sake

Davo, get a grip. You look like an idiot', seemed to do the trick, and gradually my composure returned so that I was at least able to answer the learned judge. After I'd finished my explanation, he praised those officers most directly connected with the case, particularly PC Dennison for 'accurately recording what Little had said at the time of his arrest and for closely observing the Police and Criminal Evidence Act'. What the judge said next, was music to my ears:

"The evidence of James Danby, which was admitted at the eleventh hour, was dealt with in a manner in accordance with the highest traditions of the force."

He concluded by inviting the Chief Constable to note his praise of the investigation and by thanking the jury for their, 'diligence, patience and thoroughness'. Lisa found me and after a brief hug of congratulations, told me that the world's press were waiting to interview me on the court steps outside. I wanted to find Wanda and Ray but there was no time. Lisa hadn't been kidding, about a million cameras flashed as the questions came. I'd prepared something for all possible verdicts. I was looking forward to this version though, because I wanted to tell the press what I believed had happened, to try and recover some of Rachel's damaged reputation.

"Rachel Moran was an innocent victim of the evil perpetrated by Little. I believe that his motive was lust and the only way that he could get Rachel to come to his flat was by force. She wouldn't have stood a chance. After he'd dragged her off the street and into his hallway, he grabbed a knife and stabbed her until she was dead and then he stabbed her again and again in the head and shoulders. I believe that he had sex with her after she was dead, when she could not resist or fight back."

I said much more of course before leaving them behind. I joined Maly and the rest of my colleagues in the Three John Scotts pub. The drink was only to celebrate the guilty verdict. They'd watched the press conference through the window with a well-earned pint in their hands. It would be the last time we'd all be together like this. Tomorrow, we'd all go our own separate ways, although Maly would remain as my DCI at Division.

I didn't stay long. I wanted to walk the cobbled streets to the waterfront again. I stood on the jetty and thought about my Dad. I wish he'd still been alive, we'd have gone for a pint together in the Minnerva pub behind me and I would have been at peace. I had the sense that this might well be the end of my time as a SIO. The case had taken its toll, and although I knew that I could live for a thousand years and never come across a case as heart-wrenching as this, there would be more post-mortems, and more battles to fight in a callous criminal justice system.

How much more had I left to give, how much more could I endure, I wondered, as I caught sight of Marge, the lady who used to run my old tea spot. She was walking her dog, a scraggy-coated crossbreed that didn't look too friendly. It was good to see her again with her strong Hull accent that was a natural consequence of being brought up on Hessle Road. Her husband had been a hard-drinking trawlerman, a part of Hull life that had sadly gone forever. Marge had been kind to me as a young constable walking a lonely beat during

354

the winter months, by providing refuge from the pouring rain and howling winds. In many ways, I owed my career to her. I'd decided to quit the force towards the end of my probation; I'd had enough of the dim-witted, piss-taking police culture to last me a lifetime. I'd come to say goodbye when she'd sat me down and talked me out of leaving. It was something she'd said that struck a chord.

"You've a good heart and you'll make a bloody brilliant copper someday. Tell them piss-taking bastards to go fuck themselves. Anyway, you can't go 'cos I'll miss you."

I told her that it was because of her that I'd decided to stay in the force and that I'd taken her advice. I went straight back to the station, and in front of the whole shift, I grabbed the worst offending culprit by the throat, lifted him off the floor and told him to go and stick his bullying head up his arse. I duly received a round of applause from my startled colleagues. It did the trick though, my reputation as someone not to be crossed had been considerably enhanced. The piss-taking stopped and I was left alone, thereafter.

We both laughed at the thought but she refused to take the credit. She asked me how the trial was going and when I told her that Little had just been found guilty, with a big smile on her face, she said,

"Told you you'd do OK, bloody proud of you."

She gave me a hug, and I wondered whether I'd ever see her again as I watched her disappear into the distance with her old-fashioned headscarf flapping in the wind. The coincidence of meeting Marge at exactly the time that I needed to see a friendly face wasn't lost on me, but for Rachel, a coincidence had led to her death and lifelong devastation to her family. It'd led to the world being privy to every intimate detail of Rachel's life and those of her family, for all to see and for all to judge. I gave up long ago trying to figure out just how long we had before the evil perpetrated by others would eventually overwhelm us all, like an avalanche of hatred, but it wouldn't be today at least as Little looked forward to a life of incarceration.

On the way home, I thought about how we still didn't know much about Little, the cold-blooded killer, who'd showed no remorse for what he'd done. I'd read some of his letters to his family whilst he was on remand on the segregation wing at Doncaster prison, hoping to gain an insight into his mind. They were surprisingly upbeat, laden with jokes that he found amusing. They could've been letters sent to family members parted by living in different parts of the country, not by prison walls awaiting trial for murder. In one letter to his sister he told her, 'I've just got a radio so I've been singing + dancing around my cell. I bet the guards think I'm crazy'. He was now going to have years to sing and dance within the four walls of his tiny cell, I thought, and a lifetime to contemplate how he'd brutally cut short the life of a beautiful young woman and brought unimaginable devastation to Rachel's family.

TWENTY-NINE

'I just hoped that their strong Catholic faith would be of some comfort to them both'

After the trial, the police culture didn't disappoint. It was as if it hadn't happened, apart from a call from the Chief Constable. Lord Justice Hooper had told the Chief over dinner that he was impressed with the investigation, but even more impressed with the integrity I'd displayed in bringing Danby's evidence to his attention at the eleventh hour. I wrote down what he'd said so that I could look back in years to come at a compliment from a Crown Court judge. It was something to be proud of.

DS Penman called to congratulate me on the outcome of the trial and to tell me that my search of Orchard Park Estate by consent was being held up as national best practice. She told me to expect calls from other SIOs across the country asking for my advice. Suddenly, it seemed as though I'd won back some of my lost reputation and that I actually mattered. Other SIOs would be asking me for advice - who would've thought it, a kid from an east Hull council estate influencing the way that searches are conducted across the country. DS Penman's news was an example of the brighter side of the police culture. I'd done something positive and bold, and it'd been recognised nationally by the Crime Faculty. And as I resumed my day job at Division, it seemed as though even my fiercest critics were acknowledging what had been achieved. The general opinion amongst my peers was something like, 'Fair play to him, made a fucking ballsy decision and it paid off'.

A week or so after the trial, I took Alan with me to visit Janet Devine at her home on Greenwich Avenue. I bought her some flowers, and because it was Marc Fuller's birthday, we took him some cans of beer. Janet Devine opened the front door and when I looked into her eyes, my heart sank, the all too familiar signs of a person on the edge of despair, were clear to see. I told her that I was sorry for the way she and her family had been treated under cross-examination. She tried to hold back the tears but they came anyway. Marc Fuller came downstairs and, on seeing his distraught mother, he began shaking with rage no doubt assuming that we'd upset her in some way. Eventually, he realised his mistake when he saw the flowers and cans of beer. What he had difficulty understanding though, was the fact that we'd come in the first place.

"Fucking unreal, two coppers coming on my birthday with some tinnies, nice one."

We didn't stay long. Janet Devine asked for some privacy so that she could compose herself. I wasn't sure that we'd done the right thing, although it felt like the right thing to do. I just wanted to her to know that she hadn't been forgotten. As we drove back to the station, I wondered how long it'd take for her to overcome the experience of being wrongly accused of conspiring, with her family, to pervert the course of justice. Maybe she never would.

A few months later, I received a call at home from the head of CID asking me if I'd be the SIO for a death in custody in another force. I accepted because it was something that I hadn't done before. Part of me wondered why me. I'd convinced myself that perhaps it was because I'd done well in securing Little's conviction. But it didn't take long for me to realise that it was a way of getting me out of the force for a prolonged period. I was mid-way through the post-mortem on an elderly lady, who'd died in police custody following her arrest in a secure unit for the mentally ill, when I received a phone call from a trusted colleague,

"Davo, you're not going to believe it. There's been three temporary promotions to Chief Superintendent and you're not one of them."

Even though I was angry at being overlooked, I wasn't surprised because I'd already accepted long ago that my career was at a standstill. Fortunately, I'd taken Alan Dorning with me and he listened patiently, pint in hand, to me ranting until I'd got it out of my system.

Back in my hotel room, I pulled out some books I'd brought with me and it was something that I read by Goethe, the German poet, that fitted precisely the mood I was in, 'Only where you were on foot, have you truly been'. I took comfort from the path I'd chosen to walk as a SIO, a path that allowed me the highest privilege of all: to investigate the death of another human being and witness at first hand, the incredible bravery, courage and fortitude displayed by Wanda and Ray. Sure, promotion to Chief Superintendent would've given me a fleeting sense of satisfaction, but it would also condemn me to a life far less interesting defined by endless management meetings, and exposure to an even higher degree of personal scrutiny. It would just be a matter of time before I offended some poor, sensitive soul, and Maggie Bloom would be ready and waiting, grievance forms in hand. No, my own wellbeing was more important than promotion, I thought, as I took another swig of whisky.

On the plus side, being away from the force would give me time to reflect on how I was going to find peace in an organisation ruled by political correctness. I still had ten years until retirement and, with my direct and demanding style of leadership, I knew that it was going to be an uphill struggle. My burning desire to make a difference as a police officer though, remained undimmed, and I was more determined and bullish than ever to make a positive contribution to the force. Just how I was going to achieve that was a challenge that would have to wait until I returned.

My immediate future was committed to establishing the truth of how the patient had died, and who was responsible for letting that happen. It was already proving to be a challenge of a very different kind. Walking into another force to investigate police officers for gross negligence manslaughter, as I was beginning to realise, demanded diplomacy and sensitivity. And being the face of the police service responsible for failing to protect a vulnerable and frail detainee from taking her own life, was a position that I'd never been in before. Accordingly, there was a high degree of anger and resentment towards me from the victim's only daughter that I could understand, but I'd no idea how to deal with. Yet again, I was privy to indescribable heartbreak and loss, just as I'd been with Wanda and Ray, who were never far from my thoughts. I'd been close enough to witness at first hand the suffering and utter devastation caused by the loss of Rachel. I knew that it had only been a glimpse into their world where every second would seem like a lifetime of torture, with no end in sight. How they'd managed to conduct themselves with such dignity and composure, had been a shining example to us all. I just hoped that their strong Catholic faith would be of some comfort to them both as they faced a bleak and desolate future without Rachel.

Looking back, I'd been lucky to have had the privilege of working with so many outstanding individuals, who'd been part of the search for Rachel and subsequent fight to secure Little's conviction. I couldn't have done it without them. They'd raised the bar for Rachel, in terms of their skill, commitment and professionalism, forming a formidable investigative machine, that was truly a sight to behold. They were humble, unassuming heroes, and if I were asked to describe what qualities they all had in common, it would be their natural instinct to look for the good in others, have no need of gossip, and always strive to do the right thing. It was as if they carried the torch of human kindness, to light the way, so that others may follow their lead.

In life, even though I never knew Rachel, I felt as though I'd come to know her through the eyes of her family and friends. They painted a vivid picture of a gentle soul, blessed with a passion for life that touched everyone around her. She radiated warmth, happiness and joy as if that was why she'd been put on this earth - to make it a better place for the rest of us. In death, it was of some comfort to know that we couldn't have done any more for her.

EPILOUGE

Michael Little remains in prison serving a life sentence for the abduction and murder of Rachel Moran. He has never shown any remorse for what he did to Rachel, and to date, he has not accepted his guilt.

ABOUT THE AUTHOR

Paul was born and raised on a council estate in Hull. He initially studied to become a chemical engineer and was awarded a PhD degree before working as a post-doctoral fellow at the University of Toronto, Canada.

He joined the police service in 1982, and served for thirty years reaching the rank of Chief Superintendent. Most of his career was spent in the CID and he led many high-profile murder investigations both as a Detective Chief Inspector and Detective Superintendent.

Paul is retired and lives in East Yorkshire. This is his second book. His first book, NATALIE, is a true account of the police investigation Paul led into the brutal murder and dismemberment of a working prostitute in 1998, in Hull.

COPYRIGHT

This book is copyright material and must not be copied, reproduced, transferred, distributed, leased, licensed or publicly performed or used in any way except as specifically permitted in writing by the author. Any unauthorised distribution or use of this text may be a direct infringement of the author's rights and those responsible may be liable in law accordingly.

Although this book is based on real people and real events, some names, places, and identifying features have been changed in order to preserve their privacy. The author has tried to reproduce, as faithfully and accurately as possible, what was said by individuals in the book. Court proceedings were based on the author's observations. Court transcripts were not used.

Printed in Great Britain
by Amazon